Thomas Wilkinson Speight

The Loudwater Tragedy

Thomas Wilkinson Speight

The Loudwater Tragedy

ISBN/EAN: 9783744649483

Printed in Europe, USA, Canada, Australia, Japan

Cover: Foto ©ninafisch / pixelio.de

More available books at **www.hansebooks.com**

Presented to

The Library

of the

University of Toronto

by

Miss Beatrice Corrigan

POPULAR TWO-SHILLING NOVELS.

is is a SELECTION only.—FULL LISTS of nearly 600 NOVELS free.

By GRANT ALLEN.
ories.	The Beckoning Hand.
ies.	The Devil's Die.
e's Sake.	This Mortal Coil.
Babylon.	The Tents of Shem.
Taboo.	Dumaresq's Daughter.

ER ARNOLD.—Phra the Phœnician
ΛUS WARD'S Complete Works.
Rev. S. BARING GOULD.
r. | Eve.

y FRANK BARRETT.
lty.	For Love and Honour.
or Life.	John Ford; and His
ife & Death.	Helpmate.
Olga Zassou-	Honest Davie.
	Folly Morrison.
l's Progress.	Lieut. Barnabas.
g Vengeance	Little Lady Linton.

y BESANT AND RICE.
ney Mortiboy	By Celia's Arbour.
and Crown.	The Monks of Thelema
f Vulcan.	'Twas in Trafalgar's Bay
Girl	The Seamy Side.
Mr. Lucraft	Ten Years' Tenant.
Butterfly.	Chaplain of the Fleet.

y WALTER BESANT.
t Conditions.	World went well then.
na' Room.	Herr Paulus.
rden Fair.	For Faith & Freedom.
rster.	To Call her Mine.
	The Bell of St. Paul's.
Gibeon.	The Holy Rose.
Armorel of Lyonesse.	
Katherine's by the Tower.	

E BIERCE.—In the Midst of Life.

By BRET HARTE.
of Red Dog.	Gabriel Conroy.
aring Camp.	Maruja.	Flip.
Stories.	A Phyllis of the Sierras

ROBERT BUCHANAN.
the Sword.	Martyrdom of Madeline
Nature.	Love Me for Ever.
e Man.	Foxglove Manor.
er.	Matt.	Master of the Mine.
belard.	The Heir of Linne.

By HALL CAINE.
w of a Crime. | A Son of Hagar.
The Deemster.

OMMANDER CAMERON.
"ise of the "Black Prince."

WER & FRANCES COLLINS.
age.	Transmigration.
Midnight.	A Fight with Fortune.
wenty.	The Village Comedy.
	You Play me False.
Blacksmith and Scholar.

y WILKIE COLLINS.
After Dark	The Frozen Deep.
No Name.	The Law and the Lady.
eek	Basil.	The Two Destinies.
Iecret.	The Haunted Hotel.
earts.	The Fallen Leaves.
anies.	Jezebel's Daughter.
in White.	The Black Robe.
Legacy of	Heart and Science.
Ae. [Cain.	"I say No."
inch.	The Evil Genius.
a.?	Little Novels.
agdalen.	A Rogue's Life.

). EGBERT CRADDOCK.
et of the Great Smoky M untains.

By B. M. CROKER.
| Neville. | A Bird of Passage. |
| e. | Diana Barrington. |

DAUDET.—The Evangelist.
ERASMUS DAWSON.
The Fountain of Youth.

By DICK DONOVAN.
The Man-Hunter.	Detective's Triumphs
Caught at Last!	In the Grip of the Law.
Tracked and Taken.	Wanted!
Man from Manchester.	From Information Received.
Who Poisoned Hetty Duncan?	Tracked to Doom.

By Mrs. ANNIE EDWARDES.
A Point of Honour. | Archie Lovell.

By M. BETHAM-EDWARDS.
Kitty. | Felicia.

By EDWARD EGGLESTON.—Roxy.
G. MANVILLE FENN.—The New Mistress

By PERCY FITZGERALD.
Bella Donna.	75 Brooke Street.
Polly.	Fatal Zero.	Never Forgotten.
Second Mrs. Tillotson.	The Lady of Brantome.

By R. E. FRANCILLON.
Olympia.	A Real Queen.
One by One.	King or Knave?
Queen Cophetua.	Romances of the Law.

By HAROLD FREDERIC.
Seth's Brother's Wife. | The Lawton Girl

By CHARLES GIBBON.
Robin Gray.	A Heart's Problem.
For Lack of Gold.	The Braes of Yarrow.
What will World Say?	The Golden Shaft.
In Honour Bound.	Of High Degree.
In Love and War.	Loving a Dream.
For the King.	By Mead and Stream.
In Pastures Green.	A Hard Knot.
Queen of the Meadow.	Heart's Delight.
Flower of the Forest.	The Dead Heart.
Fancy Free.	Blood-Money.

By ERNEST GLANVILLE.
The Lost Heiress. | The Fossicker.

By HENRY GREVILLE.
A Noble Woman. | Nikanor.

By JOHN HABBERTON.
Brueton's Bayou. | Country Luck.

By THOMAS HARDY.
Under the Greenwood Tree.

By JULIAN HAWTHORNE.
Garth.	Dust.	Fortune's Fool.
Ellice Quentin.	Beatrix Randolph.
Sebastian Strome.	Miss Cadogna.
Spectre of Camera.	Love—or a Name!
David Poindexter's Disappearance.

By HENRY HERMAN—A Leading Lady.
Mrs. CASHEL HOEY.—The Lover's Creed.

By Mrs. HUNGERFORD.
| A Modern Circe. | A Maiden all Forlorn. |
| In Durance Vile. | Marvel. |
A Mental Struggle.

By Mrs. ALFRED HUNT.
| Thornicroft's Model. | The Leaden Casket. |
| Self-Condemned. | That Other Person. |

By JEAN INGELOW.—Fated to be Free.

By HARRIETT JAY.
The Dark Colleen. | Queen of Connaught.

By R. ASHE KING.
| A Drawn Game. | The Wearing of the Green |
| Passion's Slave. | Bell Barry. |

By E. LYNN LINTON.
Patricia Kemball.	With a Silken Thread.
Atonement of Leam Dundas.	Rebel of the Family "My Love!"
The World Well Lost.	Ione.	Paston Carew.
Under which Lord?	Sowing the Wind.

By HENRY W. LUCY.—Gideon Fleyce.

By JUSTIN McCARTHY.
Dear Lady Disdain.	Linley Rochford.
Waterdale Neighbours.	Donna Quixote.
My Enemy's Daughter.	The Comet of a Season.
A Fair Saxon.	Maid of Athens.
Miss Misanthrope.	Camiola.

By HUGH MacCOLL.
Mr. Stranger's Sealed Packet.

London: CHATTO & WINDUS, 214, Piccadilly, W.

POPULAR TWO-SHILLING NOVELS.

** This is a SELECTION only.—FULL LISTS of nearly 600 NOVELS free.

By KATHARINE S. MACQUOID.
The Evil Eye. | Lost Rose.

By W. H. MALLOCK.—The New Republic.

By FLORENCE MARRYAT.
Open! Sesame! | Written in Fire.
Fighting the Air. | A Harvest of Wild Oats.

By LEONARD MERRICK.
The Man who was Good.

By JEAN MIDDLEMASS.
Touch and Go. | Mr. Dorillion.

By Mrs. MOLESWORTH.
Hathercourt Rectory.

J. E. MUDDOCK.—The Dead Man's Secret.

By CHRISTIE MURRAY.
A Life's Atonement. | By the Gate of the Sea.
A Model Father. | Val Strange. | Hearts.
Joseph's Coat. | The Way of the World.
Coals of Fire. | Bit of Human Nature.
First Person Singular. | Cynic Fortune.
Old Blazer's Hero.

CHRISTIE MURRAY and H. HERMAN.
One Traveller Returns. | Paul Jones's Alias.
The Bishops' Bible.

By HUME NISBET.
"Bail Up!" | Dr. Bernard St. Vincent.

By GEORGES OHNET.
Doctor Rameau. | A Last Love. | A Weird Gift.

By Mrs. OLIPHANT.
Whiteladies. | The Primrose Path.
The Greatest Heiress in England.

By OUIDA.
Held in Bondage. | In a Winter City.
Strathmore. | Ariadne. | Moths.
Chandos. | Idalia. | Friendship | Pipistrello.
Under Two Flags. | A Village Commune.
Cecil Castlemaine. | Bimbi. | In Maremma.
Tricotrin. | Puck. | Wanda. | Frescoes.
Folle Farine. | Princess Napraxine.
A Dog of Flanders. | Othmar. | Guilderoy.
Two Wooden Shoes. | Ruffino. | Syrlin.
Pascarel. | Signa. | Wisdom, Wit, & Pathos.

By JAMES PAYN.
Lost Sir Massingberd. | Mirk Abbey.
A Perfect Treasure. | Not Wooed, but Won.
Bentinck's Tutor. | £200 Reward.
Murphy's Master. | Less Black than We're
A County Family. | By Proxy. [Painted.
At Her Mercy. | Under One Roof.
A Woman's Vengeance. | High Spirits.
Cecil's Tryst. | Carlyon's Year.
The Clyffards of Clyffe. | A Confidential Agent.
The Family Scapegrace. | Some Private Views.
The Foster Brothers. | From Exile.
Found Dead. | Halves. | A Grape from a Thorn.
The Best of Husbands. | For Cash Only.
Walter's Word. | Kit.
Fallen Fortunes. | The Canon's Ward.
What He Cost Her. | Holiday Tasks.
Humorous Stories. | Glow-worm Tales.
Gwendoline's Harvest. | Mystery of Mirbridge.
The Talk of the Town. | The Burnt Million.
Like Father, Like Son. | The Word & the Will.
A Marine Residence. | A Prince of the Blood.
Married Beneath Him. | Sunny Stories.

By Mrs. CAMPBELL PRAED.
The Romance of a Station.
The Soul of Countess Adrian.

By E. C. PRYCE.
Valentina. | The Foreigners.
Mrs. Lancaster's Rival | Gerald.

By RICHARD PRICE.
Miss Maxwell's Affections.

By Mrs. J. H. RIDDELL.
Her Mother's Darling. | Fairy Water.
Uninhabited House. | The Prince of Wales's
The Mystery in Palace | Garden Party.
Gardens. | The Nun's Curse.
Weird Stories. | Idle Tales.

By F. W. ROBINSON.
Women are Strange. | The Hands of Justice.

By CHARLES READE.
Never too Late to Mend | Course of True Love.
Hard Cash. | Autobiog. of a Thief.
Peg Woffington. | A Terrible Temptation.
Christie Johnstone. | The Wandering Heir
Griffith Gaunt. | A Woman-Hater
Put Y'rself in His Place | A Simpleton. [face.
The Double Marriage. | Singleheart & Double-
Love Little, Love Long. | Good Stories.
Foul Play. | The Jilt | Readiana.
Cloister and the Hearth | A Perilous Secret.

By JAMES RUNCIMAN.
Skippers and Shellbacks | Schools and Scholars.
Grace Balmaign's Sweetheart.

By W. CLARK RUSSELL.
Round the Galley Fire. | On the Fo'k'sle Head.
In the Middle Watch. | A Voyage to the Cape.
Book for the Hammock. | Jenny Harlowe.
Mystery of 'Ocean Star.' | An Ocean Tragedy.
My Shipmate Louise | Alone on a Wide Wide Sea.

By ALAN ST. AUBYN.
A Fellow of Trinity. | The Junior Dean.

By G. A. SALA.—Gaslight and Daylight.

By JOHN SAUNDERS.
Bound to the Wheel. | The Lion in the Path.
One Against the World. | The Two Dreamers.
Guy Waterman.

By KATHARINE SAUNDERS.
Joan Merryweather. | Sebastian.
The High Mills. | Heart Salvage.
Margaret and Elizabeth.

By GEORGE R. SIMS.
Rogues and Vagabonds. | Tales of To-day.
Mary Jane's Memoirs. | Dramas of Life.
The Ring o' Bells. | Tinkletop's Crime.
Mary Jane Married. | Zeph: A Circus Story.

By HAWLEY SMART.
Without Love or Licence.

By T. W. SPEIGHT.
Mysteries of Heron Dyke. | By Devious Ways.
The Golden Hoop. | Hoodwinked.
Back to Life.

R. A. STERNDALE.—The Afghan Knife.

By R. LOUIS STEVENSON.
New Arabian Nights. | Prince Otto.

By BERTHA THOMAS.
Cressida. | Proud Maisie. | The Violin-Player.

By WALTER THORNBURY.
Tales for the Marines. | Old Stories Re-told.

By ANTHONY TROLLOPE.
The Way We Live Now. | The Land-Leaguers.
American Senator. | Mr. Scarborough's
Frau Frohmann. | Family.
Marion Fay. | John Caldigate.
Kept in the Dark. | The Golden Lion.

T. A. TROLLOPE.—Diamond Cut Diamond.

By FRANCES ELEANOR TROLLOPE.
Anne Furness. | Mabel's Progress.
Like Ships upon the Sea.

By MARK TWAIN.
Tom Sawyer. | Huckleberry Finn.
A Tramp Abroad. | Prince and the Pauper.
Stolen White Elephant | Mark Twain's Sketches.
Life on the Mississippi. | The Gilded Age.
A Pleasure Trip on the | A Yankee at the Court
Continent of Europe. | of King Arthur.

By SARAH TYTLER.
What She Came Through | St. Mungo's City.
Beauty and the Beast. | Lady Bell.
Noblesse Oblige. | Disappeared.
Citoyenne Jacqueline. | Buried Diamonds.
The Bride's Pass. | The Blackhall Ghosts.

By J. S. WINTER.
Cavalry Life. | Regimental Legends.

By H. F. WOOD.
The Passenger from Scotland Yard.
The Englishman of the Rue Cain.

By EDMUND YATES.
Forlorn Hope. | Land at Last. | Castaway.

London: CHATTO & WINDUS, 214, Piccadilly, W.

UDWATER TRAGEDY

POPULAR TWO-SHILLING NOVELS.

⁎ *This is a SELECTION only.—FULL LISTS of nearly 600 NOVELS free.*

By KATHARINE S. MACQUOID.
The Evil Eye. | Lost Rose.

By W. H. MALLOCK.—The New Republic.

By FLORENCE MARRYAT.
Open! Sesame! | Written in Fire.
Fighting the Air. | A Harvest of Wild Oats.

By LEONARD MERRICK.
The Man who was Good.

By JEAN MIDDLEMASS.
Touch and Go. | Mr. Dorillion.

By Mrs. MOLESWORTH.
Hathercourt Rectory.

J. E. MUDDOCK.—The Dead Man's Secret.

By CHRISTIE MURRAY.
A Life's Atonement. | By the Gate of the Sea.
A Model Father. | Val Strange. | Hearts.
Joseph's Coat. | The Way of the World.
Coals of Fire. | Bit of Human Nature.
First Person Singular. | Cynic Fortune.
Old Blazer's Hero.

CHRISTIE MURRAY and H. HERMAN.
One Traveller Returns. | Paul Jones's Alias.
The Bishops' Bible.

By HUME NISBET.
"Bail Up!" | Dr. Bernard St. Vincent.

By GEORGES OHNET.
Doctor Rameau. | A Last Love. | A Weird Gift.

By Mrs. OLIPHANT.
Whiteladies. | The Primrose Path.
The Greatest Heiress in England.

By OUIDA.
Held in Bondage. | In a Winter City.
Strathmore. | Ariadne. | Moths.
Chandos. | Idalia. | Friendship | Pipistrello.
Under Two Flags. | A Village Commune.
Cecil Castlemaine. | Bimbi. | In Maremma.
Tricotrin. | Puck. | Wanda. | Frescoes.
Folle Farine. | Princess Napraxine.
A Dog of Flanders. | Othmar. | Guilderoy.
Two Wooden Shoes. | Ruffino. | Syrlin.
Pascarel. | Signa. | Wisdom, Wit, & Pathos.

By JAMES PAYN.
Lost Sir Massingberd. | Mirk Abbey.
A Perfect Treasure. | Not Wooed, but Won.
Bentinck's Tutor. | £200 Reward.
Murphy's Master. | Less Black than We're
A County Family. | By Proxy. [Painted.
At Her Mercy. | Under One Roof.
A Woman's Vengeance. | High Spirits.
Cecil's Tryst. | Carlyon's Year.
The Clyffards of Clyffe. | A Confidential Agent.
The Family Scapegrace. | Some Private Views.
The Foster Brothers. | From Exile.
Found Dead. | Halves. | A Grape from a Thorn.
The Best of Husbands. | For Cash Only.
Walter's Word. | Kit.
Fallen Fortunes. | The Canon's Ward.
What He Cost Her. | Holiday Tasks.
Humorous Stories. | Glow-worm Tales.
Gwendoline's Harvest. | Mystery of Mirbridge.
The Talk of the Town. | The Burnt Million.
Like Father, Like Son. | The Word & the Will.
A Marine Residence. | A Prince of the Blood.
Married Beneath Him | Sunny Stories.

By Mrs. CAMPBELL PRAED.
The Romance of a Station.
The Soul of Countess Adrian.

By E. C. PRYCE.
Valentina.

By CHARLES READE.
Never too Late to Mend | Course of True Love.
Hard Cash. | Autobiog. of a Thief.
Peg Woffington. | A Terrible Temptation.
Christie Johnstone. | The Wandering Heir.
Griffith Gaunt. | A Woman-Hater
Put Y'rself in His Place | A Simpleton. [face.
The Double Marriage. | Singleheart & Double-
Love Little, Love Long. | Good Stories.
Foul Play. | The Jilt. | Readiana.
Cloister and the Hearth | A Perilous Secret.

By JAMES RUNCIMAN.
Skippers and Shellbacks | Schools and Scholars.
Grace Balmaign's Sweetheart.

By W. CLARK RUSSELL.
Round the Galley Fire. | On the Fo'k'sle Head.
In the Middle Watch. | A Voyage to the Cape.
Book for the Hammock. | Jenny Harlowe.
Mystery of 'Ocean Star.' | An Ocean Tragedy.
My Shipmate Louise | Alone on a Wide Wide Sea.

By ALAN ST. AUBYN.
A Fellow of Trinity. | The Junior Dean.

By G. A. SALA.—Gaslight and Daylight.

By JOHN SAUNDERS.
Bound to the Wheel. | The Lion in the Path.
One Against the World. | The Two Dreamers.
Guy Waterman.

By KATHARINE SAUNDERS.
Joan Merryweather. | Sebastian.
The High Mills. | Heart Salvage.
Margaret and Elizabeth.

By GEORGE R. SIMS.
Rogues and Vagabonds. | Tales of To-day.
Mary Jane's Memoirs. | Dramas of Life.
The Ring o' Bells. | Tinkletop's Crime.
Mary Jane Married. | Zeph: A Circus Story.

By HAWLEY SMART.
Without Love or Licence.

By T. W. SPEIGHT.
Mysteries of Heron Dyke. | By Devious Ways.
The Golden Hoop. | Hoodwinked.
Back to Life.

R. A. STERNDALE.—The Afghan Knife.

By R. LOUIS STEVENSON.
New Arabian Nights. | Prince Otto.

By BERTHA THOMAS.
Cressida. | Proud Maisie. | The Violin-Player.

By WALTER THORNBURY.
Tales for the Marines. | Old Stories Re-told.

By ANTHONY TROLLOPE.
The Way We Live Now. | The Land-Leaguers.
American Senator. | Mr. Scarborough's
Frau Frohmann. | Family.
Marion Fay. | John Caldigate.
Kept in the Dark. | The Golden Lion.

T. A. TROLLOPE.—Diamond Cut Diamond.

By FRANCES ELEANOR TROLLOPE.
Anne Furness. | Mabel's Progress.
Like Ships upon the Sea.

By MARK TWAIN.
Tom Sawyer. | Huckleberry Finn.
A Tramp Abroad. | Prince and the Pauper.
Stolen White Elephant | Mark Twain's Sketches.
Life on the Mississippi. | The Gilded Age.
A Pleasure Trip on the | A Yankee at the Court
Continent of Europe. | of King Arthur.

By SARAH TYTLER.

THE LOUDWATER TRAGEDY

PRINTED BY
SPOTTISWOODE AND CO., NEW-STREET SQUARE
LONDON

THE
LOUDWATER TRAGEDY

BY
T. W. SPEIGHT
(Thomas Wilkinson)

AUTHOR OF 'THE MYSTERIES OF HERON DYKE' 'HOODWINKED'
'BACK TO LIFE' ETC.

London
CHATTO & WINDUS, PICCADILLY
1893

PR
5470
S35 L6

807345

CONTENTS

CHAP.		PAGE
	Prologue	1
I.	ON THE EDGE OF A SECRET	17
II.	WHO IS MRS. WINSLADE?	35
III.	THE SECRET TOLD	46
IV.	IN WHICH MISS SUDLOW SPEAKS HER MIND	61
V.	A FAMILY CONFERENCE AND WHAT CAME OF IT	75
VI.	IN WHICH MISS SUDLOW HAS HER WAY	92
VII.	PERSONAL TO PHIL	98
VIII.	PHIL TAKES UP THE TRAIL AFRESH	106
IX.	A DEADLOCK	122
X.	UNCHRISTIAN CHARITY	128
XI.	FANNY AT LOUDWATER HOUSE	136
XII.	MRS. MELRAY THE YOUNGER IN A NEW LIGHT	145
XIII.	MRS. MELRAY'S STATEMENT	161
XIV.	THE STATEMENT CONCLUDED	173
XV.	A SCRAP OF PAPER	182

CHAP.		PAGE
XVI.	A FRESH LINE OF INQUIRY	198
XVII.	'A MAN I AM, CROSS'D WITH ADVERSITY'	217
XVIII.	AN UNLOOKED-FOR DEVELOPMENT	225
XIX.	AN UNAVOIDABLE NECESSITY	240
XX.	'WE MUST SPEAK BY THE CARD'	245
XXI.	THE TRUTH AT LAST	257
XXII.	ALL'S WELL THAT ENDS WELL	266

THE LOUDWATER TRAGEDY

PROLOGUE

THE STORY OF THE CRIME

12 Leighton Place, Worthing.
Thursday.

'My dear Phil.—By this post I send you a copy of a certain penny weekly journal entitled *The Family Cornucopia*, which, for lack of something better to read, I picked up the other day at a bookstall while on my way to the beach.

'Naturally, you will at once say to yourself (for you cannot deny, dear, that you occasionally express yourself with somewhat unnecessary emphasis over trifles), "What the dickens does the girl mean by bothering me with her trumpery penny rubbish?" Well, that is just the point about which "the girl" is going to enlighten you.

'Of course you have not forgotten "The Loudwater Tragedy," as most of the newspapers called it at the time (although some there were who wrote of it as the "Merehampton Mystery"). Neither, perhaps, has it escaped your memory how, with the object of helping to interest and carry out of herself for a little while, a young woman who, just then, was staying at a dull Devonshire village with the captious, but much-to-be-pitied, invalid in whose service she was, you wrote her a number of letters, dated from the very roof under which the tragedy in question had been enacted, in which you recapitulated for her information all the details of the crime as gathered by you on the spot; nor how you sketched for her the old mansion and its inmates, with the view from its windows, and all the quaint features of the sleepy little seaport, so that, after a time, she could almost have persuaded herself that what you had written formed a part of her personal experiences. If you have forgotten those letters, I have not. Yesterday I refreshed my memory by reading them again, and the reason I did so is this.

'In the periodical I am sending you there is an article extending over five pages, entitled, "How, and Why" which, strange to say, not merely seems to be based on the Loudwater Tragedy, but, under the guise of fiction, tells the story of the crime down to its minutest details; and not only does that, but, with almost photographic fidelity, limns for its readers the portraits of the various persons who were in any way mixed up with that mysterious affair.

'But the writer of "How, and Why"—he or she, as the case may be—does more, much more, than merely retell the story of the crime and describe the people who had to do with it. The article in question purports to be the confession of the murderer of Mr. Melray, written on the eve of his suicide, and professes to trace, step by step, how he was led on to the commission of the crime, and, in point of fact, sets the whole affair in an entirely fresh and startling light. To prove to you that this is so, it will only be necessary to say that the writer of the confession describes himself as having been a lover, before her marriage, of the old merchant's "girl-wife," and that it was owing to his inadvertently interrupting an assignation between the young people that "Mr. Melville" came by his death. High words passed between the elder man and the younger; there was a scuffle; a blow was given in the heat of passion, and in a moment the irrevocable deed was done. I have omitted to say that, according to the story, after the police have given up the case as hopeless, suspicion unexpectedly attaches itself to the head-clerk, (who figures as "Mr. Day"), and that, in the result, circumstantial evidence is brought to bear against him sufficiently strong to ensure his conviction on the capital charge. It is after "Mr. Day" is left for execution that the writer of the confession—who, although he acknowledges to the crime of which he has been guilty, is careful to impress upon his readers that he is not without his fine qualities—overcome by remorse, determines to avow the truth and thereby save the life of an innocent man, albeit at the expense of his own. He pens a farewell message to the "Ernestine" of the story—that is to say, to the murdered man's widow—and then gives his readers to understand that the moment after the last word of his confession shall have been written he will swallow the poison which he has procured in readiness for that purpose.

'Now, all this seems to me sufficiently remarkable. Of course, the question is, how much truth and how much fiction underlies the supposititious confession? That the whole of the latter part of it is purely fictitious we know already. We know, for instance, that not an iota of suspicion ever attached itself to Mr. Melray's managing clerk. Consequently that he has never been arrested, tried, or condemned.

Further than that, we know that the crime remains an unexplained mystery to this day.

'In view, then, of the fact that the latter half of the self-styled confession is proved to be a sheer invention, might it not reasonably be assumed that the first half pertains to the same class of narrative? Such would seem to be a common-sense way of looking at the affair, were it not that there is so much of actual fact as regards the commission of the crime itself mixed up with the narrative, and so many real persons under assumed names introduced therein, as to create a suspicion (in my mind, at least) that there may be some substratum of truth in that part of it which attributes the death of Mr. Melray to a quarrel with a former lover of his young and attractive wife.

'That you will read "How, and Why," after what I have here said about it, I do not doubt; after which I think you will agree with me that the story refers to "The Loudwater Tragedy" and to no other crime, and that the writer of it, whoever he may be, displays a singularly minute and intimate acquaintance with all the details of that still unsolved mystery.

'You will say to yourself that this is a strange letter for a young woman to write to her lover, and so it is, but then the circumstances of the case are peculiar. However, I promise you that my next letter shall be a very different kind of composition.

'Miss Mawby's bell has just rung, so I will conclude without a word more, except that, now and always, I am yours and yours only,

'FANNY SUDLOW.'

Such was the letter which Philip Winslade found one morning on his breakfast-table. But before introducing either the writer or the recipient of it to the reader's notice, it may be as well to give a brief *résumé* of the main facts in connection with the affair known as 'The Loudwater Tragedy,' so far as they had hitherto been brought to light, as also of certain of the events which led up to it.

Those who are acquainted with the once thriving port of Merehampton know what a pleasant, but withal dull, little town it is. No business firm in it is, or rather was a few years ago, more widely known or highly respected than that of Melray Brothers, ship-brokers and general merchants. Of the two brothers who made up the firm, James, the elder, was, to all intents and purposes, the sole representative. Robert, the younger brother, had been delicate from boyhood, and found it to the advantage of his health to winter abroad. Indeed, whenever he happened to be in England his visits to Merehampton were few and perfunctory, and while retaining a monetary interest in the business, he never concerned himself with the details, but willingly left the entire management to James, who, on his part, being a masterful kind of man and one who would have felt it irksome to have to put up with a partner who might chance to hold independent views—was quite content that matters should remain as they were. At this time James Melray was fifty years old, Robert being his junior by some ten or eleven years.

The house in which James dwelt, and under the roof of which both the brothers had been born, was known as Loudwater House, through having, once on a time, been the domicile of an old county family of that name. It was a handsome and substantial red-brick structure of the early Georgian period, with a good deal of ornamental stonework about it, and stood fronting the river Laming (for Merehampton is between three and four miles up stream from the sea) on what in these latter days was known as the Quay-side, but which at the time the house was built had doubtless been either green fields or private grounds pertaining to it. So long ago, however, was it since that part of the river had been banked in and the Quay-side called into existence, and since its row of ugly warehouses had been erected, each with its crane protruding from its second or third storey, and each with its suite of gloomy offices on the ground floor, that not even the oldest inhabitant of Merehampton could remember the place as being other than it was now. It was only a matter of course that, having become the home of a commercial family, the Georgian mansion should, to some extent, be put to commercial uses. Thus it had come to pass that the ground-floor rooms had been turned in part into offices and in part into a warehouse, with an additional room in which were stored cordage, blocks, sails, spars, chains and tools of various kinds, together with a miscellaneous assortment of maritime gear and appliances.

There could be but little doubt that Merehampton had passed the zenith of its prosperity as a seaport. With the opening of the railway a vital blow had been struck at the shipping interests of the little town. The coasting trade had dwindled by degrees to less than half of what it had been a few years before; some of the merchants and shippers had become bankrupt; others had taken themselves and their capital elsewhere; others, on the principle of half a loaf being better than none, had made the best of what could not be helped; half the warehouses on the Quay-side were untenanted; but through it all the firm of Melray Brothers had held manfully on its way, although in the face of a sorely diminished trade.

James Melray's household was a small one, comprising, as it did, only himself, his mother—a venerable lady between seventy and eighty years of age—who had her own suite of rooms and her own maid and companion, and, lastly, the merchant's girl-wife, who at the time the tragedy took place had been married to him some two and a half years.

Mr. Melray was a widower of some years' standing, but without family, when he first met Denia Lidington, who was the orphan niece and ward of one of his oldest friends. This friend dying, left Denia and her small fortune to his charge till the girl should come of age—a charge which Mr. Melray willingly undertook. How and by what degrees the kindly semi-paternal feeling with which he at first regarded the lonely girl changed to a sentiment of a far different texture is not within the scope of this narrative to describe. It is enough to say that about a year after his friend's death James Melray proposed to Denia Lidington, and, somewhat to his own surprise, was accepted without the slightest demur.

The marriage took place at Solchester, an inland town about a dozen miles from Merehampton, where, after her uncle's death, Denia had found a home in the house of a widowed lady of good family, but limited means, in whom Mr. Melray had implicit confidence. A month later the bride entered upon her new duties as the mistress of Loudwater House.

That she was an exceedingly pretty and attractive-looking young woman everybody was agreed; indeed, there were not wanting some who went so far as to call her beautiful. Her figure was slight, but full of grace, and was rather under the medium height of her sex. She had eyes of the clearest April blue, shaded by heavy lashes, finely-arched eyebrows, and a mass of silky maize-coloured hair. Her complexion was a pure creamy white, with only the very faintest flush of colour showing through it. There was nothing striking or pronounced about her features; indeed, considered in detail, they might have been termed insignificant, but, regarded as a whole, their effect was undeniably charming.

It was a matter of course, in view of the disparity in the ages of bride and bridegroom, that there should be no lack of croakers and prophets of the pessimistic school, who, one and all, took upon themselves to predict that such an union could be productive of nothing but discord and unhappiness, if not of evils still more dire. Time went on, however, and these and all such vaticinations remained unfulfilled. Nowhere, to all seeming, could there have been found a more contented or cosily happy wedded pair. Mrs. Melray fell in with her husband's tastes and mode of life with an easy adaptability which was as delightful as it was surprising in one so many years his junior. She made his friends her friends, and never seemed to long or care for any other society than that to which he chose to introduce her. She dressed soberly, but in excellent taste, and after a fashion which caused her to look half-a-dozen years older than her age. James Melray's first marriage had not been a happy one. His wife, a woman of an intractable temper, had been addicted to secret dram-drinking, and had thereby hastened her end. All the greater seemed the contrast between his life as it was now and as it had been then. In all Merehampton there was no happier man than he.

We now come to the fatal evening of Friday, September 18.

Twice every week, on the evenings of Tuesday and Friday, it had for years been Mr. Melray's custom to leave home as the clock was striking eight and make his way to the house of his friend Mr. Arbour, for the purpose of forming one at a sober rubber of whist. It was a custom which he had seen no reason for pretermitting after his second marriage, more especially in view of the fact that Mrs. Melray number two had never expressed the slightest desire that he should do so, and although she was thereby left alone for two or three hours on the evenings in question, she never failed to part from him with a kiss and a smile, nor greet him after the same fashion on his return.

On the aforesaid 18th of September Mr. Melray set out for his friend's house as usual. His wife accompanied him downstairs as far as the entrance hall and helped him to induct himself into his overcoat, and then, before she let him go, and because the evening was chilly, she insisted on tying a white silk muffler round his throat as a further protection against the weather. Then came the customary parting kiss, after which Mrs. Melray stood in the open doorway for a half a minute, watching her husband's retreating form. Then she shut the door and hurried back upstairs to the cosy drawing-room.

That evening Mr. Arbour and his friends waited in vain for the coming of James Melray. He never reached No. 5 Presbury Crescent.

Her husband had been gone a little over an hour

when Mrs. Melray rang the bell for Charlotte, the housemaid, and on the latter's appearance asked her to take a lighted candle and go down to her master's private office and bring thence an envelope out of the stationery case, which she would find on his table. Mrs. Melray had been writing to one of her friends, and finding that she was out of envelopes of her own, was under the necessity of using one of her husband's.

Charlotte went her way, leaving her young mistress seated at the davenport with the letter in front of her. A few moments later a piercing shriek rang through Loudwater House. The girl, holding the lighted candle aloft in one hand, had suddenly come upon the dead body of her master lying prone along the office floor between the fireplace and the table.

As already stated, Mr. Melray's business premises were on the ground-floor of Loudwater House. Although such was the case, the main entrance to the old mansion had in no way been interfered with. There, as for generations past, was the massive oaken door with its heavy lion's-head knocker and its overhanging porch—also of oak, and elaborately carved. This door gave admittance to a spacious flagged hall, whence a wide staircase led to the rooms on the upper floors. From the entrance hall a door opened directly into Mr. Melray's private office, in which room there were also two other doors, the first giving access to the outer office where sat Mr. Cray, the head clerk, and his three subordinates, while the second door opened on a narrow side alley leading from the back premises to the Quay-side, so that the merchant, when so inclined, could go in and out without having to pass through the general office.

The girl Charlotte's shrieks at the discovery of her master's body were heard not merely by the inmates of Loudwater House, but by a constable who happened at the time to be standing at the entrance to the side alley, as also by a couple of passing strangers. The three men in question were on the scene of the crime within a few seconds after Charlotte had given the alarm; for the outer door, on being tried, was found to be unfastened. Of what thereupon ensued it is not needful that we should dwell.

At the inquest it was shown that Mr. Melray's death had resulted from a blow from some blunt instrument just above the left ear. The only hypothesis which could be deduced from the scanty evidence elicited at the inquiry was to the effect that while on his way to Mr. Arbour's house, Mr. Melray had unexpectedly encountered some person, or persons with whom he was in some way connected by transactions of either a business or a private nature, and that, in company with the same, he had gone back to his office, admittance to which he would obtain by means of his pass-key, after which he had lighted the gas and opened the safe. What had happened after that, beyond the fact that Mr. Melray had come by his death by foul play, there was not the slightest evidence to show. The body had not been robbed; neither, as the head-clerk's after investigation proved, had the contents of the safe been tampered with. As far as was known, the dead man had not an enemy in the world. Where, then, was the motive for the crime? By whom had it been perpetrated? Days and weeks went on without bringing an answer to either one question or the other. Within a few hours of the discovery of the murder Mr. Robert Melray, the dead man's brother and partner, was telegraphed for, and as, just then, he happened to be no further away than London, he was promptly on the spot. He it was who, a little later, and after all the efforts of Scotland Yard to unravel the mystery had proved unavailing, offered a reward of 500*l.* in connection with the affair, which, however, still remained unclaimed.

So much having been stated by way of prelusion,

it becomes needful, for a due understanding of the way in which Philip Winslade came to be mixed up with the Loudwater Tragedy, that our narrative should revert to a date several months anterior to that of Fanny Sudlow's letter to her lover.

THE NARRATIVE

CHAPTER I

ON THE EDGE OF A SECRET

PROBABLY there was no happier man in all England than Philip Winslade on the particular afternoon on which we make his acquaintance.

At this time he had just turned his twenty-eighth birthday. He was a thin, active, keen-faced gentlemanly young fellow, with an aquiline nose and very bright and piercing steel-gray eyes. In colour his hair was a light brown, and it was perhaps owing to the fact that he was clean shaven, except for an inch of whisker on either cheek, that he looked younger than his years; that he did look so was, however, undisputable.

The cause of his felicity was not far to seek. The fact was that, while on his way down from London that afternoon, the man of all others whom he was desirous of seeing, and who for the past week or more had never been out of his thoughts for long at a time, had recognised him as the train drew up at a roadside station, and having thereupon joined him in his compartment, had, by so doing, afforded him the opportunity to seek which had been the main object of his journey. The person in question was the Rev. Louth Sudlow, vicar of St. Michael's, Iselford—a portly, handsome man of middle age, and a dignitary of some importance among that section of provincial society in which he habitually moved. Just now, however, the Vicar's sole importance in the eyes of Philip Winslade lay in the fact that he was the father of a very charming daughter with whom that young man had seen fit to fall in love.

The chance which had not only landed the Vicar in the same compartment, but had left it free from the intrusion of other passengers, was too opportune a one not to be seized on by Winslade. For one thing, and with him it went for much, their accidental encounter would do away with the need for a formal call at the Vicarage as a preliminary to a request for a private interview—a species of cold-blooded proceeding which struck him with a chill as often as he contemplated it. Further, it would obviate the risk of his being seen and questioned by Mrs. Sudlow, an ordeal to which he was far from desirous of submitting himself.

'So you have got back safe and sound from your trip,' began the Vicar, as he shook hands with Phil and proceeded to settle himself in the opposite corner of the carriage. 'I hope you had what our cousins across the water call a "good time" while you were away.'

'On that score, sir, I had nothing to complain of; and, if I may be allowed to mention such a thing, it is gratifying to me to know that I was enabled to transact the special business which took me to the States to the satisfaction of those who sent me.'

'The knowledge of duties well and conscientiously performed can scarcely be other than gratifying to anyone,' remarked the Vicar with a touch of professional unction.

This being a remark which called for no reply, Phil remained judiciously silent. He was considering in what terms he could most diplomatically lead up to the subject which lay so close to his heart.

'When I tell you, sir,' he resumed with a little touch of hesitation, 'that I came back from New York to Liverpool by the *Parthenia*, you will guess at once whom I had the pleasure of having for a travelling companion.'

The Vicar rubbed a thoughtful finger against his nose. 'Really,' he began dubiously. Then his face brightened. 'Stay, though. The *Parthenia* did you say? Why, now I call it to mind, that is the boat Fanny and her aunt were to cross by. So you and she came over together, eh? It would beguile the tedium of the voyage for both of you.'

Phil smiled inwardly. The meeting of the two young people had indeed served to beguile the tedium of the voyage, but in a way the Vicar as yet had no prevision of.

'If I recollect rightly,' resumed the latter, 'my sister was always a poor sailor, but I hope that in that respect at least Fan does not take after her aunt.'

'Miss Sudlow proved herself a capital sailor, sir; but, as far as I am aware, Mrs. Empson was invisible from the time we passed Sandy Hook till we sighted the mouth of the Mersey.'

'Fan dropped a line to her mother as soon as she landed, but we have not seen her yet. We hope to have that pleasure a week hence, when, doubtless, we shall be treated to quite a budget of traveller's tales.'

So far the conversation had kept on the lines most desired by Winslade, but having reached this point, there seemed a danger of its being diverted by the Vicar to some less personal topic, in which case the coveted opportunity would be gone past recall. He pulled himself together. One breathless moment on the brink and then the plunge!

Philip Winslade, although in the ordinary affairs of life there were few men more self-possessed than he, could never afterwards call to mind the exact terms in which he contrived to blurt forth his confession. All he was conscious of was that he stammered and hesitated like a man afflicted with an impediment in his speech; that physically he turned first hot and then cold, and that by the time he had done he had worked himself back into a state of fever. The pith of the matter was that he sought the Vicar's permission to be received as Miss Sudlow's accepted suitor. When he had come to an end he gasped once or twice like a fish out of its proper element, and then sat staring helplessly at his *vis-à-vis*, who, on his part, returned the stare with interest through his gold-rimmed spectacles.

The Rev. Louth Sudlow had listened to Winslade's confession with very mixed emotions. Once or twice he ran his fingers through his short silvery hair and murmured an ejaculation under his breath; but he did not interrupt Phil by so much as a word, preferring to wait till the latter should cease of his own accord.

Then he said: 'My dear young friend, what you have just told me has, metaphorically speaking, taken my breath away. I—I am really at a loss what to say in reply. In any case, you must not look for a definite answer from me just now. I shall require a little time to consider the matter in all its bearings. To me, just at present, one of the strangest features of the affair is having the fact thus suddenly brought home to me that my little girl, whom I used to dandle on my knee as it might be only the other day is old enough to—to—well, as the homely phrase has it—to have a sweetheart of her own. Do you know, now, I had never thought of her in that light. So easy is it to shut one's eyes, and that not intentionally, to the flight of time.' He sighed gently, and again ran his fingers through his hair.

'One of my first proceedings on reaching home,' he presently went on, 'will be to lay your request before the dear partner of my joys and sorrows, even as you have laid it before me; for in the settlement of a question so momentous, and one which so nearly concerns a daughter's happiness, the views of one parent ought to carry an equal weight with those of the other. It is certainly in your favour that both

Mrs. Sudlow and myself have been acquainted with you for a number of years; indeed, it may almost be said that we have watched you grow up; to which I may add that we know nothing of you but what is pleasant and of good report.'

There was no time for more. As the Vicar ceased speaking the train drew up at Iselford station. Both men alighted. As the elder held the hand of the younger for a moment before each went his way, he said, 'You will find me in the vestry at eleven on Monday morning. Come to me then and there. It may be that I shall have something to say to you by that time.'

Small wonder was it that Philip Winslade deemed himself one of the happiest of men as he made his way through the soft April twilight in the direction of his mother's house. His disposition was of that hopeful and sanguine cast which refuses to see difficulties in advance, or, at any rate, to take but scant account of them till they absolutely block the way. Nothing, as he told himself again and again, could have been more kind and encouraging than the reception accorded by the Vicar to his suit; and, although he was vaguely conscious that he stood by no means so high in the estimation of Mrs. Sudlow as in that of her husband, he did not for a moment allow himself to be discouraged thereby. As he walked along the quiet road, humming to himself, Love's golden shuttle was at work in his brain, weaving the things of common life through and through with gorgeous and many-coloured threads, till they became clothed with beauty like a poet's dream.

Philip had not seen his mother since his return from the States. Neither in the note he had written her announcing his arrival, nor in the later one in which he told her that he looked to see her at Whiteash Cottage in the course of Saturday, had he made any mention of Miss Sudlow's name; consequently, he could not help trying to picture in advance the mode in which his news would be received by her. That she would be astonished he did not doubt; but that her pleasure would nearly, if not quite, equal her surprise, he scarcely doubted more. Dear good mother that she was! Had not his happiness been her constant study ever since he could remember anything? And it was absurd to suppose that, in a matter like the present one, where so much was at stake, she would set up any wish of her own in opposition to his wishes, or raise a host of futile objections, as some mothers have a habit of doing, merely that they may afterwards be knocked over like so many ninepins.

Although Mrs. Winslade was a woman who was singularly self-centred, who made a point of going very little into society, and, as a consequence, of seeing very little company in return, it had not been possible for her to live so many years in Iselford without making a certain number of acquaintances; but in all cases she had been careful to keep them so much at arm's length, that not one of them could with truth have arrogated to herself the warmer title of friend. Of such acquaintances Mrs. Sudlow was one; but not even she—pushing, undaunted, inquisitive little body though she was, with a faculty educated by long practice for fishing out the private concerns of those with whom she was brought in contact—not even she had been able to pierce the fine armour of reserve which Mrs. Winslade habitually wore, although some there were who never as much as suspected its existence. Like an alert fencer, the latter was ever on her guard, and the most innocent question, or innocent-seeming innuendo, never found her unprepared with a counter thrust. Her tactics, however, were far more those of defence than offence; and it was only when she felt she was being pressed unduly that she retorted by pricking back on her own account. Few were those who had the hardihood to try conclusions with her a second time.

But it was during the earlier period of her residence at Iselford, rather than latterly, that she had found it needful when in society never to be caught off her guard. During the dozen years which had elapsed since she settled down at Whiteash Cottage, coming from nobody knew where, and bringing no introductions with her, people had had time to get accustomed to her, to accept her as she was, and not to look for more from her than she was prepared to give.

Little by little all curiosity about her had died out. Society at Iselford had stamped her with its *cachet*, and had come to accept her (without professing to understand her) as one of its elect. Only in the heart of Mrs. Sudlow did a tiny mustard-seed, so to call it, of spite and dull resentment continue to rankle, which, occasion being given it, would not fail to strike downward and upward, and force its way to the light, as such baleful germs, even after having been buried out of sight for years, sooner or later contrive to do.

For be it known that Mrs. Sudlow was not merely the wife of the Vicar of St. Michael's—which of itself was a matter of no great moment—but was, besides, second cousin to Lord Beaumaris, and, consequently, an offshoot of the noble house of Penmarthen. Hence it was that not only did she claim to have a certain standing in county society, but she was also in a position to form a little coterie of her own among the lesser luminaries of the neighbourhood, of which she was the recognised chief; and it was Mrs. Winslade's suave, but persistent, refusal to pose as one of the coterie in question which had been the original head and front of her offending. Still, it is possible that the 'Vicaress'—as many people irreverently termed her —could have forgiven even that, if, on the other hand, the widow of Whiteash Cottage would but have made a confidante of her, and have revealed to her all those particulars anent her antecedents and family history which she was secretly dying to be told. But Mrs. Winslade, always smilingly, declined to do anything of the kind. She kept the Vicaress as completely at arm's length as she did her parlour-maid, and took one into her confidence no more than the other. Mrs. Sudlow believed herself to be a thoroughly good woman, and one by whose walk and conduct many might take example with profit to themselves; but it was almost too much to expect that poor human nature could quite forgive the way in which Mrs. Winslade had thought fit to repel her advances. This secret grievance, however, if such it could be termed, was of old date by now, and one might naturally have expected that, whatever virus had been distilled from it in days gone by, would have been rendered innocuous by the simple efflux of time; but it sometimes happens that a pin-prick takes longer to heal than a gaping wound.

When Philip reached home, in place of his mother he found a note written by her awaiting him. Mrs. Winslade had gone to attend the funeral of an old woman, who, when younger, had been for many years in her service. She expected to be back at Iselford by the train due to arrive there at ten o'clock P.M. Meanwhile Phil would have to dine alone, and afterwards, if he had nothing better to do, he might meet the train in question. It was annoying to him to find that he would be compelled to keep his news to himself for four or five hours longer, after having counted confidently on being able to pour it into his mother's sympathetic ears within five minutes of his arrival at the cottage.

When his solitary meal was over he lighted a cigar, and went for a stroll in the starlit garden; first, however, paying a visit to Leo in the backyard —who recognised him by his footsteps even before he spoke, and barked a boisterous welcome—and freeing him from his chain. All Phil's thoughts this evening were happy ones. More than once he took a certain letter from his pocket and pressed it fervently to his lips; more than once in his abstraction his cigar was unwittingly allowed to go out. It was abundantly evident that he was in very bad case indeed.

At half-past nine he set out for the station, taking Leo with him. He had debated with himself whether he should take the pony-chaise, but finally decided against doing so. His mother would probably prefer to engage a fly at the station rather than have Doxie put into harness at that late hour. He took the road to the railway mechanically, swinging his cane as he went. He was hundreds of miles away in fancy. Once more he was pacing the deck of the *Parthenia* with Fanny by his side.

Mother and son kissed each other with effusion at the moment of meeting. Then Mrs. Winslade drew back a step and took a long look at Phil by the light of the station lamps.

'You know, dear, it's two months—two whole months—since I saw you last,' she said, as if by way of apology for her scrutiny. 'A long time to me; but I don't see that you are a bit changed.'

Phil laughed. 'The only change, *madre mia*, is that I know a good deal more of the world than I did eight weeks ago.'

'A sort of knowledge, my dear, that is of little or

no value unless you have learnt how to put it to a good use. Of course I know already from your letters that you were thoroughly successful in the mission which took you to the States.'

'Most successful. But I will tell you all particulars later on.'

For the mother of a son who numbered eight-and-twenty summers Mrs. Winslade might be called a young-looking woman. Her figure was tall, and had not yet lost the fine proportions for which it had been noticeable in years gone by. Both hair and eyes were dark, the latter large and shining usually with a soft clear lustre which most people found singularly attractive. She had a rather long, straight nose, a mouth indicative of firmness and self-possession, and a well-rounded chin. All her movements, if touched with a certain stateliness, were easy and gracious, and if she was not in the habit of smiling very often, when her face did light up the smile brought out a hidden sweetness of which one had only been vaguely conscious before.

Phil engaged a fly, and presently they were being driven leisurely homeward, Leo trotting contentedly behind.

'Although it is so many years since Martha Dobson left my service, I hope, Phil, that you have not forgotten her,' said Mrs. Winslade presently.

'Why, certainly not, mother! My memory is not quite so treacherous as that. I was remarkably fond of Martha, as, I am quite sure, she was of me, and although I could not have been more than six or seven years old when she left us, I am not likely to forget her.'

'She belonged to that race of faithful, staunch-hearted domestics of which, I am afraid, there are very few specimens to be found nowadays, and I don't believe she would ever have left me had not her brother sent for her to keep house for himself and his six motherless little ones. I shall always respect and cherish her memory. She stood by me like the true-hearted woman she was through the great trouble of my life—and she died as she had lived, without breathing a word to anyone of the secret she had kept for so many years.' Mrs. Winslade spoke the latter words as if to herself—as if for the moment she had forgotten that her son was by her side.

Ever since he could remember Phil had been conscious, although he could not have told how or when the consciousness first came to him, that there was a secret in his mother's life, the particulars of which were kept as carefully from him as they were from the rest of the world. He had often speculated and wondered in his own mind as to the possible nature of it; but never had he ventured to hint, even in the most roundabout way, his wish to penetrate the mystery. To-night, however, there seemed something in his mother's mood different from any mood he had ever seen her in before. The death of her old servant had evidently affected her very deeply; hidden chords had been touched, and it might well be that scenes and incidents which time had robbed of their pristine sharpness of outline had for a little while been quickened into vivid life. In any case, it seemed to Phil that now, if ever, was the moment when he might look to be taken into his mother's confidence. He put forth his fingers in the dark, and having found one of her hands, he stroked it caressingly.

'I am well aware, mother dear,' he began, 'and I seem always to have been, that many years ago your life was darkened by some great trouble, as to the particulars of which I know nothing. You have just told me that in Martha Dobson you have lost the one person to whom was known the secret of your life, and such having been the tie between you, its severance cannot but touch you keenly. But, mamsie dear, I want you not to forget that you have a son, and that if one confidant has been taken from you, there is another ready to your hand. That your trouble was over and past long ago I am quite aware, but I am equally as convinced that it entailed effects from which you are suffering now and probably will continue to suffer as long as you live. Why, then, not——?'

'My dear Phil, you don't in the least know what you are asking me to do,' broke in Mrs. Winslade, her fingers returning her son's pressure. 'If I have hitherto kept this thing from you, and if I still continue to do so, I must ask you to believe that the motives by which I have been and am still actuated are such as I am fully able to justify to my own conscience. Trust me, you are happier, far happier, in your ignorance than you could hope to be if I made you as sadly wise as myself.'

'But, mother——'

'Is another word needed, Phil?' asked Mrs. Winslade gently; but that very gentleness, as the young man was well aware, veiled a firmness not to be shaken. 'Scarcely so, I think—unless it be this: that I only know of one contingency which would induce me to break the rule of silence I have hitherto imposed on myself with regard to a certain matter.'

'May I ask to be enlightened as to the nature of the contingency of which you speak?'

'You may ask, my dear boy, but you must pardon me if I decline to satisfy your curiosity. Be content to rest in ignorance. Believe me, it is better so.'

CHAPTER II

WHO IS MRS. WINSLADE?

ALTHOUGH the Vicar of St. Michael's, in the exuberance of his good nature, had allowed Philip Winslade to infer that there was no reason why Mrs. Sudlow might not be expected to look upon the young man's suit with eyes as favourable as those with which he himself was inclined to regard it, he felt far from sure in his own mind that such would really be the case. He knew that his wife was a woman of strong prejudices and narrow sympathies, who had a habit of nourishing petty resentments till they swelled out of all proportion to the original cause of offence, whether it chanced to be real or merely suppositious. For his own part, he would have gladly welcomed Phil for a son-in-law. He—the Rev. Louth—was, comparatively speaking, a poor man. There seemed little prospect of any further preferment for him; he had eight younger olive-branches to provide for, who were growing more expensive year by year; and to be able to get his eldest daughter off his hands, and married to one who he felt sure would make her a good husband, seemed to him one of those things devoutly to be wished. He was not a man of strong will, nor even one of those who contrive to mask their moral cowardice under the bluster of self-assertion. Dear to his heart were peace and quietness, more especially on the domestic hearth. As he rang the vicarage bell this evening his courage sank a little at the prospect before him. His conscience was too sensitive to allow him to shirk what he deemed to be a duty, how disagreeable soever it might be to him; but that did not render its discharge any the easier.

Dinner came as a brief respite. It was not till later, after the younger members of the family had retired for the night and husband and wife were left alone in the drawing-room, that the Vicar braced himself to the task before him.

Mrs. Sudlow was a small, slight, fair woman, with chilly blue eyes, pinched features, and a somewhat worn and acid expression; but whether the latter was due to the fact that she found the cares of a numerous family weigh heavily upon her, or whether it had its origin in those fictitious troubles which some women make a point of creating for themselves, hugging them all the more fondly in that they have no substantial existence, was a moot point, and one which, happily, no one was called upon to decide.

The Vicar laid down the *Times*, which he had been making a pretence of reading, hemmed and gave a tug at the bottom of his waistcoat. His wife was seated opposite him, busy with some fancy embroidery.

'My dear, I picked up young Winslade this afternoon, or, to speak more accurately, he picked me up, at Downhills station. He was on his way from London to spend a few days with his mother.'

Not the slightest notice took Mrs. Sudlow. Her husband might have been addressing himself to the chimney-piece for any heed vouchsafed by her.

Again the Vicar cleared his voice.

'From what he told me, it appears that he has been over to America on some special matter for his employer, and, by a rather singular coincidence, it so happened that he crossed from New York in the same steamer that brought my sister and Fanny. By the way, I don't think that Fan, in the letter she wrote us after landing, as much as mentioned young Winslade's name.'

'Why should she? Doubtless to her such a detail seemed too insignificant to be worth recording.'

This was not a very promising beginning, but there could be no drawing back now; whatever might be the result, he must go through with that which he had made up his mind to say.

'There may, perhaps, have been another and a totally opposite reason why Fan made no mention of Philip Winslade in her letter.'

'What *do* you mean? The older you get, Louth, the fonder you become of beating about the bush when you have anything to say.'

'That's your opinion, is it, my love?' he demanded, not without a shade of irritation. 'Well, then, in what I am about to tell you there shall be no beating about the bush—none whatever. Here, in a few words, is the long and the short of it. Fan and young Winslade met on board the *Parthenia*, doubtless as old acquaintances, they having known each other for years. My sister being prostrated by sea-sickness, they were naturally thrown much together, and by the time Liverpool was reached had contrived to fall in love with each other, and come to some sort of a mutual understanding in the affair. Had Winslade and I not met in the train, it was his intention to have sought an interview with me in the course of Monday next.'

Mrs. Sudlow's needle came to a halt midway in a

stitch, and the line of her lips hardened till the division between them was scarcely perceptible.

There was a brief space of silence when the Vicar had brought his statement to an end. Then Mrs. Sudlow said in her chilliest accents : ' And what, pray, might be Mr. Philip Winslade's purpose in seeking an interview with you on Monday next ? '

' What purpose but one can a young man in such circumstances have? What he is anxious to obtain is my consent—or rather, I ought to say, *our* consent —to his engagement with Fanny. Indeed, he went so far as to put the question to me this afternoon ; but of course I told him that it was impossible for me to give him an answer on the spur of the moment, or, in point of fact, till I had consulted with you in the matter.'

' I fail to see why you could not have given him an answer on the spur of the moment, as you term it.'

' Surely, surely, my dear, in a matter which so nearly concerns the welfare of our child, some little time for consideration is imperatively demanded.'

' None whatever, as it seems to me, where a person like Philip Winslade is in question. You might have given him his answer there and then, and thereby have saved him the necessity of seeking a further interview with you.'

'Um! That would certainly have been rather an arbitrary mode of procedure. But there is another view of the affair which does not seem to have struck you. As I understand it, Winslade and Fanny have already come to some sort of an agreement, in which case——'

'There is no need whatever why you should trouble yourself on that score. Fanny will be home in a week from now. I shall know how to deal with her.'

'And yet Fan is a girl of spirit,' remarked the Vicar drily, 'and when once she has made up her mind, sticks to her point like a limpet to its rock. I rather doubt, my dear, whether you will find her as easy to manage in this affair as you seem to anticipate.'

'I have not the least doubt in the world that, to serve his own ends, Philip Winslade has exaggerated a mere passing flirtation, such as is so often indulged in on board ship, into something far more formidable than it really is. In any case, as I said before, you may leave me to deal with Fanny, and, if needful, to —to bring her to her senses.'

'With all my heart. But why this display of animosity as regards young Winslade? More than once I have heard you hint that it would be a good thing if Fan were to make an early marriage.'

'I am not aware that I have imported any animosity into the conversation. I have merely brought to bear a modicum of that wordly prudence and common sense which it behoves all parents to exercise where the future of their children is in question, but in which, I am sorry to say, you are lamentably deficient.'

She paused to re-thread her needle.

'After all,' she resumed, 'if one may ask, who and what is this Mr. Philip Winslade with whom you seem to be so taken up?'

'Come, come, Kitty, you can't pretend that you are altogether ignorant of his antecedents. He is a clear-headed, energetic, clever young man, and, as it seems to me, sure to make his way in the world. He is a good son——'

'*Cela va sans dire.* It would be more to the purpose if you were to ascertain the amount of his income and the nature of his prospects—provided he has any.'

'Those were points, my dear, which there was no opportunity of entering upon in the train. But had he not conceived himself to be in a position to marry, if not just yet, in the not distant future, I do not suppose he would have spoken to me as he did.'

'Would you not be nearer the mark if you were to say that such "mercenary considerations," as I have no doubt you term them to yourself, never entered your mind?'

The Vicar coughed and proceeded to polish his spectacles with his handkerchief.

'You seem to forget,' resumed Mrs. Sudlow, a little inconsequentially it might have been thought, ' or, rather, you never care to remember, that Fanny is second cousin once removed to the Earl of Beaumaris. But there! I have known for years, to my sorrow, that you have not a morsel of proper pride in your composition.'

The Vicar's shoulders went up deprecatingly. 'My dear,' he said, 'if the noble Earl, your second cousin, had ever done anything for us, or had interested himself in our fortunes in any way, it might have been politic to bear the family connection in mind. But, seeing that neither he nor his daughters, the Lady Mary and the Lady Anne, care a stiver about us, it may be as well to leave the "claims of long descent" out of the discussion.'

Again Mrs. Sudlow's lips compressed themselves into a thin straight line. She felt that it had become necessary for her to shift her basis of attack. She had reserved one barbed arrow till the last. 'After all, you have contrived to shuffle out of the question I put to you, which was, Who is Philip Winslade?'

'My dear, you know as well as I do that he is the only son of Mrs. Winslade, who has been a neighbour of ours for the last dozen years, and who, in addition, is a lady for whom I have the highest possible regard.'

'Oh, I am quite aware that you always had a sneaking *penchant* for Mrs. W. She is what is vulgarly called a "fine woman," and I have not forgotten that your tastes always did run in that direction.'

The Vicar held up his hands. 'My love, you are forgetting yourself!'

'Not at all. If I may push my question further —Who is Mrs. Winslade?'

'You know precisely as much about her as I do.'

'Which is equivalent to saying I know nothing about her.'

'Her life for the past twelve years is before you to bear witness for her.'

'As much of it as she has allowed to be seen, and that, as you must admit, is very little. In the first place, Who was she before she made her appearance at Iselford? She planted herself among us without a single introduction. To this day nobody knows where she sprang from. She passes herself off as a widow—who can say with certainty whether she ever had a husband?'

This was too much for the Vicar. He got up abruptly, his face very red, and an unwonted sparkle in his eyes. 'For shame, Kitty; for shame!' he exclaimed. 'I never thought to hear such words from the lips of my wife. I will leave you to your uncharitable thoughts and retire to my study.'

It was not often in their little skirmishes that the worthy Vicar ventured to offer such a bold front of opposition to his wife as he had this evening, and through all the irritation and annoyance into which she had stung him he could not help pluming himself somewhat on his unwonted display of pugnacity. Still, nothing had been settled, no course decided upon as between husband and wife, and it was quite evident that the question would have to be reopened by one or the other of them. And reopened it was next morning as soon as breakfast was over, with the result that the following note, addressed to Philip, was delivered by Quince, the sexton, at Whiteash Cottage early on Sunday afternoon:

'My dear young Friend,—With reference to what passed between us yesterday afternoon, Mrs. Sudlow and I have come to the decision that, pending my daughter's arrival at home about a week hence, when an opportunity will be afforded us of ascertaining her views and wishes, the question at issue had better remain precisely where it is at present. Such being the case, it seems to me advisable that our interview, as arranged for to-morrow, should be postponed till a future date. You may, however, rely upon it that as soon as I have any communication to make you shall hear further from me.

'Pray present my remembrances to Mrs. Winslade, and believe me,

'Sincerely yours,
'LOUTH SUDLOW.'

CHAPTER III

THE SECRET TOLD

On their arrival at the cottage on Saturday evening it was manifest to Phil that his mother was very tired, and he debated with himself as to whether it would not be better to delay breaking his news to her till the morrow. But he felt that it would be hard to have to do so; so, after waiting till she had rested awhile, and had partaken of some refreshment, he drew his chair a little closer to hers and began.

'Mother,' he said abruptly, feeling at the same time a hot flush of colour mount to his face, 'I have not only brought you myself to-day, but some very special news into the bargain.'

'Indeed, my dear boy. By very special news I presume you mean news which I shall be glad to hear. Don't keep me on tenterhooks longer than you can help.'

'The fact is, mamsie, that I've fallen in love with

Fanny Sudlow (you know Fanny—have known her for years), and—and although it may seem egotistical to say so, I've every reason to believe she doesn't dislike me—indeed, far from it. My intention was to call on the Vicar while down here, and ask his consent to our engagement; but, by great good fortune, I encountered him in the train this afternoon so I took advantage of the opportunity to tell him what I am now telling you, and I must say that the dear old boy listened to me most kindly, and, in short, I'm to meet him at the vestry at eleven on Monday, when—— But, good gracious, mother, you are ill! What can I get you? What can I do for you?'

Mrs. Winslade had been lying back in her easy-chair; but the moment the confession that he was in love escaped Phil's lips her frame seemed to become suddenly rigid, while her face blanched to the hue of one at the point of death. Slowly her figure rose from its half-recumbent position till it sat stiffly upright, her long slender hands grasping each an arm of the chair. It was at that moment Phil lifted his eyes and caught sight of her face. He sprang to his feet in alarm, but his mother put up her hand with a restraining gesture, and he sank back in his chair, unable to take his eyes off her face.

'It has come at last—that which I have so long

dreaded!' said Mrs. Winslade, speaking in a hard dry voice, wholly different from her customary low and mellow tones. 'Of course it was folly to hope that the blow could be much longer delayed, and if it had not come now it must have come a little later.' She paused, as if to crush down the emotion which she found it so hard to keep back. 'To-day, when you asked me to reveal to you my life's secret, I told you that you knew not what you asked, and for your own sake I refused to tell it you. Now, however, you *must* be told. There is no help for it—would to heaven there were! My poor boy, you are about to pass from the land of sunshine into that of shadow, and it is my hand that perforce must thrust you there.'

'Mother,' said Phil, a little proudly, 'it seems to me that you underrate both my strength and my courage. If you, a woman, have been able uncomplainingly to carry this dark secret (whatever its nature may be) all these years, why should you fear that I, a man, may sink under the burden of it?' Next moment he was on his knees in front of her and her arms were round his neck. 'Forgive me,' he added, 'I know that in this, as in everything, you have acted for the best.'

'Mine is a terrible confession for a mother to

have to make to her son,' began Mrs. Winslade a few minutes later, when she and Phil had in some measure recovered their composure. 'As you are aware,' she went on, 'I have never talked to you much about your father. He died when you were about three years old, and to you he is nothing more than a name.'

'That is all, mother—a name. Whenever I have ventured to speak of him, which has not been often, you have seemed so distressed, so unaccountably put about, that I have refrained from questioning you about him, and have been glad to turn our talk to other things.'

'That I had ample cause for my reticence you will presently learn.' She paused, and sat gazing into the glowing embers in the grate for what, to Phil, seemed a long time. Then she roused herself with a sigh, and, turning her eyes full upon him, said slowly: 'Do you happen ever to have heard of a certain criminal, who was notorious enough in his day, but who by this time is happily well-nigh forgotten—Philip Cordery by name?'

'Why, it was only the other day, so to speak, that I met with a magazine article giving an account of his career, which had a strange fascination for me. He was known as "The Prince of Forgers." But what of him?'

'Merely this—that Philip Cordery, the so-called Prince of Forgers, was your father.'

'Mother!' was the only word that broke from the young man's lips. It was the half-stifled cry of one struck suddenly in some vital part. Horror, incredulity, and shame the most bitter, all seemed to appeal to her out of his dilated eyes to take back her words. Then with an abrupt gesture he rose. As he crossed the room a groan forced its way from his lips. Although the lamp had been lighted long before, the curtains were still undrawn; on these pleasant spring evenings it was the custom to leave them so till bedtime. Phil opened the long window and stepped out into the veranda. A fine rain had begun to fall; sweet fresh odours seemed to be wandering aimlessly to and fro; there was a sense of silent gratitude in the air, for all nature had been athirst. Phil stood there minute after minute, resting his head against the cool pillar of the veranda. His soul was sick within him, his mind was in a tumult in which nothing formulated itself clearly save the one hideous, overwhelming fact that Philip Cordery was his father, and that he was the son of a felon. As yet he only suffered vaguely, like one who, having been suddenly struck down, comes back to consciousness by degrees. He was stunned, he was dazed, the real anguish had yet to come. A dash of cold rain in his face recalled him in some measure to himself. He stepped back into the room and shut the window, and, crossing to his mother, he stooped and pressed his damp cheek for a moment against hers.

In Mrs. Winslade's eyes, as she sat fronting the fire, pale, erect, with that absolute quietude which comes from the intensity of restrained emotion, there was nothing to be read but infinite compassion—compassion for the son whom hard circumstance had forced her to smite thus sorely.

'So that is the secret you have kept from me for so long a time,' said Phil quietly, as he resumed his seat.

'That is the secret.'

'Well, mother, being what it was, I can't wonder at your locking it up in your own breast, at your safeguarding it from the world; still, it might, perhaps—I only say perhaps—have been better if you had told me years ago.'

'Ah, my son, do not say that! Should I not have been a wretch to cast a blight over your young life one hour before I was absolutely compelled to do so? But you know, or, at least, you can guess, why I have at length broken the seal of silence which I imposed on myself so many years ago, and have told you this to-night.'

'Yes, I think I know,' he said with a sort of slow sadness. 'After what I told you just now—that I had won the love of one of the dearest girls on earth—you felt that the time had come when I must walk blindfold no longer, when, at every risk, the bandage must be plucked from my eyes.'

'The necessity was a hard one, but there seemed to me no help for it.'

'None whatever. It will be a hard thing and a bitter to have to tell the Vicar on Monday morning.'

'After all these years, is there no other way than that?'

'None that I can see. The understanding between Fanny and myself has gone so far that I could not withdraw from it honourably, even were I wishful of doing so. No, mother, there is nothing left me save to tell everything to the Vicar and leave him to decide the matter in whatever way may seem best to himself.'

For a little while neither of them spoke.

Then Phil said: 'Mr. Sudlow is an honourable man, no one more so, and I feel sure, and so must you, mother, that your secret—or ours, as I must now call it—will be as safe with him as though it were still unspoken.'

Mrs. Winslade did not reply; only to herself she said: 'My poor Phil, you forget that there is such a person as Mrs. Sudlow to be reckoned with.'

Phil was bending forward, staring into the fire with gloomy eyes, his elbows resting on his knees, and his chin supported by his hands. 'Of course it is too much, altogether too much to expect,' he went on disconsolately, 'however good and kind-hearted a man Mr. Sudlow may be and is, that he will ever consent to accept me in the light of a prospective son-in-law. No; he will insist on the engagement being at once broken off; and, under the circumstances, how can anyone blame him?'

Mrs. Winslade still sat without speaking. Not a word of what her son had said could she controvert. His life was wrecked so far as his love for Fanny Sudlow was concerned, and she had not even a solitary spar to fling to him. Far more clearly than he she realised what must inevitably come to pass when once her life's secret had passed beyond her keeping and his.

After a little space Phil's sombre thoughts found a vent for themselves in another channel.

'Mother,' he said abruptly, 'it seems to me something incredible that I should really be the son of such a man as Philip Cordery.'

'It is none the less a fact which cannot be gainsaid.'

'He—he died in prison, did he not?'

'He did, years before we came to live at Iselford.'

Again for a little while the silence remained unbroken. Then Mrs. Winslade drew herself together like a woman who has nerved herself for the performance of a duty which, however painful it may be, must yet be gone through with.

'Now that you have been told so much it is only right that you should be told more,' she presently said. 'You shall hear my story once for all. After to-night I trust there will be no need for either you or I ever to refer to it again.' She closed her lids for a few moments like one conjuring up in memory the scenes of bygone years.

Then with her still beautiful eyes—large, dark, and just now charged with a pathos too deep for words—fixed on her son, she began: 'My mother was dead and I was living at home with my father, who was rector of Long Dritton, in Midlandshire, when I first set eyes on Philip Cordery. At that time he was a man of two or three and thirty—handsome, plausible, well-read, or so to all seeming; master of more than one showy accomplishment, and, in addition, a man who had been, or professed to have been, nearly everywhere. No wonder that I, a simple country-bred girl, who knew nothing whatever of the world, felt mightily flattered when this grand gentleman, for such he appeared in my eyes, began by complimenting me on my looks, and, a little later, went on to pay me attentions of a kind which could scarcely be misunderstood. Such being the case, it is almost needless to add that I presently ended by falling in love with him.

'Ours was a famous hunting county, and Mr. Cordery, who kept a couple of horses, had taken rooms for the season in the neighbouring town of Baxwade Regis. He was hand and glove with the master, Lord Packbridge, and was made welcome at several of the best houses round about. He won my father's heart, in the first instance, by putting down his name for a very handsome subscription to the Church Restoration Fund. I hardly know how it came about, but before long he began to be a frequent guest at the rectory. I suppose my father was taken by him, as most people seemed to be, and certainly I have never met anyone more gifted with the faculty of attracting others than he was. Well, there came a day when Philip Cordery asked my father to bestow on him the hand of his only child. Before doing so, however, he had drawn from my lips the avowal that I loved him. In what way he contrived to satisfy my father as to his means and position in life, I never heard; but that he did satisfy him is certain, seeing that my father gave his unqualified sanction to our engagement. I deemed myself the happiest of girls. We were married in the early summer and went for a month's tour on the Continent.

'On one point I must do Philip Cordery justice. He did not marry me for the sake of my fortune, which, indeed, was only a matter of a few hundreds of pounds left me by my mother's sister. Neither could he expect anything at my father's death, for the living of Long Dritton was a very poor one, and my father's purse was never shut against the claims of charity. It was a great blow to me when, within a couple of months of my marriage, my father died after a few days' illness; but when, eighteen months later, my other great trouble fell upon me, I no longer grieved that he had been taken.

'My husband had hired a small furnished house at St. John's Wood, London, which stood in its own grounds and was surrounded by a high wall. Its position was a very secluded one, so much so that it could not be overlooked from any other house. Your father had never enlightened me in definite terms as to the nature of the business in which he was engaged, but I had a vague notion that he was connected, although in what capacity I was wholly ignorant, with some important firm in the City. Sometimes his duties took him from home for a week or ten days at a time. At other times there would be days when he never went beyond the precincts of his own garden. He had given me to understand that his great hobby was experimental chemistry, and he had fitted up a room on the top floor of the house as a laboratory where he often worked till far into the night, and the door of which, whether he was engaged there or not, was always kept locked. Considering the number of people whose acquaintance he had made in the shires, it seemed strange that he should know so few people in London, but so it was. He belonged to no club, we saw very little company, and he rarely took me anywhere except now and then to the theatre. Such callers as we had were all men, many of them being foreigners of different nationalities. I usually got away from them to my own room as soon as possible, and Philip seemed pleased that I should do so.

'All this time, although many of my illusions

had taken to themselves wings, I was by no means unhappy. Philip, while never demonstrative, was kind in his careless, easy-going fashion; in fact, I may say that I believe he was as fond of me as it was in his nature to be of anyone. And then, by-and-by, you were born, and life seemed to me a sweeter thing than it had ever been before.

'It was when you were about four months old that the crash came. There is no need for me to dwell on that time, nor to recapitulate in detail all I had to go through. It is enough to say—and it may now be said once for all—that Philip Cordery was proved to have been the leader and guiding spirit of one of the most notorious gangs of bank-note forgers with which the present century has had to do. I saw him but twice after his conviction. A month or two after my second interview with him he died. A little later, through the death of an uncle, I came in for a legacy (taking his name at the same time), the income derivable from which has enabled me to keep up a home such as you have known as long as you can remember. At my death the capitalised amount will become yours to deal with as you may deem best.'

Philip had refrained from interrupting his

mother's narrative by a word; indeed, his interest in the tragic story she had to tell was too intense to allow of his willingly breaking in upon it even for a moment. When she had come to an end the silence that ensued was broken by a deep-drawn sigh from him. 'Poor mother! poor mother!' he murmured half aloud. It was on her and on all she had undergone that his thoughts were dwelling just then, rather than on that mysterious entity—to him he would remain for ever a mystery and a wonder—Philip Cordery, the author of his being; or even on the effect which his mother's revelation might have on his own future.

Presently Mrs. Winslade spoke again. 'You will now be able to comprehend one thing which has doubtless puzzled you more than enough in days gone by, and that is why I have led so persistently secluded a life, seeing so little company under my own roof and scarcely ever visiting anywhere. Never feeling sure from day to day that the secret of my past might not by some mischance become public property, I was determined that the good folk of Iselford should not have it in their power to say that I forced my way into their society under false pretences—that I had sought them out and sat by their firesides, being conscious all the time there was that in my history which I would be ashamed to have them know. It is they who have sought me out; it is they who have thrust themselves on me. In so far my conscience holds me free from blame.'

CHAPTER IV

IN WHICH MISS SUDLOW SPEAKS HER MIND

PHILIP WINSLADE did not accompany his mother to church on Sunday morning. His heart was still so sore, he was still so mentally shaken by his mother's revelation that, like the stricken deer, he craved for solitude the most absolute. It was a craving Mrs. Winslade was too wise to combat. She herself had suffered in like manner in years gone by, and her heart bled for her boy.

Phil still held firmly by his overnight determination to make a clean breast of it to the Vicar at their interview on the morrow, and it was so evidently the right thing to do that on no account would his mother have breathed a syllable in any effort to dissuade him therefrom. In the course of the afternoon the Vicar's note was delivered at the Cottage, and after a first reading it seemed both to Phil and Mrs. Winslade as if a brief providential breathing-space had been accorded them. The evil day was only put off for a time; but it was a respite, and they were grateful for it.

Further consideration of the note, however, made it evident that, although the Vicar expressed a wish to defer the Monday's interview till he should have had an opportunity of consulting his daughter, that was no sufficient reason why Phil should take on himself to delay his confession. Was it not, rather, his duty to tell everything to the Vicar before the meeting in question took place? With the latter in possession beforehand of all the facts of the case, it could not afterwards be alleged that any unfair advantage had been taken of either his or his daughter's ignorance of them. Clearly here also was the right thing to do.

Next morning after breakfast—such a breakfast as either mother or son had the appetite to partake of—Phil set out for the vestry. His mother kissed him and bade him be of good cheer; her eyes were dry, but there was a wistfulness in the smile with which she followed him as he left the house which seemed to have its origin in emotions too profound for tears. As it fell out, however, the Vicar and Phil were not destined to meet that day. The latter, on reaching the vestry, was told by Jabez Drew, the parish clerk, that 'his reverence' had been summoned from home by telegram and was not expected back till next day. Now, Philip Winslade was due back in London at nine o'clock on Tuesday morning. Evidently there was no help for it. He must defer what he had to say till the Vicar should appoint a meeting at his own time and place.

At this stage another difficulty confronted him. He had promised that he would write to Miss Sudlow and let her know the result of his interview with her father, by which means she would be forewarned as to the attitude her parents would be likely to adopt towards her when she should see them a few days later. But, as Philip asked himself, how was it possible, under the circumstances, that he should write to her at all? Nothing would have been easier than for him to tell her in so many words that the Vicar had postponed all decision in the affair till he should have seen Fanny herself; but how could he tell her so much without telling her more? He had written to her twice already such letters as it is a lover's happiness to indite, but how dare he mention such a word as love now with that hideous secret crushing him down like a veritable Old Man of the Sea? Neither could he tell his tale to her before telling it to her father. To have done so would have been to take advantage of the Vicar in a way his pride would not allow him to stoop to, and would, in addition, have the appearance of trying to secure, through Fanny's compassion and womanly pity, a promise to continue true to him which she might see cause to regret after the influence of her parents should have been brought to bear on her. Even at the risk of having hard things thought of him by her he loved so fondly, he would keep an unbroken silence till he had made his confession to the person who was entitled to hear it first of all.

Miss Sudlow went down to Iselford on Saturday by the same train that her lover had travelled by a week before. She had been puzzled and somewhat put about when day passed after day without bringing her the expected letter, or a word of any kind from Phil. That she put a score of questions to herself goes without saying, to none of which, however, was any answer forthcoming; and it was not without a certain vague uneasiness and dread of what the next day or two might have in store for her that she travelled down home. Nothing of this, however, did she betray to her mother, who, with one of her sisters, she found awaiting her arrival at the station.

Fanny Sudlow, unlike her mother, was a brunette.

She had brown eyes, frank and vivacious, a great quantity of dark wavy hair, and a face that depended more on character for its attractiveness than on any special charm of feature. As we shall presently discover, she was a young woman of spirit, with a strong sense of independence and considerable fixity of will, which latter characteristic her mother called by another name.

'My dear,' said Mrs. Sudlow, after she had embraced her daughter, eyeing Fanny's Saratoga trunk with evident dismay, 'pleased as I am, of course, to see you again, my hope was that you had only come to pay us a flying visit, and that, in point of fact, you had contrived to make yourself so indispensable to your aunt that she would ask you to stay with her altogether.'

'I am sorry to disappoint you, mamma, but I have left Aunt Charlotte for good and all. When I went to her you know it was only as a makeshift till her companion, Miss Pudsey, whose health had broken down (and I don't wonder at it) was able to resume her duties. Then poor Pudsey is terribly afraid of the sea, and Aunt Charlotte having made up her mind to go in person to America and look after some property she was afraid she was being swindled out of, probably thought that I should be of more use to her during the voyage out and home. Now, however, Pudsey is back in harness, so aunt and I have said good-bye, mutually glad to have seen the last of each other for at least a considerable time to come.'

'It is a pity, a very great pity, that you were not at more pains to conciliate your aunt; and she with so many thousands to leave behind her.'

By this time they had packed themselves into one of the station flies and were being jolted homeward.

'It is just possible that if Aunt Charlotte had been a poor woman instead of a rich one, I might have been at more pains to please her than I was. But, for my part, I've no inclination to fill the *rôle* of toady to a cross-grained and abominably selfish old woman, however well-to-do she may be.' Then, a moment later, she added: 'Not for a thousand a year would I willingly degenerate into a Pudsey.'

'Still, I cannot help repeating that it is a great pity you could not bring yourself to put up with your aunt's whims and little infirmities of temper, especially knowing, as you do, what a number of mouths there are at home to be fed, and what a little money there is to do it on. But of course it was too much to expect that you would sacrifice any of your ridiculous prejudices, whatever might be the gain to others from your doing so.'

Fanny did not reply; she was already debating a certain scheme in her mind which would reduce the number of mouths to be fed at home by one.

It was not till rather a late hour, and after the younger members of the family circle had retired for the night, that Mrs. Sudlow found an opportunity of being alone with her daughter. The Vicar, with a prevision of what was coming, had shut himself in his study on the plea of having to put the finishing touches to his morrow's sermon.

Mrs. Sudlow was not without her misgivings as to the success of the task she proposed to herself. Her preliminary skirmish with Fanny in the afternoon had proved to her of what stuff the girl was made. But the little woman was not deficient in pugnacity, and rather relished a battle-royal now and again, as tending to diversify the monotony of everyday existence. Only she would much rather that her antagonist should have been someone other than her daughter. In the present instance, however, there was no help for it.

'Your father accidentally encountered young Winslade the other day, when he was down here over the week-end,' began the Vicaress. 'From what

I gathered, it would seem that you and he met on the steamer which brought yourself and your aunt over from New York.'

The clear olive of Fanny's cheek flushed to the tint of a damask rose at the sudden mention of her lover's name. There was something in her mother's tone, an added flavour of acidity, as it were, which warned her that she was about to be attacked. A moment later her coolness came back to her in full measure.

'What you gathered was no more than the truth, mamma,' she said. 'Philip Winslade and I met on board the *Parthenia*, and seeing that Aunt Charlotte was confined to her state-room the whole way across, I was glad to have someone to talk to other than strangers.'

'I can quite understand that, my dear; and if the matter had only ended there no harm would have been done. Mr. Winslade, however, would seem to be gifted with an amazing amount of effrontery and self-conceit.'

'You surprise me, mamma. That he is occasionally a little audacious, I am willing to admit; but of the other qualities which you attribute to him I know nothing.'

'In any case, it would seem that you have studied him to some purpose.'

'There is so little to do on board ship except study one's fellow-passengers.'

Mrs. Sudlow was becoming slightly nettled.

'There is all the difference between a general study and an individual one. I have good reason for speaking of young Winslade as I did. May I ask, Fanny—and I trust you will give me a straightforward answer—whether you were aware of the particular object which brought him to Iselford a week ago?'

Again that tell-tale colour dyed Fanny's cheeks, but she answered her mother as calmly as before.

'I was quite aware, mamma, of the nature of the business which brought him here. He came to see papa and to ask him for his sanction to our engagement.'

'Your engagement! Can it be possible that the wretched affair has gone as far as that?'

'That is just as far as the "wretched affair" has gone.'

'You—you astonish me. I can't find words to express a tithe of what I feel. Do you mean to tell me that you have been cozened into an engagement with this young man?—that you have allowed him to extort from you a promise which——'

'Pardon me, mamma, but there has been no

cozening, as you term it, either on one side or the other. Quite the contrary, I assure you. My engagement with Philip Winslade is the outcome of my own free action. It was entered into deliberately and with my eyes wide open.'

'Oh, this is too much!' cried Mrs. Sudlow, her hands quivering with the excitement which she had some ado to keep under. At that moment she would dearly have liked to box her daughter's ears, as she had been used to do in days gone by. 'But, thank goodness, it is not too late,' she went on. 'Your father must interfere. The affair must be broken off at the earliest possible moment.'

'Did papa give Mr. Winslade to understand as much at their interview last week?'

Mrs. Sudlow paused before answering. She had taken it for granted that Fanny was acquainted with what had passed between the two men, but in so thinking she had evidently assumed what was not the fact. She would have given much to be able to assure the girl that the Vicar had already sent Phil to the right-about; but, with all her faults, she was a truthful woman where a question of fact was involved, and Fanny's question demanded a truthful answer.

'No, Fanny,' she replied; 'your father, instead of

giving Mr. Winslade his *congé* there and then, as he ought to have done, was weak enough to defer his final decision till after your arrival at home.'

'Dear, dear papa!' murmured Fanny under her breath. Mrs. Sudlow saw the added sparkle that flashed suddenly out of her eyes, but did not hear the words.

'Not that the result will be in any way different,' resumed the latter lady dogmatically. 'Your father must write the young man a note on Monday, informing him that the affair is finally broken off.'

'Indeed, and indeed, mamma, he must do nothing of the kind.'

'Why not, pray?'

'Because the affair, as you call it, is not broken off —in point of fact, it is quite a long way from being broken off.'

'Disobedient girl! And would you, then, persist in this—this entanglement in direct opposition to the wishes of your parents?'

'Pardon me, mamma, but I have not yet heard from papa's lips that he is so wholly opposed to my engagement as you seem desirous of making him out to be.'

'For all that, I tell you that he will write to the purport just now stated by me.'

'I should be very sorry for him to do so. The writing of such a note would simply have the effect of putting things in more of a tangle than they are already; and that is hardly necessary, I think.'

'Perhaps you won't mind telling me what you really mean.'

'Simply this, mamma. Even if papa were to write such a note as you speak of, it would not have the effect of breaking off my engagement. I have given my word to Philip, and only he himself could induce me to take it back, and I am quite sure he is not likely to attempt anything of the kind. So long as I remain under age my obedience, up to a certain point, is due to my parents, and I will do nothing in direct opposition to their wishes. But my engagement will continue to stand good just the same, and in two years and two months from now I shall be twenty-one.'

It was gall and wormwood to Mrs. Sudlow to be compelled to listen to this outspoken statement without seeing any means by which it might be gainsaid. 'You are a wilful, headstrong, disobedient girl,' was all she could find for the moment to say. It was a statement which Fanny made no attempt to refute.

'Neither you nor your father have an atom of proper pride about you,' resumed Mrs. Sudlow in a tone of cold acidity. 'Little did I think that any daughter of mine—the daughter of a woman who can trace back her ancestry for upwards of three hundred years—would ever condescend to marry anyone so low down in the social scale as Philip Winslade. I know quite well what his Lordship will say when he hears of it—for hear of it he must. He will say that you have disgraced the family from which (on your mother's side) you spring, and he will beg that your name may never be mentioned in his hearing again.' For once the little woman seemed on the verge of tears. For her the picture her imagination had conjured up was full of pathos.

Fanny bit her lip and waited for a few moments before trusting herself to reply. Then she said: 'With all deference to you, mamma, I don't care the snap of a finger what his Lordship may choose either to think or say—indeed, if it comes to that, I very much doubt whether he remembers that there is such a person as poor me in existence, and certainly I am not going to make a fetich of him. I have not forgotten that day when the Earl and his daughters drove over from Raven Towers, where they were staying on a visit, and condescended to partake of luncheon at the Vicarage. As for his Lordship, I remember that both in manners and appearance he struck me as being more like a small shopkeeper than a nobleman with a long line of ancestry, and the way he once or twice snubbed papa, who is much the finer gentleman of the two, made my blood boil, young as I was at the time. And then, when I was asked to show the Lady Anna and the Lady Mary round the garden, I have not forgotten with what frosty condescension they listened to my remarks, nor how they stared at my sunburnt cheeks, and my country-made shoes and my poor print frock—as if, taken altogether, I were a creature who had strayed by chance from another sphere. Do you think, mamma, that to themselves, or to each other, they would acknowledge that the same blood runs in my veins as in their own? No, I am quite sure they would not.'

Mrs. Sudlow cast up her eyes and shook her head. She could not but acknowledge to herself that she had come off second best in the encounter. All she could find to say was: 'You are incorrigible—yes, perfectly incorrigible; and I am at a loss to know why Providence has seen fit to afflict me with such a child.'

CHAPTER V

A FAMILY CONFERENCE AND WHAT CAME OF IT

It was quite by chance that Philip Winslade did not travel down to Iselford on the second Saturday by the same train that Fanny went by. As it fell out, however, he was detained at the last moment and had to wait for a later train. On Sunday morning his mother went to church without him. If Fanny had reached home she would be sure to be there, and it seemed better not to run the risk of a chance meeting with her on the way to or from church, in view of his impending interview with her father.

When morning service was over and the Rev. Louth Sudlow retired to the vestry to disrobe himself, he found his wife and eldest daughter there before him. Mrs. Sudlow had just taken up a note addressed to her husband which she had found on the table. ' Now, who can this be from ? ' she was saying as the Vicar entered. Fanny, who had recognised the writing, blushed and turned away, but did not answer her mother. The Vicar took the note, opened it, read it in silence, and then handed it to his wife. It was from Philip Winslade, asking the Vicar to name an hour when it would be convenient for him to see the writer on the morrow about ' a matter of urgent moment.'

'A matter of urgent moment!' repeated Mrs. Sudlow. ' What can that be, I wonder ? '

The Vicar did not reply, but there and then he sat down and wrote an answer to the note, naming, as before, the vestry for the place of meeting, and the hour of eleven.

It was only natural that, as Fanny walked home with her parents, she should feel somewhat disquieted. Why had her lover not written to her in the course of the week, as he had promised to do ? That he was at Whiteash Cottage was proved by his note ; why, then, had he omitted to accompany his mother to church ? Above all, what could be the matter of urgent moment he was so anxious to see her father about ?

As yet the Vicar had not mentioned her lover's name, nor as much as hinted at any knowledge of her engagement. But that did not surprise her. Probably he did not care to enter upon the subject on the Sabbath. Doubtless he would say what he had to say on the morrow. His manner towards her had been, or so she fancied, more than commonly kind and affectionate, and how could she accept that as anything but a happy augury? Had the news of her engagement displeased him, or proved a source of annoyance to him, he would scarcely have failed to make the fact patent to her in one way or another. She longed for the morrow to come, as young people have a way of doing. Never had the even-paced hours seemed to drag themselves to so wearisome a length. She was glad when bedtime had come, and gladder still when, after a restless night, she saw the April dawn begin to brighten in the eastern sky.

It wanted a quarter to eleven when the Vicar left home, and the clock had just struck twelve when Fanny, from the window of the morning-room, saw him coming back across the lawn. Her heart sank, so grave and preoccupied did he look. She would fain have opened the long window and have run to meet him, but her mother's cold eyes were upon her, and she refrained. When the Vicar entered the room two minutes later his first act was to cross to where his daughter was sitting, and taking her head gently between his hands, to kiss her on the forehead.

'Papa!' exclaimed Fanny, looking up into his

face with frightened eyes, and laying her hand for a moment on his sleeve. That he was the messenger of ill news her heart portended but too surely.

Mrs. Sudlow was too accustomed to reading her husband's looks not to know that something was amiss; but although her curiosity was keen to hear whatever news he might be the bearer of, she set her thin lips tight and seemed to be intent on her sewing and on nothing beyond it. The Vicar sat down in his easy-chair and proceeded to rub his spectacles with his handkerchief.

'Little did I dream when I left home this morning,' he began, sighing as he did so, 'that I should have such a strange and distressing story to tell on my return. Dear me—dear me! Who could have believed in the possibility of such a thing?'

'My dear, if you would but endeavour to be a little less prolix!' said Mrs. Sudlow. 'If you cannot see that Fanny is dying of impatience, I can.'

The Vicar hemmed and fidgeted in his chair.

'Really, my love,' he murmured deprecatingly. Then turning to Fanny and addressing himself directly to her, he said: 'I am afraid, my child, that what I am about to tell you will distress you greatly, but unfortunately the blow is one which there are no means of averting. The reason Philip Winslade wished to see me this morning was that he might impart to me, in strict confidence, a certain circumstance connected with his personal history which only came to his own knowledge a few days ago. It appears that when Mrs. Winslade became aware of the existence of some sort of an engagement between her son and you, and was told he was about to seek your parents' sanction thereto, she revealed to him the circumstance in question, which had hitherto been kept carefully from him. What she had to tell him was that her husband and his father was a certain notorious bank-note forger, Philip Cordery by name, who was tried and convicted upwards of twenty years ago, and who died in prison a little while afterwards.'

'Ah!' was the sole comment vouchsafed by Mrs. Sudlow; but although a word of two letters only, it can be made to convey a variety of meanings, and on the present occasion what it conveyed to the Vicar was, 'I always felt sure that there was something discreditable in that woman's past, and now you see how right I was.'

Fanny's cheek had turned a shade paler, but as yet she scarcely realised the full significance of her father's news. After the silence had lasted a few moments she said, 'But why, after keeping the fact a secret for so many years, should Mrs. Winslade have thought it needful to speak of it now?'

'Whatever may have been her trials and misfortunes, Mrs. Winslade is a high-principled woman,' replied the Vicar. 'When informed that her son was seeking to become engaged to a certain young lady, she revealed to him the story of his parentage as a measure of simple right both to the person in question and her parents. It would rest with them to accept or dismiss him as they might deem best, when the truth about him had been told; but in any case Mrs. Winslade was determined that there should be no risk of accepting him blindfold and under a cloak of false pretence.'

'It seems to me,' said Fanny, with a little glow of colour, 'that it was a very magnanimous thing of Mrs. Winslade to do.'

'You talk like a school-girl,' broke in Mrs. Sudlow. 'For very shame the woman could not do otherwise than as she did.'

'On that point, my dear, I must venture to differ from you,' remarked her husband in his blandest accents. 'I fully believe there are many women who would have continued to keep silence in the future as they had in the past rather than run the risk of spoiling their son's chance of marrying into a reputable family. Such persons might not unreasonably allege that the fact of their having been able to keep their secret for so long a time might be taken as a strong argument that they would be able to keep it for ever.' Then, a moment later, he added: 'Poor young fellow! I felt truly sorry for him. There was a touch of manly pathos in the way he told his tale, which affected me more than anything it has been my lot to listen to for a very long time.'

'It is an extremely disagreeable episode well ended,' remarked Mrs. Sudlow with an air of satisfaction, as her sharp teeth bit in two the thread she was sewing. 'Of course, you gave the young man his *congé* there and then?'

Fanny stared at her mother as if doubting whether she had heard aright.

'I told him that I would write to him in the course of a day or two—nothing more.'

'I think it a great pity you did not send him packing at once. I have no patience with such temporising ways.'

'But, mamma——' began Fanny, and then stopped at sight of her father's uplifted hand.

'My dear, it was not for me to dismiss the young man after so summary a fashion. It seemed to me due to Fanny that before arriving at any decision in

G

the matter, the whole of the circumstances should be made known to her.'

'There I differ from you *in toto*,' said Mrs. Sudlow with accentuated acidity. 'You are Fanny's father, and as such it was your bounden duty to give young Winslade clearly to understand that all is at an end between him and her, now and for ever.'

'But, mamma, all is not at an end between us. Far from it,' said Fanny, with that little air of determination which her mother was learning to know so well.

Mrs. Sudlow turned quickly on her.

'Girl, are you mad?' she demanded with a stamp of her foot. 'What way but one can there be of dealing with a man whose father was a forger and a felon, and whose mother for years has been passing under a name not her own? Why, even to shake hands with such a person would make me feel as if there was a gaol taint about me for days to come.'

The Vicar coughed uneasily. 'Pardon me, my dear, but your sentiments are scarcely such as become the wife of a minister of the Gospel.'

Mrs. Sudlow sniffed, but did not condescend to any reply.

'That Philip Winslade's father was what he was,' said Fanny, 'is Philip's misfortune, but in no wise his fault; and why such a fact should be allowed to affect anyone's estimate of him is what, so far, I fail to understand.'

Mrs. Sudlow's dull eyes flamed out as they did on rare occasions only. 'Do you mean to tell me, Fanny Sudlow,' she said with a cold, slow emphasis, which was the more effective in that her anger was so evidently at white-heat—' do you wish me for one moment to credit that, after what you have been told, it is not your intention at once to break off whatever engagement (oh, how rashly entered into!) may heretofore have existed between yourself and this unhappy young man?'

'You are right, mamma, when you term him an unhappy young man. But is not that the very reason why our engagement, instead of being broken off, should, if possible, be riveted more firmly than before? Who should stand by him now this great trouble has come upon him if not I, to whom he has given the greatest treasure a man has to give?' Her cheeks glowed, her eyes shone with an inner radiance—never, to her father's thinking, had she looked so beautiful as at that moment.

Mrs. Sudlow turned upon her husband. 'Louth, speak to her!' she commanded. 'If she has so far forgotten herself and the lessons of her upbringing as no longer to heed her mother's wishes and commands, it is to be hoped that this new evil influence has not yet obtained such complete control over her as to induce her to treat her father's admonitions as contemptuously as she has seen fit to treat mine.'

The Rev. Louth Sudlow felt that his position was anything but an enviable one. His sympathies were altogether with his daughter; but to a man who loved peace and quietness as he loved them, to sanction the unfurling of the flag of rebellion on the domestic hearth might well represent itself as a very serious thing indeed. Such being the case, he did what weak men nearly always do when they find themselves in a corner—he resolved to play the timid game of expediency, and to attempt the impossible feat of steering a straight course between two strongly opposite currents.

Addressing himself to Fanny, he said: 'My dear girl, while fully agreeing with you that in the case of a person who has been overtaken by a misfortune which he has had no hand in bringing on himself, and yet from the consequences of which it is impossible for him to escape, it is the duty of those who know him and respect him—and—and like him—to rally round him, and prove to him that though the world at large may look askance on him, he will find no change in them, it is still possible, I think, to push even so admirable a sentiment to a point at which it not only becomes Quixotic, but—but, so to speak, indefensible. And this, my dear, as it appears to me, is just what you seem inclined to do in the case under discussion. Young Winslade by his action in coming to me first of all has proved his entire willingness to release you from any promise you may have made him—such promise having been given in ignorance of what has since become known, and accepted by him in equal ignorance. The question therefore now is, whether you ought not at once to reclaim your promise, and release him from any he may have given you. Although at present, as far as we are aware, the knowledge of this painful episode is confined to us three, there is no knowing how soon, nor by what mischance, it may become common property. Think, then—consider, I beg of you most seriously—what in such a case would be your position as a member of a family which society (always terribly unrelenting in such cases) would shun and contemn almost as if it were plague-smitten. Are you willing for the sake of a passing girlish fancy—(you shake your head; but, knowing the world far better than you know it, I hold by the phrase)—to run the risk of overshadowing and embittering your whole future life? Strive to realise all that you would sacrifice by such a step, and then ask yourself what compensation you can reasonably expect in return. The wrench of parting might be a sharp one, and just at first the pain might seem almost intolerable, but time would heal the wound, as it does the wounds of all of us, and before long life would again look as bright to you, and as full of promise, as ever it had done.'

When the Vicar ceased he rubbed his white hands softly one within the other like a man well satisfied with himself. He had not been oblivious of certain contemptuous sniffs on the part of his wife during the progress of his little oration; but he was too familiar with such tokens of disparagement to allow himself to be affected thereby. Fanny felt that one of the most important moments of her life had come. Drawing a deep breath she said:

'Papa, when I gave my promise to Philip Winslade that I would one day become his wife, it was with no intention of ever taking it back, and far less than ever should I think of doing so now that a shadow has crept over his life of which neither he nor I knew anything when my promise was given. As for the world, or that small section of it which, as you say, would look askance at him and his if his story were to become known, it seems to me not worth a moment's consideration when weighed in the balance against other things. Disgrace comes but as we bring it on ourselves. Papa—and you too, mamma—permit me, therefore, with all due deference and respect, to say, once for all, that I have given my heart into the keeping of Philip Winslade, and in his keeping I mean it to remain.'

'If such be the case, my dear child, there is nothing more to be said,' remarked the Vicar.

'Nothing more to be said? Oh!' said Mrs. Sudlow, as she started to her feet, a vivid spot of colour flaming in either cheek. Then staring her husband full in the face, she said, in quiet, venomous accents, 'Louth Sudlow, you are a fool!' After which emphatic asseveration she swept slowly from the room with all the dignity of which so little a woman was capable, leaving father and daughter gazing blankly at each other.

A couple of hours after the somewhat stormy scene detailed above, the following note was delivered at Whiteash Cottage :

'Dear Phil,—Papa has told me *everything*. The only effect has been to make me love you the more, if, indeed, that be possible. This afternoon I am going to Frimpton to see my old nurse, who is ill, and I shall return by the footpath through the meadows between six and seven o'clock. You may come part of the way and meet me if you like.

'Always and always yours,

'F. S.'

They met at the stile where the footpath through the fields loses itself in the high road, about a quarter of a mile on the hither side of Frimpton—Phil being determined that the walk back to Iselford should be as long a one as possible. They had only seen each other once since their parting on the landing-stage at Liverpool, and they now stood for a moment or two, hand clasped in hand and eyes gazing into eyes, trying to read whatever secrets of the heart might perchance be revealed therein, and feeling their inmost being flooded with a gladness which, for the little while they stood thus, made speech seem an impertinence.

Fanny was the first to find her tongue. She withdrew her hand from Phil's grasp, and, instead, slipped it under his arm. Then they set their faces towards Iselford.

'Do you know, Phil,' began Miss Fan, ' it was very noble of you to come to my father and tell him what you did.'

'It was simply my duty. No other course was open to me.'

'But we don't, some of us, always care to do our duty, even when we see it clearly before us. And, in your case, I am by no means sure that it was a duty, or, indeed, anything more than a piece of modern-day chivalry, beyond the reach of folk of ordinary stature.'

'I am afraid you rate what I have done far more highly than it deserves.'

'I can, at least, think my own thoughts about it,' replied Fan softly. 'But poor Mrs. Winslade—what she must have suffered at finding herself driven to make such a confession! My heart bleeds for her.' As she spoke she could feel a shiver run through the arm on which her hand was resting.

For a minute or two they walked on in silence. Phil felt that it was now his turn to speak. 'My dear,' he began, 'in the note I received from you this afternoon you tell me that you only love me the more after what I said to your father.'

'I told you no more than the truth.'

He lifted her hand and pressed it passionately to his lips.

'But there are your parents to think of,' he went on. 'It is your place, your duty to consider them first of all. It is too much to expect that they should welcome to their fireside, or be willing to allow their daughter to ally herself to, the son of a felon. They would deem both her and themselves disgraced by so doing.' Here an involuntary sigh broke from him. 'Listen, then, dearest. Let the cost to myself be what it may, I here and now cancel the promise you gave me three weeks ago on board ship. Take it back and try to forget that it ever had an existence. We did not know then all that we have learnt since. To you a far different fate is due than to wed the son of Philip Cordery the forger.'

Fanny laughed a little laugh that had in it more of tears than mirth. 'You foolish, foolish Phil!' she exclaimed. 'And is that the sort of young woman you take me for? What a low opinion you must have formed of me! How strangely you must have misread me! No, sir, you not only have my promise, but I have yours, and I mean to keep it fast—fast—fast! So "no more of that, Hal, an' thou lovest me." As for papa, I feel sure that in his heart he admires and likes you to-day far more than he ever did before. He will never as much as lift his little finger in opposition to our engagement. With mamma I admit that it is different. She is not without her opinions, and there is always that fetich of our noble relations to block the way. But this she knows from me and clearly understands, that neither on account of our relatives (who care nothing for us), nor for any other cause—certainly not by reason of anything you told papa—will I take back my plighted word. I am yours, and you are mine.' Then, a moment later, she added: 'Beyond my father and mother, there is no one else to consider, for that your and Mrs. Winslade's secret is safe in their keeping cannot for one moment be doubted. The world will never be any wiser than it is now.'

In the face of such a declaration of unwavering love, so unfalteringly given, so instinct with loyalty and determination, what could Philip, what could any lover, have done save that which he did? The place was solitary, not a creature was in sight; his arms encircled her, he drew her to him, and then his lips pressed hers in a lingering kiss which was repeated again and again. 'O my love—my love!' he murmured. 'I am not worthy, indeed I am not, of all that you are sacrificing for my sake.'

With her head resting against his shoulder, she looked up into his face with a heavenly smile. 'Where true love exists there can be no such thing as a sacrifice.'

CHAPTER VI

IN WHICH MISS SUDLOW HAS HER WAY

ALTHOUGH Mrs. Empson, the Rev. Louth Sudlow's widowed sister, was a cross-grained, selfish old woman, to whom existence, unseasoned by the fulsome flatteries of Miss Pudsey, or one of her genus, would have seemed barely tolerable, she was not quite oblivious of the claims of relationship. She knew that, for his position in life, her brother was a poor man, encumbered with a numerous and increasingly expensive family, and it was probably her knowledge of those facts that was her inducement for writing the following letter:

'My dear Louth,—That you rarely trouble yourself so far as to inquire whether I am alive or dead is a fact which, with that regard for truth which is supposed to pertain to your cloth, but does not invariably do so, you would find it difficult to deny; still, it does not on that account follow that I should treat you and your interests with an equal amount of indifference.

'Although your eldest daughter, who, as far as I can judge, must, when young, have been allowed to have far too much her own way, and cannot now help betraying the results of her defective bringing-up, chose to quit my roof in a very abrupt and off-hand fashion, after flouting certain suggestions which, entirely for her own good, I was at pains to lay before her, I bear no ill-feeling towards her on that account. Indeed, were you here, Miss Pudsey, my *dame-de compagnie*, would tell you that one of the most marked traits of my character is that I invariably strive to return good for evil.

'As a proof that such is the case, I write these few lines to inform you that Lady Charlotte Mawby is looking out for a companion (who must be a young gentlewoman) for her daughter, who is somewhat of an invalid; and should you think it worth your while to allow Fanny to leave home in the capacity in question, I have little doubt about being able to secure the position for her. The salary would be thirty-five guineas a year.

'Don't shilly-shally over this offer, as you have

a way of doing over most things, but let me have a positive " yes " or " no " by return of post.

     'Your affectionate sister,

         'Charlotte Empson.'

'P.S.—Pray remember me to Mrs. Sudlow.'

 This characteristic effusion was like another apple of discord dropped among the inmates of the Vicarage. Needless to say, Mrs. Sudlow's indignation took immediate flame. What business, she should like to know, had Mrs. Empson to assume that *her* daughter, who was second cousin once removed (on her mother's side) to the Earl of Beaumaris, was desirous on her own account, or would be permitted by her parents, to accept the position of companion to any one?—much less to the daughter of a woman whose husband was nothing more than a rich tallow-chandler who had been created a baronet, for what reason nobody seemed to know, at the close of his year of office as Lord Mayor. It was like Mrs. Empson's low-bred impertinence to dare to propose such a thing.

 But fully one-half of Mrs. Sudlow's indignation was due to the tone in which the letter was written. It was gall and wormwood to her to have to submit to reflections on the manner in which her daughter had been brought up. And then, too, the way in which all reference to herself was relegated to a postscript! Yet she dared not, by way of retort courteous, wing even the tiniest of envenomed shafts in return. For her children's sake she could not afford to quarrel with their rich, but odious, old aunt. It was very hard.

But what was Mrs. Sudlow's amazement and bitter indignation when Fanny remarked in her calmly aggravating way that she felt greatly obliged to her aunt, whose offer had come at a most opportune moment, seeing that she had been on the point of asking her parents to allow her to look out for some such situation as the one in question. She was quite aware, she went on to say, that her father's means were cramped, and it seemed to her that she was now of an age when she ought no longer to be a burden to him, but in a position to earn her own living. Her next sister, Winifred, was quite old enough to help her mother with the younger children and to take that position in the household which had heretofore been filled by her—Fanny. In short, this self-opinionated young person made it clearly manifest that she was possessed by a strong desire to work out an independent position for herself, pending a certain event which just now was only dimly discernible as something which pertained to a far-distant future.

As regards this little episode it is enough to add that, in the result, Fanny had her way, and a fortnight later was duly installed as companion to Miss Mawby.

In her encounter with her daughter Mrs. Sudlow had been beaten 'all along the line,' but even in her defeat she contrived to extract a grain of comfort from the fact that, as Miss Mawby rarely visited London, but spent nearly all her time at one or another watering-place, either in England or on the Continent, it would not be possible for Fanny and her lover to see much, if anything, of each other. That they would correspond was a foregone conclusion, but Mrs. Sudlow had seen something of the world, and had very limited faith in the axiom that ' absence makes the heart grow fonder.' Within her experience she had not infrequently found that absence has a precisely opposite effect, and that young men—and young maidens too, for that matter—lacking the presence of the object on whom their affections are supposed to be fixed, have a habit of gradually cooling down and of being drawn, as by a magnetic influence which they are unable to resist, to worship at some other shrine, and to conveniently forget, or ignore, the vows they have already whispered in the ear of another. Fanny had told her parents that, as regarded her engagement, no further steps should be taken by her till she was of age; therefore did Mrs. Sudlow derive some barren comfort from the thought that in two years many things might happen.

She found it far easier to forgive Philip Winslade than to forgive his mother; indeed, the latter was a piece of magnanimity which transcended the scope of her limited nature. After all, the young man had not been so much to blame. Fanny was an attractive girl, and it was small wonder that he had fallen in love with her. The head and front of his offending lay in the fact that he had been presumptuous enough to aspire to the hand of one in whose veins ran the blood of the ennobled Penmarthens.

CHAPTER VII

PERSONAL TO PHIL

PHILIP WINSLADE had been educated at the Iselford Grammar School, whence he had gone, with a scholarship, to Cambridge. As he did not conceive himself adapted for either the Church or the Bar, after taking his degree he had cast about for an opening in a tutorial capacity by way of making a start in life. This he had not been long in finding in the family of a certain Mr. Layland, a wealthy London merchant, who engaged him to take charge of the education of his two sons—backward boys who had been spoiled by their mother, lately dead. Under Phil's supervision the lads soon began to make marked progress, and Mr. Layland had every reason to congratulate himself on his choice.

It was when his engagement with the merchant was about two years old that, as a matter of curiosity and more in order to kill a few idle hours than with any ulterior purpose, he took up and began to study the details of a recent mysterious robbery of bonds and securities of which his employer had been the victim, and which had baffled all the efforts of policedom to bring the criminals to justice. As it was, Winslade presently found that the task he had taken in hand had an absorbing interest for him, as also that it brought into play a certain faculty of analysis of the possession of which he had been only half conscious before, as well as a gift for the sifting of contradictory evidence and the marshalling in orderly sequence of a complicated array of apparently disconnected details, thereby enabling him to build up a theory which indicated how and where the missing clue should be looked for. The result was that Winslade succeeded in doing that which Scotland Yard had failed to effect. As a consequence, his success got talked about in certain City circles, and, a little later, he was asked to take another case in hand which so far had proved to be as great a puzzle as the previous one. Here again Phil was successful in evolving a clue which in the result proved to be the right one.

Such was Mr. Layland's belief in his tutor's abilities that when Phil's engagement came to an end, in consequence of the departure of his pupils for a public school, the merchant requested him to go to the States and there carry out a certain diplomatic business commission which, for reasons of his own, he did not care to entrust to any recognised member of his staff. It was while on his voyage back to England that he encountered Miss Sudlow and her aunt, and thereby brought about a crisis in the affairs of Fanny and himself such as had entered into the dreams of neither.

So unwilling was Mr. Layland to dispense with Phil's services that on his return from America he offered him an influential position in his counting-house at a liberal salary to start with, and with a promise of promotion before he should be much older. But tempting as the offer was in some ways, Phil, feeling that he had neither liking nor aptitude for a commercial career, found himself compelled to decline it. As the next best thing the merchant could do for his *protégé*, he recommended him to his friend Mr. Robert Melray, who just then happened to be in need of the services of a secretary and amanuensis.

Mr. Melray had lately returned from an expedition into the interior of Borneo, and Winslade's duties consisted chiefly in transcribing his diary, together with a miscellaneous collection of notes written in all sorts of places and under all sorts of circumstances, and in working up the whole into a connected narrative of travel with a view to its proximate publication in volume form.

Winslade, working at his employer's rooms in London, had only been engaged a few weeks at his new duties when news came to hand of the tragic and mysterious death of Mr. James Melray. Robert Melray at once hurried down to Merehampton, and Phil was left to go on with his task alone.

One day, about a month later, Robert Melray being up in town for the first time since his brother's death, seized the opportunity to call on his friend Mr. Layland. Naturally their talk gravitated to the strange circumstances connected with the death of the elder Mr. Melray, the younger brother deploring in forcible terms the fact that, despite his offer of a reward of five hundred pounds, so far not the slightest clue to the perpetrator of the crime was forthcoming. Then it was that Mr. Layland brought Winslade's name on the carpet, instancing the able way in which he had succeeded in tracking down the criminals in the case of the bond robbery, as also in the second case he had taken in hand, and strongly advising his friend to induce Phil to take up the affair *sub rosâ* and see what *he* could make of it. Robert Melray, who was ready to catch at the slightest straw in his burning desire to bring his brother's murderer to justice, did not fail to act on the merchant's advice. He went direct to Winslade, told him what he had heard with reference to his abilities in a certain line, and begged of him, as a great favour, to take the Loudwater Case in hand and bring all his efforts to bear on its unravelment.

It was not without reluctance that Phil acceded to his employer's request. He had a strong objection to being regarded in the light of a private detective, but the circumstances of the affair being such as they were, it would have seemed a very ungracious act on his part to refuse his aid, whether it might prove worth much or little, in the elucidation of the mystery of James Melray's death.

Accordingly, a few hours later found him at Merehampton duly installed in Loudwater House in the position of Mr. Robert Melray's amanuensis. Not a syllable was breathed to anyone that any ulterior motive was at the bottom of his sojourn under the roof of the old mansion.

But, as we have already seen, all Winslade's efforts proved, as those of the police had already done, wholly unavailing to trace the assassin of James Melray. The mystery baffled him as it had baffled them, and at the end of a month he went back to London no wiser in one respect than he had left it. A month or two later his services with Mr. Melray came to an end.

While he was taking a brief holiday and considering in what way he could best put to account such talents and experience as he possessed, a communication reached him from Mr. Layland. That gentleman was the chief promoter, financially, of a new weekly newspaper which was on the eve of making its appearance, and he was good enough to offer Phil an appointment on the staff. It was an offer which was gratefully accepted. The new venture proved to be a success from every point of view. Phil was still engaged on it, and was likely to be so for an indefinite time to come. He had at length found the *métier* which seemed best suited to his tastes and abilities, and that of itself ought to afford a large measure of content to any reasonable being.

A close correspondence had been kept up all this time between himself and Miss Sudlow. Only twice had they met, and that for an hour only on each occasion. Miss Mawby, the semi-invalid to whom Fanny filled the office of companion, as a rule detested London, but there were times when she was seized by an irresistible longing to do a day's shopping at the West-end, on which occasions she would rush up to town from wherever she might be, dragging Fanny with her, only to go back, exhausted and worn out, a couple of days later. On two such occasions it was that Fanny and her lover had contrived to meet.

Philip Winslade had never felt quite the same man from the date of his mother's confession. It seemed to him as if he had grown half-a-dozen years older in the course of the first few hours after he was told. Circumstances had forced him to confront the skeleton which for long years had been his mother's companion, and it seemed to him that its grisly presence would haunt him till the last day of his life. With it ever in the background, only felt to be there while he was mixing among the crowd of his fellow-men, but intruding itself as a ghastly reality on his hours of solitude, a measure of that sunshine which his life's morning had heretofore held had vanished, never to return. It was only his supreme love for Fanny which strengthened him and nerved him to oppose with all the power of his will the insidious encroachment of that baleful shadow which, but for that, would have gradually enfolded him in its chill embrace, and have darkened the issues of his life through all the years to come.

We now come to the date of the letter written by Fanny to her lover, the contents of which are already known to the reader. That letter was answered to the following effect a week later.

CHAPTER VIII

PHIL TAKES UP THE TRAIL AFRESH

'My darling Fanny,—That your letter, with its accompanying number of *The Family Cornucopia*, was a great surprise to me I at once admit. After reading it, I turned to the story, which I went through very carefully, some parts of it more than once, and I quite agree with you that the writer of it seems to have been mixed up in some, to me, inexplicable way with the Loudwater Tragedy.

'So much, indeed, was I impressed with several points in the narrative, so startling was the new theory of possibilities which it had the effect of opening up, so minute did the writer's acquaintance seem to be with the details of the crime, that a strong desire to find out some particulars about him, and, if it were possible, to make his acquaintance, took possession of me. All the more strongly did I feel myself urged thereto in that it was impossible for me to forget how thoroughly the case had baffled all my attempts at its elucidation.

'Accordingly, the following forenoon found me at the office of *The Family Cornucopia*, where, after having sent in my card, I was presently asked into the presence of the editor—a pleasant, middle-aged gentleman, Mr. Philpot by name. When I told him that my object in calling on him was to obtain the name and address of the writer of an article in such and such a number of his magazine, he shook his head and said with a smile that I was asking for a kind of information which he was not prepared to give save in very exceptional cases. To this I replied that my case was a very exceptional one indeed, and thereupon I went on to tell him of my connection with the Loudwater affair (leaving him to infer that I was still in the service of Mr. Melray), how struck I had been by the perusal of the story entitled "How, and Why," and proceeded to detail some of my reasons for wishing to make the author's acquaintance. After that there was no further difficulty. "Here is what you ask for," he said a couple of minutes later, as he handed me a slip of paper.

'"May I ask, Mr. Philpot, whether you have had any previous contributions from Mr. Frank Timmins?" I queried, after a glance at the name on the paper.

'"None that we have seen our way to accept. From time to time he has sent us several little things, none of which, however, have proved to be quite up to our mark; but the story entitled ' How, and Why,' was so far superior to anything Mr. Timmins had sent us before that we were glad to retain it."

'There being nothing further to learn from Mr. Philpot, I presently went my way. A hansom took me to the address in Pentonville which the editor had given me. Mr. Timmins, however, proved to be not at home. He was a single man, his landlady told me, and I further elicited from her that he was a reporter for certain newspapers, as also that the most likely time for finding him at home was after seven o'clock in the evening.

'Seven-thirty sharp saw me again at Pentonville. This time, fortunately, Mr. Timmins was at home, and I was at once shown to his sitting-room, which, I may add, was also his bedroom. He had just finished his tea and was in the act of charging his pipe as I was shown in. When his landlady disappeared she took the tea-tray with her.

' Mr. Timmins is a man of four or five and twenty, with a fair but somewhat freckled face, straw-coloured hair, and weak eyes. By the time I had been ten minutes in his company I had discovered him to be one of that numerous class of young men who have a very excellent opinion of themselves and their abilities, without having anything to offer the world in justification thereof.

'The first thing I did was to hand him my card.

'"To what may I attribute the honour of this visit, Mr. Winslade?" he asked, as, after glancing at the card, he laid it on the table.

'"I am given to understand by the editor of *The Family Cornucopia* that you are the author of a story entitled 'How, and Why' which appeared in a recent number of that magazine. May I assume, Mr. Timmins, that such is the fact?"

'He changed colour and hesitated for a second or two before answering. Then he said: "Really, Mr. Winslade, I am at a loss to imagine how it can possibly matter to you whether I am, or am not, the author of the story in question. Still, if, as you state, Mr. Philpot has seen fit to acknowledge the fact, I am not going to run counter to his statement."

'"Thank you for your frankness, Mr. Timmins," I replied, as I drew my chair a little closer to the table which divided us. "You may take it for granted that the information I am here to seek at your hands has not for its object the satisfaction of an idle curiosity; very far indeed is that from being the case. What I should like you to tell me first of all is, whence and how you obtained the information, in other words, the basis of fact, on which your story is built up."

'As before, there was the same hesitation prior to answering. Then he said: "I fail to understand why you should assume that my story has any, even the slightest substratum of fact, or that it is anything more than a specimen of purely imaginative writing."

'"That is a point as to which I can speedily enlighten you," was my reply.

'Thereupon I entered into the reasons, one by one, which had sufficed to convince me that, whoever the writer of the story might be, he was someone who had not merely a suspiciously intimate knowledge of all the details of the Loudwater Tragedy, but one who professed to account for the crime after a fashion so startling and original that I, as a person connected to some extent with the case, felt bound to ascertain what amount of truth, if any, underlaid his statements.

'Mr. Timmins listened with growing wonder, and when I had come to an end he lay back in his chair, and for several seconds could do nothing but stare blankly at me. At length he said: "It is, perhaps, a fortunate thing for me, Mr. Winslade, that my share in the story, or whatever it may be called, is one that can very readily be explained. To begin with, I am only part author of it. But perhaps I had better, first of all, explain by what a singular conjunction of circumstances the original MS. came into my hands. Possibly you may remember that, some months ago, several people were killed owing to a railway accident about a couple of miles beyond Eastwich?" I nodded. "I, sir, happened to be in the train when the accident took place, but was fortunate enough to escape with nothing worse than a few bruises and a severe shaking, while the only other passenger in the same compartment with me was killed on the spot. I had been to report the speeches at a great political meeting in the country, and was on my way back to London by the night mail, travelling first-class in order that I might be the better enabled to transcribe my notes *en route*. For a part of the time I was alone, but at some station, I forget which, I was joined by another passenger. I was too immersed in my work to take more than the most casual notice of him, and all I can remember is that he was young and dark-complexioned and had a black moustache. I did notice, however, and I had occasion to remember the fact later on, that after he had been some time in the carriage he took out of his pocket a number of loose sheets of paper covered with writing, and began to read them with what seemed to me the closest attention, making an occasional pencil memorandum in the margin of one or another of them as he went on. We were both at work, each in his own fashion, when, without any other warning than a prolonged shriek of the engine, of which neither of us took any notice, the crash came. All I knew, or felt, of it was a momentary shock, as if all my limbs had been suddenly dislocated, after which came an utter blank.

'" When consciousness returned, and I was able to realise what had happened, I found myself lying on the sloping embankment of the line, where I had been laid by the men who had extricated me from the wrecked carriage. A yard or two away lay stretched the body of my travelling companion, stone dead. A little brandy, administered by I know not whom, revived me wonderfully, and thereupon I woke to the necessity of recovering my missing shorthand notes, which doubtless were somewhere among the *débris* of the carriage. Feeling still too shaken and bruised to go in search of them myself, I gave a platelayer half-a-crown to find them for me by the aid of his hand-lamp. After a quarter of an hour he returned with a jumble of loose papers, which he said were all that he could find. Without looking at them, I thrust them into my pocket, and it was not till after I reached home, some five or six hours later, and came to examine them, that I found among them the sheets which my dead travelling companion had been reading at the moment of the accident, which the platelayer, in ignorance of their not being my property, had rescued from the wreck together with my own.

'" For the time being I laid them aside, but later in the day, when my own work had been despatched, I sat down to read them ; and next day, when I went down by train to attend the inquest to which I had been summoned as a witness, I took the papers with me. And now comes a very singular feature of the affair. The body of my travelling companion was never identified; nor, so far as I am aware, is it known to this day who he was; nor, beyond such information on the point as the railway-ticket found in one of his pockets afforded, whence he had come or for what place other than London—which is a big address—he was bound. He seemed to have been travelling without luggage of any kind ; his linen was unmarked, and there was nothing whatever found on him by the aid of which his identity could be established. Under those circumstances, I kept the dead man's papers by me, saying no word about them to anybody. As a matter of course, I took the precaution of looking carefully through them with a view of ascertaining whether they furnished any clue to the personality of the writer, but none such could I find. When I tell you this, Mr. Winslade, you will at once understand in what light I regarded the MS. To me it seemed neither more nor less than a rather clever little magazine story—a piece of pure fiction, in point of fact. As such I read it, and such I should have still believed it to be but for what you have told me this evening.

'"Well, sir, some three or four months after the unknown writer of the MS. had been buried, I said to myself one day, 'Why not write it out in my own hand, invent an ending to it, give it a name, and send it to one of the magazines? If it comes back it will only be one failure the more.' And failures in that line were things to which I was becoming pretty well used."

'Here I interrupted Mr. Timmins for the first time.

'"You say 'invent an ending to it,'" I remarked. "Had the MS., then, a different ending from that which it has in the printed story?"

'"I ought, perhaps, to have remarked before that it had no ending of any kind," replied Timmins, "but broke off abruptly at the bottom of a page. Whether the writer had never finished it, or whether, if a more thorough search had been made in the carriage, the continuation of it would have been found, I am, of course, unable to say. In any case, as far as I am concerned, unfinished it was; consequently all the latter part of the story, as printed, is from my pen."

'I at once saw how important a knowledge of this fact might prove to be, should the Loudwater Case ever come to be reopened. Laying the open periodical before him on the table, I said, "Will you be good enough, Mr. Timmins, to point out the place where the original MS. left off, and your pen took up the running?"

'After drawing the magazine to him and casting his eye over the columns, he said presently, marking a certain place with his thumb-nail as he did so, "Here is where the original writer ends and I begin."

'"May I take it, then, as a fact that up to the point indicated by you the printed story follows exactly on the lines of the MS.?"

'"As nearly so as makes no matter. Here and there a word may have been changed or transposed, or the turn of a sentence altered, but it may be accepted as being to all intents and purposes a faithful copy of the MS."

'You, my dear Fan, have read the story; so, when I tell you that the point at which the break occurs is where "Ernestine" and her former lover find themselves together in the old merchant's office, you will not fail to call to mind what a very important share of the narrative proves to be wholly due to the inventive genius of Mr. Timmins. And yet, perhaps, on further consideration, it is not really so important as at first sight it seems. You and I knew, the moment we read it, that the latter half of the narrative was nothing more than a farrago of fiction; but who, in view of the little that is really known of the causes which led to Mr. Melray's death, dare venture to assert that the incidents, as detailed in the early part of it, may not be based on fact? That is just what one would like to be in a position to determine.

'But to return.

'"By the way, Mr. Timmins," I said, "I should like very particularly to inspect the original MS.; indeed, I may add that I should like to take possession of it for a little while."

'"I am sorry to say that it is no longer in existence. I kept it till I heard that my story was accepted; then I burnt it."

'"Oh, you idiot!" was my mental exclamation; but aloud I only said it was a great pity he had done so.

'"Judging from what you have told me," I went on presently, " I suppose I may take it for a fact that there was no hint whatever in the MS. about suspicion fixing itself on 'Mr. Day,' the head clerk, nor anything about his arrest and subsequent trial and conviction? Neither, I presume, was there any mention made of the writer's intention to commit suicide?"

'"All those portions of the narrative were of my own invention. The thing needed an ending of some kind in order to render it acceptable to a magazine editor, and, to tell you the truth, I rather prided myself on the way in which I got over the difficulty."

'Evidently there was nothing more to be got out of Mr. Timmins. The truthfulness of what he had told me I did not for a moment doubt. He made no difficulty, before I left him, about pledging me his word not to speak of our interview to anyone.

'The first thing I did next day was to hunt through a file of old newspapers for the particulars of the Eastwich railway accident. What I there read confirmed Timmins's statement in every respect. One of the four victims of the accident was buried without having been identified. Still, it was just possible that someone might have since come forward and, by means of his clothes and the minute personal description of him which would doubtless be taken prior to his interment, have been able to claim him as the missing relative, or friend, of whom they were in search, in which case his name and address when living, with, possibly, other particulars concerning him, would doubtless be now in the possession of the railway authorities.

'But my hope that such might prove to be the case was doomed to disappointment. The next post took a note from me to the railway company, to which they promptly replied. No one, they informed me, had ever come forward to claim, or identify, the unknown victim of the Eastwich accident.

'My next step was to write to Mr. Robert Melray and ask him to inform me when and where I could have half an hour's talk with him. His reply was to the effect that he should be in town a couple of days later and would call upon me.

'My justification for so doing lay in the fact that in the MS.—supposing that any value was to be attached to its statements—there were certain allegations so seriously affecting the reputation of the widow of the murdered man that it seemed to me absolutely essential that the present head of the family should be made acquainted with them. It would then rest with him to decide whether any further action, and if so, of what kind, should be taken in the affair, or whether it should be allowed to rest where it does and remain an unsolved mystery till the end of time.

'Well, my interview with Mr. Melray came off in due course. As I think I have told you before, he is a man of strong feelings, although he shows little of them on the surface, and his burning desire to bring to justice the unknown person, or persons, who were concerned in his brother's tragic fate remains just as strong as ever it was. I found him more inclined than I confess I am to look upon the MS. (so to term that portion of the narrative found in the railway carriage) as a genuine recital of facts. To him it seems by no means unlikely that the assassin of his brother may, in very truth, have been a former lover of Mrs. Melray. Of course the question did not fail to put itself to him, as it had already put itself to me: Were the murderer and the unknown man who was killed in the railway accident one and the same person? And if so, was he also the writer of the MS.? But those were questions which he was no more able to answer than I had been.

'I had already cause for believing that the feeling with which Mr. Robert Melray regards his brother's widow is not of the most friendly kind. That to a certain extent she is inimical to him I cannot doubt. Consequently I was not much surprised when he avowed his intention of having the case reopened—to the extent, at least, if such a thing should prove possible, of testing the accuracy of the MS. so far as it concerned itself with the relations between " Ernestine," otherwise the wife, and her lover. But such a course was far easier to determine on than to carry into effect, and how to set about it was a point which puzzled both of us. Finally Mr. Melray and I parted without having come to an agreement as to any definite course of action. He has promised to call on me again three days hence. Meanwhile, at his request, I am going down to Solchester with the view of making a few cautious inquiries having reference to the existence there of any possible lover of Mrs. Melray prior to her marriage.

'And now to change the subject to something more personal to ourselves.

. . . . . .

'Yours unalterably,
'Philip Winslade.

'P.S.—If any further evidence were needed to prove that the story " How, and Why " is based on the Loudwater Tragedy, one might find it in several of the thinly-veiled names which the anonymous writer has thought fit to make use of. Thus, in the story Mr. Melray becomes "Mr. Melville"; the head clerk, Mr. Cray, is changed into "Mr. Day"; Silston, the chief constable, becomes "Dilston"; while, in place of Merehampton as the *locale* of the narrative, we are introduced to the town of "Hampton Magna."'

CHAPTER IX

A DEADLOCK

A FEW days later the train deposited Winslade at Solchester, one of those third-rate provincial towns where it is next to impossible to hide anything from one's neighbours, and where it seems to be the rule for everybody to know everything, or to assume that they do, about everybody else's business.

From this it followed that Phil experienced little difficulty in finding plenty of people ready and willing to tell him all there was to tell about the early life and antecedents of the Denia Lidington who later on became the wife of Mr. James Melray. The fact of her husband's tragical fate and the mystery which still enshrouded his death, had served to bring everything connected with her freshly to people's minds; indeed, the good folk of Solchester had come to look upon the Loudwater Tragedy as being a matter which concerned them nearly, if not quite, as much as their Merehampton neighbours.

The one fresh fact pertinent to his inquiry elicited by Winslade was that, while still little more than a school-girl, Miss Lidington had had a very pronounced flirtation with a handsome, but impecunious, ne'er-do-well, Evan Wildash by name, which had so alarmed the girl's uncle that he had sought out the young fellow and had there and then made him an offer of two hundred pounds on condition that he took himself off for good and all to one or other of the colonies. This Wildash had made no difficulty in doing, and, a couple of years later, tidings, the authenticity of which nobody had seen reason to doubt, had come to hand of his death by fever at the Cape. In any case, Evan Wildash had never been seen in Solchester again.

The information thus obtained seemed to Robert Melray to supply strong and convincing reason for accepting as an authentic record the MS. which such a strange chance had put into the hands of Mr. Timmins. To him it now appeared clearly manifest that Wildash had *not* died abroad as was reported, but had come back, had surreptitiously sought out the Denia Lidington of former days, had had more than one meeting with her, the last of which had been interrupted by the justly indignant husband, and that in the quarrel which ensued the latter had been foully murdered. Of all this Robert Melray was fully convinced in his mind. Scarcely more difficult did he find it to believe that Wildash himself was the writer of the MS. (although what his object had been in penning such a document was by no means clear), as also that he was the unknown man who was killed in the railway accident.

Winslade, while fully admitting the plausibility of the theory thus advanced, was by no means inclined to allow his judgment to be overridden by opinions so positive as those cherished by Mr. Melray. That the latter's theory might prove to be in consonance with the facts of the case, should those facts ever be brought to light, he was quite open to allow; but, on the other hand, there was a possibility that it might be at total variance with the truth. What he was willing to grant was that, had such a thing been feasible, it might have been advisable to reopen the case on the assumption that the statements embodied in the manuscript might be based on certain circumstances which all previous inquiries had failed to elicit.

But to have gone to the widow and challenged her with being cognisant of the existence and return of Wildash, as also with being an accessory after the event, if not a passive agent at the scene of her husband's death, would have been a brutal thing to do in any case, and infinitely more so in the event of the theory of her having had a former lover who was implicated in the affair turning out to be nothing more than a wild invention on the part of the writer of the manuscript. Be the truth what it might, such an accusation would only be met by an indignant denial, and one which there would be no means whatever of refuting. Finally, the two men parted without having arrived at a decision of any kind, to meet again by appointment a couple of days later.

Then Mr. Melray said to Winslade, 'It seems clear to me that I can do nothing, that I am bound hand and foot. Unless some further evidence bearing on my brother's fate, of which at present we have no cognisance, should turn up from some unexpected quarter, the mystery must rest where it does. It is a terribly unsatisfactory state of affairs, but one which I am powerless to alter.'

It was at Mr. Layland's house that the meeting took place; and now, when Phil rose to take his leave, the merchant, who had been present at the interview, pressed him so cordially to stay and dine that he could not well have refused, even had he been wishful of doing so.

As they sat after dinner over their wine, Robert Melray said to his friend: 'You have helped me from time to time in more ways than I could reckon up, and now I want you to help me once more. My mother has given me orders to look out for a governess for my little boy. He is just turned six, and I am told that his education is being shamefully neglected. Now, if you and Miss Layland will put your heads together and pick me out a likely person for the post in question, you will oblige me more than I can say.'

Phil pricked up his ears. Miss Mawby had died quite suddenly about three weeks before, and Fanny Sudlow was already looking out for another situation. After spending a few days at home she had gone to stay for a time at the house of one of her old school friends who was lately married. Her mother had not yet forgiven her for her refusal to break off her engagement to Phil, and Fanny felt that, for the sake of domestic peace and harmony, it was better that they should still remain apart; besides which she had no inclination to again become a burden on her father's resources, which were taxed to the utmost by the necessity of having to provide for those younger than herself. All these were matters within Phil's cognisance.

'There ought to be no difficulty in finding you the article you require,' said Mr. Layland. 'I will get my sister to pick out a few likely advertisements and see what can be done.'

'I hope you won't think it presumptuous on my part,' remarked Phil, addressing himself to Mr. Melray, 'but I may just mention that my mother is acquainted with a young lady, the eldest daughter of the Vicar of Iselford, who, from what I know and have heard of her, would, I imagine, exactly suit your requirements.'

'Nothing could be better. Let the young lady call upon Miss Layland, and if *she* is satisfied as to her qualifications, I am quite sure that I shall be.'

Thus it came to pass that within a fortnight from that date Miss Sudlow entered upon her new duties at Loudwater House as governess to Master Freddy Melray.

CHAPTER X

UNCHRISTIAN CHARITY

WITH all the emphasis of which he was capable, and, indeed, with far more than he had ever ventured to bring to bear before, the Rev. Louth Sudlow had impressed upon his wife the obligation they were under, as a matter of principle and honour, to keep inviolate the secret which had been entrusted to them by Philip Winslade. It was one of those things as to which it was not permissible to open their lips to a soul. It must remain with them as though it had never been spoken. To all which Mrs. Sudlow agreed; and although her agreement might be of that negative kind which is implied by the phrase that 'silence gives consent,' in her own mind she honestly meant to carry out the condition laid upon her by her husband. All that, however, could not, or, in any case did not, keep her from letting Mrs. Winslade see, whenever they chanced to encounter each other, that she knew the latter's secret, and in that fact found her justification for looking down upon her in a way she had never ventured to do before. Heretofore there had always been a certain show of cordiality between the two ladies. Whenever they met they stopped to shake hands and smile, and take stock of each other's bonnet, and make a few mutual inquiries about nothing in particular; but now Mrs. Sudlow passed Mrs. Winslade with the most frigid of bows, and a sort of drawing round her of her skirts, more metaphorical, perhaps, than actual; but none the less a palpable fact to the other. All of which said as plainly as words could have done : 'I know you for what you are—a woman passing under a name not your own ; the widow of a forger and a felon ; and, as such, not fit to move in that circle in which you have hitherto been received in ignorance of your antecedents.' These were moments of triumph to Mrs. Sudlow, and at such times she felt half inclined to condone the act which had been the means of putting such a power into her hands. Sweet to her was it to be able to stab this woman again, and yet again, who for twelve long years had so persistently kept her at arm's length, and whose airs of quiet superiority (on this point the Vicaress allowed her fancy too wide a margin) and general *noli-me-tangere* manner had been to her as a perpetual hidden sting, the existence of which was known to herself alone.

K

As time went on Mrs. Sudlow found her secret becoming more and more of a burden. If only she could have shared it with someone—if only she could have had one confidant with whom to dissect and discuss it in all its bearings. There were times when the longing to whisper it became almost irresistible; but she knew that her husband would never forgive her if she were to breathe the slightest hint of it to anyone. Weakly good-natured, and somewhat of a time-server, as the Rev. Louth Sudlow might be in some things, no man could be more rigid than he on a point of honour, or have a more genuine contempt for the mean and ungenerous motives which prompt the actions of so many people. No; however painful its continued presence might be, Mrs. Sudlow—so indifferent, as a rule, to her husband's wishes, so contemptuous of his opinions, and so habituated to having her own way—was yet in this matter afraid to take the embargo off her tongue which the Vicar (so foolishly and weakly, as it seemed to her) had seen fit to lay upon it.

One of Mrs. Sudlow's most intimate friends was a certain well-to-do maiden lady, of middle age, Miss Tuttilow by name, who, being very hospitable and fond of society, and without a grain of malice in her composition, was deservedly popular.

Miss Tuttilow had one brother, who, like herself, was unmarried, and who was a partner in a firm of London lawyers. In the spring of each year Gregory Tuttilow made a point of stealing away from business for a few days, and of spending a brief holiday with his sister, in order that he might be able to indulge in the fishing for which the neighbourhood of Iselford is so justly famed.

It was on an afternoon in the pleasant month of May that Miss Tuttilow, who never let a week go by without calling at least once at the Vicarage, said to her 'dear friend,' Mrs. Sudlow: 'Gregory has gone back home after a week of the best fishing he has had for years. By the way, the mention of his name reminds me of a rather curious circumstance which happened the other day. He and I had walked into the town together—he to buy some tobacco and I some feminine fal-lals—when whom should we meet face to face but Mrs. Winslade. She favoured me with one of her indefinite smiles, bowed slightly, and passed on. "You seem to know that lady. Who is she?" queried my brother, as he turned for a moment to look after her. Whereupon I told him as much as anybody in Iselford knows about Mrs. Winslade, which, as you and I are aware, is very little; and then, of course, asked him what *he* knew about her?

"Nothing at all," was his reply. "It was merely that she put me very strongly in mind of a person, one of your sex, whom I had occasion to meet professionally two or three and twenty years ago. The person in question was the wife of a notorious forger, Philip Cordery by name, who engaged our firm to defend him at his trial. I found Mrs. Cordery to be a very charming woman, and I pitied her from the bottom of my heart for being wedded to such a scoundrel. As it happens, I have a very excellent memory for faces, and really, allowing for the lapse of time, your friend Mrs. Winslade bears a quite startling likeness to the Mrs. Cordery of so long ago. But, of course, it can be nothing more than a coincidence." Singular, was it not, my dear friend? And it would be still more singular, would it not? should Mrs. Winslade and Mrs. Cordery turn out to be one and the same person. But even if such were the case nobody in Iselford would be able to prove it.'

'You are mistaken,' said Mrs. Sudlow, '*I* could prove it. I have known of it for the last two months.'

Miss Tuttilow jumped up as if a cracker had exploded under her chair. 'Goodness gracious me!' was all she was able to gasp out in the first access of her amazement.

Next moment Mrs. Sudlow could have bitten her tongue off with vexation. She had had no intention whatever of enlightening her visitor as to the extent of her knowledge, and it was not until the latter ventured the assertion that noboby in Iselford would be able to identify Mrs. Winslade with Mrs. Cordery, that she, all unwittingly, let slip that fatal sentence, which it was impossible to recall, and equally impossible to soften down, or twist to any other meaning than its few simple words conveyed. She felt excessively annoyed with herself; but that in nowise altered what was done. All she could now do was to minimise the effects of her indiscretion as far as it might be in her power to do so.

What passed further between the two ladies need not detain us. It is enough to say that when Miss Tuttilow left the Vicarage she was under a solemn bond of secrecy; but, whether purposely or by accident, she quite omitted to inform Mrs. Sudlow that she had already informed two other 'dear friends' of her brother's meeting with Mrs. Winslade, and of the remarkable likeness which he averred she bore to the wife of a notorious criminal.

As time went on it seemed to Mrs. Winslade that people, even some of those she had known longest, were beginning to look upon her with changed eyes.

At first she told herself that it was nothing more than fancy; but, before long, what had been a doubt deepened into a certainty. She could not be mistaken. Many with whom she had been on speaking terms for years now passed her with a curt nod, or a frigid bow, or even in some cases averted their eyes of set purpose, and made believe not to see her. Whenever an errand took her into the town she was aware that not infrequently people turned and stared at her, and sometimes whispered to one another, as if there was something about her which differentiated her from others of her sex. It was impossible for her any longer to doubt that her life's secret had become public property.

She would not blame Mrs. Sudlow even in her thoughts; she would not believe that the Vicaress, notwithstanding the veiled hostility which had existed between them for years, would, knowingly and of her own free will, do her so ill a turn. But, indeed, it would have been a matter of small moment to her to be able to ascertain by what mischance the truth had become known. The situation was an intolerable one, for beneath that calm and equable exterior lay hidden a proud and sensitive spirit, which, now that its secret armour had been pierced, lay at the world's mercy. Iselford as a home was no longer possible to her; she must seek another elsewhere.

'Where should she go but to London and keep house for her son?' demanded Phil, not without a show of reason, when the case was laid before him. She had given in her adhesion to the plan, but had not quite settled the date of her departure, when Phil came down to spend the week-end with her. Together they went to church on the Sunday morning, but, as they left after service was over, so unmistakable was the way in which they were avoided—it may be said shunned—by one group of whilom acquaintances after another, that, as they quitted the churchyard, Mrs. Winslade let her veil drop over her face, and Phil could feel that the arm resting within his was trembling. 'My dear boy,' she said presently with a pathetic quaver in her voice, 'if you can arrange to stay over to-morrow I will go back with you. The furniture and other things can follow later on.'

Thus did it come to pass that Mrs. Winslade was driven from the home which had sheltered her for so long a time by the 'look askance, the cut direct' of a number of so-called 'good' people, whose views, both mental and ethical, were as restricted and as incapable of expansion as the horizon of the petty provincial town in which their lot happened to be cast.

CHAPTER XI

FANNY AT LOUDWATER HOUSE

MISS SUDLOW and Phil made a point of writing to each other twice a week. With the ordinary run of their correspondence we have nothing to do; it concerned themselves only and was sacred to their own eyes. But there came a day, after Fanny had been about three weeks at Loudwater House, when she addressed to her lover a long epistle, which, as having an important bearing on the events of which this narrative is a record, is here transcribed in so far as it is needful to do so.

'In accordance with a promise which I made you some time ago, I now proceed to jot down a few impressions and opinions anent the new—and strange—little world and its inmates into the midst of which I was so suddenly transplanted three weeks ago.

'First of all, let me gratefully record the fact that

everybody is very kind to me, that my comfort is studied in a score of different ways, and that I am treated more like one of the family than a dependent. My pupil is a dear little fellow, quick at learning and of an affectionate disposition, and I am really becoming quite attached to him.

'I confess that for the first few days I stood somewhat in awe of Mrs. Melray the elder. You know what a stately, almost imperious, old dame she is, with a manner which at first strikes one as being reserved almost to the point of frigidity; but by degrees one discovers that it is nothing more than manner, and that under it beats a warm woman's heart, in which there is no lack of generous sympathies.

'That, at least, is how I construe her character, and I don't think that I am far out in my diagnosis. But it may be that I have been exceptionally fortunate, in view of the fact that two or three days ago Mr. Melray said to me, with one of his dry smiles: " I find that my mother has conceived quite a liking for you, Miss Sudlow. It is not often that she takes to anyone as she has taken to you." Of course it was very gratifying to me to be told this, especially as I had in no way laid myself out to conciliate the old lady.

'Of Mrs. Melray the younger what shall I say? I confess that in many respects she is an enigma to me. I was scarcely prepared to find her so attractive as she really is. Beautiful she is not, and it would be a misnomer to apply the term to her, but her face is one which I should think that seven out of every ten men would find singularly fascinating, in addition to which there is a strange but indefinable charm about her personality, which even I, one of her own sex, find it impossible wholly to resist. She is still curiously girlish, not merely in appearance, but in many of her ways, and when I first set eyes on her in her widow's weeds, it caused me the oddest sensation imaginable; indeed, I would not like to assert that a moisture, rare with me, did not dim my eyes as her tiny hand lingered for a moment or two in mine.

'To connect, even in thought, those guileless blue eyes, that milk-white brow, and that expression at once so candid and innocent, with crime of any kind, much more with a crime so mysterious and terrible as the murder of Mr. Melray, seems to me as if one were to draw up an indictment in opposition to Nature's own instincts. And yet there have been occasions when, taking her unawares, I have caught her scrutinising me with a certain indescribable something in her gaze which has not merely puzzled me, but rendered me vaguely uneasy. At such times it has seemed to me that, instead of its being I who was studying and trying to read her, it was she who was submitting me to a like process.

'I remember your giving it as your opinion that Mr. Robert Melray entertained no very friendly feeling towards his brother's widow, and the longer I stay here the more inclined I am to think you were right. But then, Mr. Melray is one of those dry, reserved, undemonstrative men, as to whose likes or dislikes it is somewhat rash to formulate too positive an opinion. Being the gentleman he is, it goes without saying that he treats her with uniform courtesy and consideration; but underlying it all there is a certain hardness and frigidity which, no doubt, are partly natural to him, but in part only as it seems to me.

'But, if one may be allowed to entertain some doubt as to the quality of the feeling with which Mr. Melray regards the youthful widow, there can be no room for doubt as far as his mother is concerned. That Mrs. Melray the younger is distinctly antipathetic to Mrs. Melray the elder unfortunately admits of no dispute. Not that they see much of each other, save at luncheon and dinner, and perhaps for an hour afterwards in the drawing-room. The dowager always breakfasts in her own apartments and spends the major part of her time there with her companion, a middle-aged spinster, Miss Armishaw by name, and an amiable nonentity. More than once young Mrs. Melray has spoken to me, in her prettily pathetic, girlish way, of the evident dislike in which the elder woman holds her: "I have done all I can in the effort to conciliate her, but in vain," she says; "so now I have given up the attempt as useless. I have been told that there are some women so constituted that they always dislike their daughters-in-law unless they themselves have had a hand in choosing them; and yet that seems a hard thing to believe."

'From this you will gather that the widow and I are on very good terms with each other; and such, indeed, is the case. On first coming here I arranged with the elder Mrs. Melray that the hour from twelve till one each day, weather permitting, should be devoted to taking Freddy out for a run in the fresh air. There is a big old-fashioned garden at the back of Loudwater House to which we sometimes limit our constitutional; but more frequently we make our way into the meadows which skirt one shore of the river and extend for miles, where the air is the purest imaginable. Well, on the third morning, as I was getting ready to go out, young Mrs. Melray came to me. "I should so much like to go out now and then with you and Freddy, Miss Sudlow, if you will kindly allow me to accompany you," she said. " Since my husband's death my life has necessarily been a very quiet one. I have hardly anyone to talk to and I go nowhere. It would be a charity to let me join you."

'What could I say except that I should be very glad of her company, and since then she has made a point of joining me in my walk every other day, or thereabouts. Usually she has not much to say on these occasions, and, as you know, I do not shine as a conversationalist, so that it sometimes happens that we pace along for a quarter of an hour, side by side, without a word passing between us; but she seems quite content that it should be so. Now and again, however, she expands a little and begins to talk of her own accord. In this way I have heard a good deal about her early home life at Solchester, together with sundry particulars concerning her school-days; but no syllable bearing, directly or indirectly, on the existence of any possible lover in the days before her late husband asked her to be his wife. Her mention of Mr. Melray is of the rarest; but when she does speak of him, it is more as if she were referring to some near and dear elderly relative than to a husband whom she has lost. I see no reason for doubting that she cherishes a very warm regard for his memory. To the tragic circumstances of his death she never alludes even in the remotest degree. One can well imagine that for her the subject is too dreadful a one to bear talking about. It is impossible to help feeling sorry for her when one calls to mind the nature of the calamity which has overshadowed her young life.

'Loudwater House has few visitors. Occasionally someone calls upon the dowager Mrs. Melray, and since my arrival two of young Mrs. Melray's former associates at Solchester have been to visit her. The people we see most of are staid, practical-minded Mr. Cray, who has been head-clerk to the firm for the last quarter of a century, and Mr. Richard Dyson, a kinsman of the Messrs. Melray, who has been in the employ of the firm since he was quite a youth. These two Mr. Melray frequently brings upstairs with him to dinner. Knowing so little of the business as he does, and liking it still less, he is almost wholly dependent on them for its conduct and efficient working. You will remember Mr. Dyson as a particularly good-looking young man, with a cool *dégagé* manner, stylishly dressed, and with the air of one who knows how to appraise his personal advantages at their full value. He is a great favourite with the elder Mrs.

Melray—a result probably due in part to his own pleasant qualities, and in part to the fact that he is the only son of a niece whom in bygone years the dowager regarded almost in the light of a daughter. As his kinsman's assistant in business, he has proved to be everything that could be wished—so Mrs. Melray herself gives me to understand—and there is little doubt that, had Mr. James Melray lived, he would, in the course of a few years, have been made a partner in the firm.

'But if Richard Dyson is a favourite with his own relatives, the same cannot be said of him with regard to his kinsman's widow. That there is a marked coolness between the two cannot escape the notice of anyone who has eyes to see. They address each other no oftener than is absolutely necessary, and on those evenings when Mr. Dyson dines with us Mrs. Melray retires to her room an hour or more before her usual time. But whatever this state of things may be the outcome of in no wise concerns me. In our frequent walks together Mr. Dyson's name is never mentioned between the widow and myself.

'And now, my dear Phil, I think I have told you all there is to tell that would be likely in any way to interest you. After having been used for a long time to Miss Mawby's restless peregrinations, life at

Loudwater House is, in comparison, pleasant and home-like. Dull I have not yet found it; indeed, on that point I have no fear whatever. It seems hard to believe that so short a time ago a tragedy so dire was enacted under the roof of this old mansion, where already the wheels of life move as noiselessly and methodically as if actuated by clockwork, and where one might easily imagine, but for the black dresses of the ladies, that nothing out of the common ever had happened or ever could happen. Has the drama, then, come to an end? Is there nothing more to follow? or has the curtain yet to rise on another act? *Chi vivra verra.* Not a word more; but, instead, a kiss—nay, a score. (Oh, fie! fie!)

'FAN.'

CHAPTER XII

MRS. MELRAY THE YOUNGER IN A NEW LIGHT

ONE morning, about a fortnight subsequently to the date of the letter embodied in our last chapter, Winslade was surprised to receive by post a somewhat bulky package addressed to him in Fanny's familiar hand. He opened it wonderingly, and his wonder was in nowise lessened by what he found therein. First of all there was a long letter from Fanny, and, secondly, a manuscript in a different writing, tied round with narrow white ribbon.

After requesting that Phil would not open the manuscript till he should have read what she had to say, Fanny went on as follows :

'From what I have already told you at different times, you will readily comprehend that Mrs. Melray the younger has a great deal of spare time on her hands which, I have no doubt, she sometimes finds it rather difficult to get through with satisfaction to herself. Previously to her husband's death (this is what she tells me), she subscribed to the local library; but, as a consequence of that event, her subscription has been allowed to lapse, and she is unwilling to take it up again just yet, feeling sure in her own mind that such a step would be disapproved of by her mother-in-law as savouring of disrespect for the dead. Now, the stock of books at Loudwater House is limited in number, and comprises but few volumes which would be likely to interest a young woman like Mrs. Melray, who has no special pursuits and no tastes in particular, unless it be a love of fiction (in its narrative form), which seems to be a part of the natural endowment of our sex. Under these circumstances, Mrs. Melray has several times asked me for the loan of whatever books or magazines I may happen to have by me (and, thanks to you, dear, I am kept pretty well supplied with both), a request with which I have very willingly complied.

'Well, in the course of the afternoon of Tuesday last, she came to me in the school-room to ask me whether I had anything by me which she had not yet read. As it happened, she had already pretty well exhausted my current supply. Then suddenly, while I stood with my finger on my lip, wondering whether I had anything left which would be likely to suit her, a great temptation assailed me. Low down in my heart a voice whispered: "Why not give her 'How, and Why' to read? That it will startle and surprise her can hardly be doubted, for whether she is as innocent as I believe her to be, or whether, if she chose to do so, she could clear up the mystery of her husband's death, the story can scarcely fail to recall vividly to her mind every circumstance connected with that event, while it is next to impossible to credit that she can be so blind as not to comprehend that, intermixed with a lot of fictitious matter, it is the story of Mr. Melray's tragical end which is being thus retold by some unknown pen. Scarcely less can she fail to see that the 'old man's darling,' who plays such an important part in the narrative, is intended for none other than herself. In any case, the reading of it by her can do no possible harm, and there is just a chance—a very faint one, I admit—that something unforeseen may result therefrom."

'(That something unforeseen *has* resulted therefrom you will presently have ample proof.)

'Such were the thoughts that flashed through my mind during the three or four seconds that I stood with my finger on my lip. Then, turning to Mrs. Melray, I said: "I am afraid that you have all but exhausted my supply till a fresh one comes to hand. However, I will see what I can find."

'I confess that my heart beat a little faster than common as I brought from my bedroom the number of *The Family Cornucopia*, and placed it in her hands. So lonely is her life that she spends an hour or two most forenoons in the school-room with Freddy and me; accordingly I was not at all surprised when she drew her chair up to the fire and settled herself for what she calls a " comfortable read."

'I watched her furtively, feeling pretty sure that, as a child picks the biggest currants out of its cake first of all, so would she pick out the story " How, and Why" from the rest of the somewhat dry and jejune contents of the magazine. First her face flushed, and then, a few seconds later, paled as suddenly; then she flashed a look at me and caught my eyes fixed on her, with, it may be, a directness in their gaze which she found somewhat disconcerting. Anyhow, hers were the first to drop. For a minute or more she sat staring into the fire, her little pearly teeth biting into the crimson of her under-lip. Then, as if she had come to some resolve, she got up suddenly, and, looking me steadily in the face, said in tones as steady as her gaze: " It is not often that I am troubled with a headache, but one has laid hold of me this afternoon. If you don't mind, dear Miss Sudlow, I will take this magazine to my own room and read it there." Of course I told her that I did not mind in the least, and that I hoped her headache would soon pass off. Whereupon, with the palm of one hand pressed to her brow, and smiling a little strangely, she went, taking the story with her.

'For the rest of the day nothing more was seen of Mrs. Melray. At dinner-time she sent down word that she had a bad headache, and apparently she had not got rid of it by next morning, seeing that she failed to appear at the breakfast-table, neither was she visible at luncheon. But a surprise was in store for me. In the course of the afternoon a note was brought me by Charlotte the housemaid. Here it is:

'"Dear Miss Sudlow,—Will you oblige me by coming to my room as soon as Freddy's lessons for the day are over?

'"Yours sincerely,
'" DENIA MELRAY."

'I am afraid that for the rest of the afternoon Master Freddy and his lessons received but a very perfunctory attention at my hands. Much to the boy's delight, I dismissed him a quarter-of-an-hour before the usual time, and five minutes later found me at the door of the widow's private sitting-room, which, during her husband's lifetime, had been known as the small drawing-room. After a preliminary tap I turned the handle and went in.

'Mrs. Melray was half sitting, half reclining on a couch. The blinds were part way down, so that the room was in semi-darkness, and as she reclined there in the glow of the firelight, with her aureole of pale gold hair, with the delicate ivory contours of her face thrown into relief against the embroidered cushion which supported her head, and with the graceful folds of her sombre draperies wrapping her round, she made indeed a charming picture.

'"I have asked you to come here," she began, "because we shall be more free from interruption than we should be anywhere else." Then, with a touch of bitterness, she added: "From morning till night no one ever intrudes upon me here. In all England there can be few more lonely mortals than I. But I am getting used to it by this time. Don't sit there, Miss Sudlow, half a mile away from me. Here is a chair that will suit itself deliciously to the curves of your back. Come and try it."

'As soon as I was settled in the chair indicated by her, she said: "That was rather a curious story you gave me to read yesterday. But before saying more about it, I want to ask you a certain question. Of course you can please yourself about answering it; but, in any case, I trust you will not be offended by my asking it."

'She paused as if expecting me to say something.

'"I don't think there's much likelihood, Mrs. Melray, of my being offended by any question you may choose to put to me."

'"It is very nice of you to say so, and yet—— But here is my question without further preface. (Now, dear, remember, no offence!) Are you, or are you not, the *fiancée* of Mr. Philip Winslade, who was here on a visit of several weeks' duration a little while ago?"

'Her question took me so by surprise that not to save my life could I have kept back the rush of telltale colour that dyed my cheeks.

'Next moment, to my surprise, Mrs. Melray clapped her hands, as a child might have done, and broke into a low rippling laugh.

'"I can see that I guessed rightly," she exclaimed, "for, after all, my question was only a guess."

'"Yes," I said, "you have guessed rightly. Mr. Winslade and I are, and have been for some time, engaged." Although I spoke gravely, I felt in no degree offended by her question, and she saw it. "But, if I may put a question in my turn, Mrs. Melray," I went on after a momentary pause, "what were the grounds which led you to the assumption that a tie of any kind existed between Mr. Winslade and myself, or even that we were as much as known to each other?"

'"The explanation is a very simple one, as you shall hear. One day last week I had just come in from my walk and was passing through the hall, when my eye was caught by some letters on the table, which had arrived by the afternoon post. Thinking that perhaps one of them might be for me (although such an event would indeed be a rarity) I took them up to examine the addresses. There was none for me, but there was one for 'Miss Sudlow,' which was sealed with wax as though it might contain something of value. I suppose it was a touch of natural curiosity that caused me to turn the letter over and examine the seal, which proved to be a representation of an Assyrian winged bull, and the same instant my memory recalled the fact that attached to Mr. Winslade's watch-guard was an intaglio which represented a winged bull. The inference to be drawn was an obvious one, at least it seemed so to me, and, as the event has proved, it was a correct one."

'It began to dawn upon me that there might be more, much more, behind those guileless blue orbs and that candid brow than either you or I had dreamed of.

'" Your powers, both of observation and deduction, seem to have been cultivated to some purpose," I remarked drily.

'" I am not quite sure that I follow you," she answered, with a puzzled look, which might be genuine, but might just as easily be assumed. " You must bear in mind that I am not clever in the way you are. But now that you have been so frank with me on one point, perhaps you will be equally so on another. What special object, may I ask, had you in view in giving me a certain story to read ? "

'This was a question the answer to which demanded some consideration. For once in a way, my dear Phil, your generally ready and quick-witted Fan was undoubtedly nonplussed.

'" Suppose I answer the question for you," said Mrs. Melray presently, with a smile which brought both rows of her pearly teeth into view ; but, for all that, it was not a pleasant smile by any means.

'" The story in question having come under the notice of my estimable brother-in-law, and he being satisfied that, as far as some of the incidents it treated of were concerned, it could refer to one case and no other, brought you, my dear Miss Sudlow, to Loudwater House, hoping, by your help (that is to say, by matching one woman against another) to be able to sift to the bottom sundry statements embodied in the opening pages of the narrative, as to the truth or falsehood of which neither he nor anyone else had any knowledge whatever. Finding, after a time, that your design was no nearer its fulfilment than at first, you took the only step left open to you—you gave me the story itself to read, hoping to gain goodness only knows what advantage thereby. Tell me, now, are my surmises, or guesses, or whatever you like to call them, very wide of the mark?"

'This, as you must admit, was very plain speaking indeed, and if I had been taken aback before, I was doubly so now. Her blue eyes were bent on me as she finished speaking with a sort of hard keenness in their concentrated gaze, such as heretofore I should not have deemed them capable of expressing. One thing was clear to me, that she was labouring under an altogether erroneous belief, of which it became my duty at once to disabuse her.

'"If you are under the impression, Mrs. Melray," I said, "as your words seem to imply, that I was invited here by your brother-in-law to act as a sort of private detective, or, in other words, to play the part of a spy on you and your actions, I can only say that you are wholly mistaken. I am here to fill the post of Freddy's governess, and with no ulterior motive of any kind. It was entirely of my own accord, and unprompted by anyone, that I yesterday gave you the story, 'How, and Why' to read. At the same time, I admit that when I put it into your hands it was with the object of enabling you, should you feel so disposed, to disprove certain allegations, which, as I take it, can refer to no other person than yourself."

'" Allegations which concern me most seriously, for I quite agree with you that, in the eyes of anyone acquainted with the case, they point unmistakably to Denia Melray. But tell me this: Should I be very wide of the mark in assuming that the story has already been read both by Mr. Winslade and Mr. Robert Melray?"

'" It has been read by both of them."

'" So much I surmised. And now, will you be good enough to enlighten me as to anything you may happen to know about the authorship of this very remarkable composition? I am also curious to learn by what chance it fell into your hands."

'Frankness being apparently the order of the

day, I at once proceeded to recount to her everything as it had happened, from my purchase of *The Family Cornucopia* onward through all the details of your interview with Mr. Timmins, ending with a mention of the letter from the railway company, in which it was stated that one out of the four people killed in the accident had never been identified. She seemed to drink in every word with an almost breathless avidity. I fancied that her face paled perceptibly when I told her how, on Mr. Timmins coming to his senses, the first thing he saw was the dead body of his unknown travelling companion stretched out beside him. Neither of us broke the silence for a little while after I had come to an end. Mrs. Melray was the first to speak.

' " Did "—here her hand went up to her throat for a moment—" did Mr. Timmins describe to Mr. Winslade—what I mean is, did he give him any description of the stranger who was killed ? "

' " The notice Mr. Timmins took of his fellow-traveller was of the most casual kind. All he could call to mind was that he was young and dark-complexioned, with a black moustache."

' " Yes—yes—young and dark-complexioned, with a black moustache," she repeated like an echo. " It must have been he—it could have been no other than he! Poor Evan! What an end—what a terrible end!"

'She turned and buried her face in the sofa-cushions, and presently her slight frame was shaken by those dry-eyed, almost silent sobs which bear witness to a grief that, for the time being, is beyond the consolation of tears.

'I knew not what to do—of no way in which I could comfort her. The conditions of the case were so exceptional that I felt myself utterly helpless. I could only sit and look dumbly on.

'"Poor Evan!" she had said. I did not forget that Evan Wildash was the name of her one-time lover, who was said to have gone to the Cape years before, and to have died there.

'After a time, without lifting her face from the cushions, she said, "Leave me now, dear Miss Sudlow. Come to me at the same time to-morrow, when I shall have more to say to you."

'I need not tell you, my dear Phil, with what impatience I awaited the afternoon of the morrow. In the interim Mrs. Melray kept closely to her rooms, being waited upon by her own maid and being present at none of the family meals.

'I found her on the second afternoon just as I had found her on the first; it might have been five minutes instead of twenty-four hours since I had left her last. She was very pale, but perfectly composed. "I want you to sit, please, where you sat yesterday," she said.

'For a little while she lay back on her cushions with drooping eye-lids and close-drawn brows.

'"When I came to think over what passed at our interview yesterday," at length she began, "I saw that two courses were open to me. I might have professed my entire ignorance of the writer of the manuscript found in the railway carriage; have averred that all that part of the narrative prior to the murder which concerns itself with the 'young wife' and her lover was sheer romance, that I had never had a lover since I was sixteen, and that he had died in Africa years ago; and, finally, I might have defied anyone to prove that I knew one iota more in connection with my husband's death than was given by me in evidence at the inquest. That was one of the two courses open to me, and to most women in my position it is the one which would have recommended itself to them.

'"The other course was to tell the truth as far as it is known to me, to reveal that which I have hitherto hidden in my own breast—and that is what I have made up my mind to do. Ah! you don't know how often I have been tempted to do this before to-day; but, like the coward I am at heart, I have hitherto shrunk from the ordeal. I am quite aware of the feeling with which both Mr. Melray and his mother regard me, and that the knowledge is very painful to me I need scarcely say. I think it very likely that if their attitude towards me had been one of greater sympathy (affection I hardly looked for), they would long ago have been made aware of all that I have to tell. But be that as it may, the truth shall now be told, whatever its effect may be on the relations between them and me in time to come. For more reasons than one, however, I have thought it advisable not to recount to you by word of mouth what there is to make known, but rather to set it down in black and white, so that you and others may be able to read it at your leisure. It took me till far into the night to accomplish my self-imposed task. Here is the result."

'As she finished speaking she thrust her hand under the sofa cushion and brought forth a thin roll of manuscript, which she handed to me.

'"Read this first yourself," she said, "and then oblige me by handing it to my brother-in-law. I should like it to be understood that I shall expect not to be cross-questioned about this, that, or the other statement comprised in it. That would simply be to torture me. The paper tells all there is to tell. I have nothing to add to it."

'The enclosed is a copy, written out by myself, of Mrs. Melray's narrative. The original was this morning placed by me in the hands of Mr. Robert Melray.'

CHAPTER XIII

MRS. MELRAY'S STATEMENT

'My mother died when I was little more than a child, and a year later I lost my father. After the latter event I went to live at Solchester with my uncle, Mr. Samuel Champneys, who was also my guardian. When I first met Evan Wildash I was sixteen years old and had just left school. He was my senior by four years and had come to Solchester to fill a vacancy in a land surveyor's office, his home, meanwhile, being with a maiden aunt whose house was only a few doors away from that of my uncle. Evan was an especially handsome young man, with large, black, lustrous eyes, a dark Italian-looking face, and a most persuasive voice; in short, just the kind of provincial Romeo to take captive the heart of a romantic school-girl. Small wonder, therefore, was it that, when he one day whispered in my ear that he loved me, he took mine captive on the spot. After that we used to met in secret two or three times a week, and, as if that were not enough, we got into the way of writing silly little love notes to each other between times, our post-office being a hollow in an old apple-tree at the bottom of my uncle's orchard.

"This went on for half a year or more, wholly without my uncle's knowledge, and never was girl more happy than I. Not for a moment did I doubt Evan's assurances that in all the world he loved but me; and, in return, he had all the girlish love I had to bestow. By-and-by rumours began to reach me of the wild and reckless kind of life he was leading—of his racing and betting propensities, of his card-playing, billiard-playing, and I know not what besides; but he was my Bayard in so far that, in my eyes, he was *sans reproche*, and I would not listen to aught that was said in his disparagement. At length, however, the crash came. He was dismissed from his situation, and, worse than all, dismissed without a character. Even then I would hear no ill spoken of him.

' It was just about this time that someone, I never discovered who, opened my uncle's eyes (good simple man!) to the state of affairs between Evan and myself. Under these circumstances five uncles out of six would have sent for their niece and have upbraided her and made things generally unpleasant for her; but he went to work after a different fashion. Instead of scolding me, he sent for my lover.

'According to Evan, as told to me later, Uncle Samuel spoke to him something to the following effect: "You have lost your situation and you have lost your character—such a one as you had to lose. Solchester and you must now part company. I am given to understand that you profess to be in love with my niece. If you are seeking her for the sake of her small fortune—and it is only a very small one —I must impress two facts upon you. The first is, that she will not be of age for three and a half years; the second, that her money is so tied up that her husband, whoever he may be, will not be able to touch a penny of it. Now, although I am my niece's guardian, and although she is legally bound to do my bidding while under age, I have no wish to quarrel with her on your account. Rather than do that I am prepared to make you an offer, which, for your own sake, I strongly advise you to accept. What I have to propose is this: That, on condition of your breaking off all future relations with my niece, and of your at once going out to one of the Colonies—I care not which— I will present you with the sum of two hundred and fifty pounds, the odd fifty to be given you at once for your passage and outfit, and the two hundred to be paid you the day after you land at Melbourne, or Halifax, or at whatever port you may decide upon consigning your worthless self to." Evan took a day to consider. On the morrow he told my uncle that he would accept the proffered sum and go.

'" So that is the price at which you and my uncle appraise me!" I whimpered, when, with his arm round my waist and my head resting against his shoulder, he told me what he had agreed upon doing. "Two hundred and fifty pounds! Oh, if I had but known before!"

'" Believe me, dearest, it is for the best," he replied as he softly fondled my cheek. Then he went on to say that his plan was to go out to the South African diamond fields, where, according to his account, fortunes, just then, were being picked up "every day of the week." Why should he be less lucky than others? What was there to hinder *him* from picking up a fortune? He had not the slightest doubt that at the end of two, or, at the most, three years, he should be back in England, worth who could say how many thousands of pounds. When that desirable state of affairs should have come to pass, he would marry me despite the opposition of all the uncles in the universe. Meanwhile, would I be true to him? Of course I would be true to him, I told him as I wept quietly on his shoulder.

'Well, he went. One letter he wrote me after landing at Cape Town, which reached me through the good offices of his aunt, Miss Pinchin, who was privy to our engagement and willing to further it to the best of her ability. After that there was a long, long silence, and finally, about a couple of years after his departure from England came the news of his death from fever.

'I cried, but not a great deal, when the news was told me. The fact was that by the time Evan had been gone three or four months I began to find, much to my surprise and hardly less to my mortification, that his image was slowly, but surely, fading and losing its vividness of outline in my memory— that I no longer thought of him by day and dreamt of him by night, as I had been wont to do, and that his unaccountable silence troubled me less and less as time went on. Love, or that which I had dignified with the name of love, had taken no real root in my heart. A few natural tears I shed when the news was told me; and a sense of what might have been, but never could be now, came over me and smote me as with a lash. But I quickly dried my eyes. Three days before I had promised to become the wife of James Melray.

'My uncle had died some time before, after having appointed Mr. Melray my guardian for the remaining term of my minority. He placed me under the care of a certain Mrs. Simpson, and there, from time to time, he used to come and see me. Before a year was out he one day took my breath away by making me an offer of marriage. I asked for a couple of days to consider my answer, at the end of which time I accepted his offer. Before doing so, however, I gave him clearly to understand that I entertained no warmer feeling for him than one of simple liking and esteem. He was quite content, he told me, to take me on those terms. Affection, he did not doubt, would follow in due course. There seemed to me no need for mentioning the name of Evan Wildash. The episode in connection with him was a thing of the past. He was dead, and therewith the promise I had given him had no longer any binding force.

'Mr. Melray and I were married. I did my best to make my husband happy, and, through all the dark days which have followed, the consciousness that I succeeded in doing so has been the greatest consolation left me. He prophesied rightly when he said that, being rooted in esteem, affection would not fail to grow. It did grow, as he knew, and he was happy in the knowledge.

'One afternoon, about a week prior to that fatal September day, having finished my shopping in the town, instead of going direct home, I was tempted by the fineness of the weather to go round by the Ladies' Walk, that fine old avenue of elms which stretches for nearly a mile along the left bank of the river, and is the only park, so to call it, of which Merehampton can boast.

'I had been strolling slowly along for some minutes, immersed in thought, when I was startled by a man who came suddenly out from behind the trunk of one of the big old trees, and stepping in front of me blocked the way. A second look was needed before I knew him again. It was Evan Wildash; but oh, how changed! With his sallow, sunken cheeks, his restless, furtive eyes, his long, unkempt hair, and his shabby, ill-fitting clothes, he looked like a vile copy of his former self. I fell back with a cry as my eyes met his. "So, traitress, you have not forgotten me!" he exclaimed through his set teeth, as he followed me up with clenched hands and raised shoulders.

'What answer I made I don't recollect, nor does it matter; but apparently it had the effect of soothing him in some measure. " Let us sit," he said, " I have much to tell you, many questions to ask." Accordingly we seated ourselves on one of the public benches. At that hour of the afternoon the walk was nearly deserted; its whole length did not hold more than half-a-dozen people.

'What passed between us may be briefly summarised.

'After that one letter written from the Cape, he had gone "up country" to the diamond fields. There he was presently smitten by sunstroke, and months passed before he was able to crawl outside the hospital-tent. So reduced was he in strength that manual labour of any kind was out of the question, and in order to keep himself from starving he was glad to accept a berth in a store; and there he had stayed till he had saved enough money to pay his passage home.

'"But when you got better, why did you not write," I asked. " I did write, again and yet again," he replied. " After that first letter not a line from you ever reached me," I said. " What conclusion could I come to save that you had forgotten me ? " " If that is so, then has there been treachery at work," he replied, with a contraction of his ebon brows. "That is a thing to be ferreted out, and I charge myself with the task. Meet me, three days from now, at the same time and place."

'On that understanding we parted. There had been little or no tenderness in his manner towards me, but only, as it were, the gloomy humour of a man who found himself despoiled by another of something which he had believed to be his own, but on which, in his heart, he had set no particular store. On my part, I felt towards him nothing but a sort of repulsion mixed with pity—pity for the so evidently forlorn condition of one whom ill-fortune had so remorselessly dogged. As for his good looks they were gone as completely as if they had never existed. I wondered at and half despised myself when I called to mind that there had been a time when I looked up to this man as the hero of my dreams.

'I met him three days later as I had promised. He had averred that there had been treachery at work, and I was curious to learn the result of his inquiry. What he had to tell was something of a shock to me. The letters he had written after his recovery from his illness had all, like the one written after landing, which duly reached me, been sent under cover to his aunt, Miss Pinchin. But by the time the second letter came to hand I was engaged to be married. Miss Pinchin, in the exercise of her discretion, instead of forwarding that and the subsequent ones direct to me, had put them into fresh envelopes and addressed them to Mr. Melray. Whether he had opened and read them, or whether, having had some hint from the spinster as to the probable nature of their contents, he had burnt them unread, is a point as to which I am as ignorant to-day as I was then. At any rate, not one of them ever reached the person for whom they were intended, and, for the time being, a dull fire of resentment was kindled in my heart.

'For all that, I was by no means prepared to look at the affair from the point of view of Evan Wildash. In brief he pressed me to elope with him. "You loved me—that you cannot deny," ran his plea. "When I was compelled to leave you, you gave me your promise to remain true to me; and that you would have kept it I fully believe, had not the report of my death been spread about, and had you not found yourself, after your uncle's decease, alone in the world. Even then, but for my aunt's treachery, it would not have been too late for you to have saved yourself from marrying a man whom you can henceforth regard with nothing but loathing and contempt. Although you have failed me, I have been true to you. To-day you are infinitely dearer to me than you were four years ago. You belong to me. You are mine and mine only. We will fly together to some land beyond the seas. I have means at command and you shall not want. Come, then—now—at once! In twelve hours we shall be far beyond pursuit."

'Such and such like were the persuasions and arguments made use of by him. But I had no longer any love for him (if, indeed, I had ever had any)—no, not the least bit! Rather was I frightened of him. His restless manner, his strange jerky movements, a peculiar twitching of one corner of his mouth, and an indescribable something which flashed out at me every now and again from the sombre depths of his eyes, made me timorous of him and involuntarily caused me to shrink from too close a proximity to him. It seemed to me then—as, with still more reason, it seems clear to me now—that he had never thoroughly recovered from the effects of his sunstroke, and that, to a certain extent, he could hardly be held accountable for what he might either say or do.

'I will not weary you with the details of all that passed between us. I was afraid to take too indignant a tone with him, lest my doing so should provoke an explosion of passion on his part, which might end in a way disastrous to one or both of us. There was, however, no lack of firmness in the way in which I gave him to understand that between himself and me all was at an end for ever, and that that must be our last interview. He pleaded and urged me to reconsider my determination, but to no purpose. Finally, finding that I had only half-an-hour left in which to get home and change my dress before dinner, I was compelled to leave him somewhat abruptly. "Shake hands before I go, and let us part as friends," I said.

'He stared at my extended hand for a moment or two with bent brows. Then, with a strange harsh laugh which seemed to me to have an echo of insanity in it, he said: "Part as friends—you and I? Never! We are lovers, not friends. You are mine and I am yours. Not even death shall have power to divide us." Then, pulling his hat over his brows and turning quickly on his heel, he flung me a parting look over his shoulder. "It is *au revoir*, and not farewell," he exclaimed with a wave of his hand, and so strode swiftly away through the gloaming.'

CHAPTER XIV

THE STATEMENT CONCLUDED

'For the next few days there was an uneasy feeling at my heart, a sense of impending misfortune, of which I could not rid myself. "It is *au revoir*," he had said, and that despite my telling him that on no account would I consent to meet him again. What motive was at the bottom of his persistence? When and how would he attempt to force his presence on me? For three days I never left the precincts of the house and garden.

'I now come to the fatal 18th of September. About ten o'clock on the morning of that day, after breakfast was over and my husband had shut himself up in his office, a note was brought me with word that the messenger had been instructed to wait for an answer. Even before I opened it I guessed but too surely who it was from. As nearly as I can recollect, it ran almost word for word as under:

'" You *must* see me once more and to-day. I have made up my mind to leave England in less than a week from now, probably never to return; but I cannot go without bidding you farewell. Besides, I have some letters of yours, written years ago, which I will give you when I see you. Should you refuse me this last request, you must abide by the consequences. To-morrow at daybreak my body will be found in front of Loudwater House. There will be a bullet in my brain and on my lifeless heart will be found your letters.—E. W."

'Such a message, coming from a man whom I believed to be half demented, was enough to frighten any woman, and it frightened me. I scribbled a line in answer, saying when and where I would meet him.

'All that day I was a prey to the most dismal forebodings. It was Friday. My husband, who was as regular in his habits as a piece of clockwork, made an invariable point of leaving home punctually at eight o'clock every Tuesday and Friday evening, in order to make one at a rubber of whist at the house of his friend, Mr. Arbour. Being thus aware that from eight till half-past ten my time would be at my own disposal, and being unwilling to meet Evan again by daylight in the Ladies' Walk, from fear lest the fact of my doing so should somehow reach my husband's ears, in my reply to him I had named nine o'clock as the time, and the corner of the graveyard of St. Mary's Church (a lonely spot at that hour and not more than three hundred yards from Loudwater House) as our place of meeting.

'I had fully made up my mind that this our last interview should be as brief a one as possible. I was morbidly anxious to regain possession of my letters. Unless I did so there was no knowing into whose hands they might fall nor what use might be made of them. And then for Evan Wildash to have committed suicide at the door of my husband's house would have been a dreadful thing indeed!

'The clock struck eight as my husband was putting on his overcoat in the hall. I tied a muffler round his throat, and at the door he kissed me, as he always did, even if he were not going to be more than an hour away. Alas and alas! how little did I dream that it was the last time he would ever press his lips to mine!

'After he was gone I scarcely know how the time passed till nine o'clock. As I look back in memory, everything that happened that night after my husband's departure seems as far removed from reality as is the recollection of some hideous nightmare. It is enough to say that I was at the corner of the churchyard within five minutes of the appointed hour, where I found Evan already waiting for me.

'Of what passed between us I have only the vaguest recollection—after-events seem almost to have blotted the record from my mind. I remember with what a feeling of relief my fingers closed over my letters, which, however, he did not yield up without evident reluctance. Half a minute later his clenched hand went up to his heart, and, with a low cry, he staggered backward, and would have fallen had not his other hand instinctively gripped one of the churchyard railings. "That accursed pain again!" he exclaimed with a groan. "Brandy!—I must have brandy! or I shall die."

'I gazed around in despair. As I have said, the place was a lonely one. There was no tavern in sight, nor, indeed, was I sure in which direction the nearest one lay. By this time he was resting his back against the railings, and even by that dim light I could discern that his features were warped by agony. Then a thought struck me. I had planned so as to leave Loudwater House unknown to anyone, having made my exit not by way of the front door, but through my husband's private office, one door of which opens into a side lane. My intention was to go back the same way, which the latch-key I had brought with me—applicable to both the front and side doors—would allow of my doing. It now struck me that if only Evan could walk as far as the office I might be able to get him some brandy from the liqueur-case upstairs unseen by anybody. I told him my idea, and he assented to it eagerly. How in the agony he was in he contrived to get as far as Loudwater House I cannot tell; but there we were at last. I opened the door with my key and went in first, he following. The place was in darkness; but I knew where matches were always to be found. "Wait by the door till I get a light," I said, being afraid lest he might stumble over something in the dark. Whether he did not heed me, or did not hear me, I have no means of knowing. In any case, he groped his way forward into the room, and a moment later an exclamation broke from his lips. He had half fallen over some obstruction on the floor. As I struck a match, and the gas-jet leapt up, I turned my head to see what had happened. By that he had recovered his footing, and, the instant the room became flooded with light, I saw that he was staring intently at his outstretched hands. Without my being aware of it, my eyes followed the direction of his. Then I saw that his hands were wet—nay, more, that they were bedabbled with blood. A moment I gazed, horror-stricken, then my eyes travelled downward, and the dread knowledge burst upon me that the object over which Evan had stumbled was none other than the murdered body of my husband!

'Frozen, I stood there gazing at the ghastly object—all the currents of life seeming, for the time being, to stand still. As for Evan, his gaze wandered from his hands to the body, and thence back to his hands. Then, all at once, he burst into a harsh, discordant, maniacal laugh, almost more dreadful to hear than was that which lay so white and still on the floor to look upon.

'"Blood!—blood on my hands—and *his* blood!" he cried with a half shriek. "They will say that *I* did it—I—I!" Again his madman's laugh rang through the room. Then, with a last stare at his crimsoned hands, he turned, and, as I verily believe, without as much as another look at me, he flung wide the door and, passing with staggering strides out into the night, vanished from my sight for ever.

'But before that I was down on my knees by the side of my dead husband. How did I know he was dead? you may possibly ask. My first glance at his face had been enough to assure me that no faintest spark of life animated the marble-like image at my feet. On it was stamped the indescribable seal of death. For all that, as I now knelt by him my hand felt for his heart, but not the slightest fluttering responded to the pressure of my palm. He must have been dead some time. Already the hand I took in mine, and the brow to which I pressed my lips, were of an icy coldness.

'Presently I stood up and asked myself what I ought to do next. An unnatural calm possessed me. My eyes were dry and burning, but it seemed to me as if my limbs were as cold as those of the corpse at my feet. Tears would come later on, tears in abundance, but just then the fountains were fast sealed. I knew, no one better, that what I ought to have done was there and then to raise an alarm and summon the police with all possible speed. "But if I do that," I said, "how can I explain away my presence at this untimely hour? And what if Evan, in his half-demented condition, and with his blood-imbrued hands, should be arrested and confronted with me? Would it not, in such a case, go hard with the pair of us, innocent though we are?" My poor dear husband was dead, of that there could be no doubt. It could do him no good, but might do me infinite harm, were the slightest shadow of suspicion to fall upon me in connection with the mystery of his murder, as would almost inevitably be the case were I found in that room at that hour with my outdoor things on, without anyone in the house dreaming that I was otherwhere than in my own chamber.

'Such were some of the thoughts that surged through my brain while one might have counted a dozen slowly. My mind was made up. After one last shuddering glance at my poor dear one, I put out the gas, opened the inner door without noise, satisfied myself that no one was about, sped upstairs and reached my own room unseen. A quarter of an hour later I rang the bell, to which Charlotte, the housemaid, responded. Under the pretence of being without an envelope in which to enclose a letter I had just written, I asked her to take a lighted candle, go down to Mr. Melray's office, and bring me one from there. The rest is known.

'As already stated, I never saw Evan Wildash after that night, nor did the slightest tidings of him ever reach me. After having read the story " How, and Why," and after having heard from Miss Sudlow by what strange chance the MS., of which the first half of the story professes to be a faithful copy, came into the hands of a certain Mr. Timmins, I can only conclude that the unknown stranger who met his death in the railway accident could have been none other than Evan. As to whether his partial derangement (for that his brain was affected I cannot doubt) was temporary or permanent, and by what motive he was possessed in describing under fictitious names, but not without sundry exaggerations and erroneous deductions, some portion of that which passed between himself and me, I am no more able to divine than the veriest stranger who may read these lines.

'Of the murder of my dear husband (surely such a crime cannot go for ever unpunished!) I know nothing more than is here set down.

'And that I aver to be the solemn truth.

'DENIA MELRAY.'

CHAPTER XV

A SCRAP OF PAPER

WITHIN twenty-four hours of the receipt by Philip Winslade of Miss Sudlow's letter enclosing the copy of Mrs. Melray's statement, he and Mr. Robert Melray were closeted together in a private room of the hotel where the latter generally stayed during his visits to town.

'What a pity, what a very great pity it is that Denia was not straightforward enough to tell me all this at first,' said Mr. Melray as he replaced the statement, which he had been glancing over afresh, in his pocket. 'As you will readily conceive, it is an immense relief to me to find that she is in no way implicated in my poor brother's tragical fate. It would indeed have been terrible had anything tending to the contrary come to light, and I am truly thankful my mother and I have been spared any such revelation. Unfortunately we seem no nearer the elucidation of the mystery of James's death than we were before.' He sighed heavily, his chin drooped forward on his breast, and he seemed lost in thought. There was a long pause. Suddenly he raised his head and, with his eyes bent searchingly on Winslade, said: 'I suppose *you* see no reason to doubt the accuracy of any of the details embodied in my sister-in-law's narrative?'

It was a question which Phil had expected to have put to him, and there was no hesitation in his reply.

'I see no valid reason for questioning the *bona fides* of Mrs. Melray's narrative. There are certain points in connection with the events of September 18, as told by her, which would undoubtedly be open to grave suspicion did she not account for them in such a seemingly straightforward and natural way. For instance, on the face of it, it seems nothing less than a most remarkable coincidence that she and Wildash should have found themselves in her husband's private office within so short a time of Mr. Melray's unaccountable return and all that must have happened immediately after.; and yet the explanation of how they came to be there is so simple and direct that, when one comes to consider, it seems by no means improbable that things should have fallen out as she asserts them to have done.'

'Does there not seem to you a possibility that my brother may have accidentally discovered the assignation of the young people—that, in point of fact, he may have come suddenly upon them while they were talking together by the corner of the churchyard, that a quarrel may thereupon have ensued, with a result that was fatal to James?'

'That is a point which I have not failed to consider; but it is one which, the more I look at it, the more I find it to bristle with difficulties. That Mr. Melray left home as usual at eight o'clock is not questioned. Supposing him to have gone there direct, he was due at the house of Mr. Arbour from ten to twelve minutes later. Mrs. Melray states that, knowing her husband would not be back before half-past ten at the soonest, she named nine o'clock for her meeting with Wildash. This seems quite feasible, seeing that by that hour most of the shops would be shut, that there would be fewer people in the streets, and, consequently, less likelihood of their meeting being observed. But, supposing Mrs. Melray to have been unwise enough to fix a quarter or half-past eight for the meeting, what then? The churchyard where the meeting is said to have taken place is in an exactly opposite direction to the road Mr. Melray would have to traverse on his way to Mr.

Arbour's; what possible reason, therefore, could take him so far out of his way? Even supposing for a moment that, by some means of which we know nothing, he had got wind of the assignation and had made up his mind to be present, that he carried out his intention, that high words passed between the two men, resulting in a quarrel fatal to one of them; supposing all this, we at once find ourselves beset with a fresh difficulty—none other, in fact, than to account for Mr. Melray's body being found in his own office, and not in the street by the churchyard, where the quarrel, had there been one, must presumably have taken place. But there is no evidence of a quarrel, nor as much as a single witness to prove that the two men ever met, while it could not for a moment be contended that Wildash, after killing Mr. Melray, could unobserved have dragged the body as far as Loudwater House. No; I confess it would be much harder for me to swallow these difficulties than it is to accept Mrs. Melray's narrative as a truthful statement of the facts of the case as far as she was concerned in them; and, looked at from her point of view, one can quite understand her anxiety to keep the whole affair a secret from everybody.'

'Your views in the main seem to tally with my

own,' said Mr. Melray, 'and I am glad to have them confirmed by you.'

'It certainly seems somewhat singular,' resumed Winslade presently, 'that no one in Solchester should have known of the return of Wildash, and that by all his old associates the tidings of his death should still be implicity believed. His aunt's evidence on the point would have been most valuable, because she, more than anyone, would have been likely to know of his return; but, unfortunately, she died some months ago. As to whether he and the stranger who was killed on the railway were one and the same person, there seems very little likelihood now of our ever being able to prove; the probability, however, would seem to be in favour of their being the same man.'

'It is a point which, I confess, has very little interest for me,' replied the other. 'But now comes the question,' he presently resumed, 'of what I ought to say to my sister-in-law, of what notice, in point of fact, it is advisable that I should take of her extraordinary statement.'

'If I may be allowed,' said Winslade, 'I would suggest that the less notice you take of it the better.

'My own opinion exactly. Indeed, if she and I were brought face to face, I scarcely know what I should find to say to her about it. For me, at least, it opens up a very different view of her character from the one I held before. But that,' he added with one of his dry smiles, 'is scarcely a point as to which it behoves me to enlighten her.' He paused for a few seconds, sitting with half-shut eyes and drumming softly on the table with one hand. Then he said: 'Perhaps, after all, my best plan will be to write her a brief note, telling her I have read her statement, and that although I am sorry she did not see her way to take me into her confidence long ago, yet, bearing in mind the uncommon circumstances surrounding the affair, that I do not feel at liberty to blame her for her reticence. Further, that I accept her statement without the shadow of a doubt as to the truth of anything there set down, and that for the future it may be as well that the subject should not be further alluded to between us. Yes,' he continued with an air of relief, 'I think that will decidedly be the best thing to do.'

At Loudwater House everything went on as before. Fanny and the younger Mrs. Melray remained on the best of terms, and the latter continued to join her and Freddy two or three times a week in their walks. Once, and once only, did the young widow refer to a certain matter which was as carefully shunned by

Fanny as by herself. One day when Freddy was out of hearing, Denia said: 'I suppose I am only telling you what you know already when I inform you that my brother-in-law's perusal of the statement which I gave into your hands resulted in his writing me a short, but extremely nice letter.'

'I was given to understand that it was Mr. Melray's intention to write to you.'

'I cannot tell you how happy his letter has made me. Ever since receiving it I have felt sorry and ashamed of myself for not having taken him into my confidence at first and told him all I had to tell. All my life long I shall think very differently of him from what I used to do.'

There was a little break in her voice as she finished speaking, and Fanny, glancing at her, saw that her blue eyes were brimmed with tears.

If, since her receipt of his letter, Mrs. Melray regarded her brother-in-law from a changed standpoint, Fanny did not fail to notice that he, on his part, now treated her with a certain show of cordiality of which there had been no sign before. Heretofore he had always addressed her ceremoniously as ' Mrs. Melray,' whereas he now as often as not spoke to her and of her by her baptismal appellation. A cloud seemed to have lifted itself off the house. The pretty widow's eyes began to sparkle again as they had not sparkled since her husband's death.

Only, Mrs. Melray the elder, when in her daughter-in-law's company, continued to be as grim and taciturn as she had always been. Nothing had happened which served to change or modify the silent, but uncompromising hostility with which she regarded the younger woman. That she could be very different when she chose was shown by her treatment of Miss Sudlow, which was not merely considerate, but had in it a certain element of cordiality, of a somewhat chill and stately kind it may be, but which, coming from the person it did, meant more than it would have meant from another.

One of the chief duties of the dowager's companion was to read aloud to her mistress. Unfortunately, about this time Miss Armishaw contracted a severe cold, which resulted, for the time being, in a partial loss of voice. In this strait Fanny offered her services as reader, an offer which Mrs. Melray was pleased to accept. This brought the two women into more confidential relations than before, for the readings always took place in the elder lady's private sitting-room, and were usually followed by half-an-hour's chat on sundry topics of the day before Fanny went back to her more immediate duties.

It was in the course of one of these after-reading talks that the dowager said: 'Not till a week ago, my dear, did Robert give me a certain document to read, which, as I understand, was placed by my daughter-in-law in your hands first of all. It is a document which serves, in my opinion, to place her conduct in a very curious light indeed, and one which she may well have shrunk from having thrown on it. On that point, however, I will say no more. She is my son's widow, and although it would be hypocrisy on my part to say that I like her, I have no desire whatever to prejudice her in the eyes of others. Nay, I will go so far as to admit that there was never the slightest fault to be found with the way she did her duty by her husband, and that since his death her conduct has been most exemplary. That her life under this roof is a very lonely and isolated one cannot be disputed, consequently that she should seek your society a good deal is not to be wondered at. I am quite willing to grant her considerable powers of attraction, and if anyone were to question me closely on the point, I should probably be at a loss to say what there is about her which repels me so. There the feeling is, however, and it is one which I have been unable to overcome. If I were to describe it as a vague instinctive distrust I should perhaps not be very wide of the mark.'

Fanny knew not what reply to make to this unwonted burst of confidence. But seeing that the dowager did not look as if any reply were expected of her she wisely held her tongue.

After a pause, during which the elder lady sat staring into the fire with a far-away look in her eyes, she spoke again.

'I suppose we may now finally give up all expectation of ever seeing my poor son's murderer brought to the bar of justice.'

'For my part, madam, I cannot go so far as to admit that,' replied Fanny. 'One never can tell from day to day what clue may turn up, or what important fact be brought to light, perhaps from a quarter the least expected, or in a way the most surprising and unthought of. I have read of cases as apparently unfathomable as that of Mr. Melray, which time has unravelled after its own fashion, and after those most experienced in such matters had given them up as hopeless.'

'Let us trust, my dear, that it may prove so in my son's case; but every day that passes tends to make it more unlikely.'

'If one could only discover by what motive Mr. Melray was influenced, or what particular object he had in view, in coming back to his office after having set out for the house of Mr. Arbour, we should, I think, lay our hands on a very important clue. I suppose there was nothing found among Mr. Melray's papers bearing on that feature of the affair?'

'So far as I am aware, nothing. Mr. Cray had the going through of my son's papers, and had there been anything of the kind among them he would surely not have overlooked it. Not only was he closely questioned at the inquest, which was twice adjourned, but, later on, he had more than one private interview with the officer from Scotland Yard who had the case specially in hand. No man, however, could have been more entirely bewildered and nonplussed than he was. Again and again he declared that, as far as his knowledge went, his master had not an enemy in the world—no, not a single enemy, but a thousand friends!'

'I presume,' said Fanny, 'there was nothing found on Mr. Melray's person after death—no letter, or memorandum of any kind—which would serve to throw even a glimmer of light on the events of the 18th of September?'

'Mine were the hands that emptied my son's pockets of their contents after death,' said the mother with a thin quaver in her voice. 'Of course she—his wife, I mean—was supposed to be too much overcome to think of anything. I knew that James was in the habit of carrying a pocket-book, and it seemed to me that there might perhaps be entries in it which it would be as well that no strange eyes should read. Accordingly I took possession of it, and it has never been out of my keeping since that time.'

'Pardon my inquisitiveness, but may I ask whether you have made yourself acquainted with the contents of the pocket-book?'

'I went carefully through it within a few hours of my son's death.'

'And there was nothing in it that would serve———?'

'Nothing whatever. Nearly the whole of the entries in it have reference to his personal or domestic expenditure, for James was methodical in all his ways, and as careful to balance his private expenses as he was his business accounts. Since that day I have never opened the book, but have kept it locked up in my writing-table. Of course I was very much upset and put about just then, and it may be as well that you, with your younger and more trained eyes, should look over it, for, now that the point has been raised, it will certainly be more satisfactory to me to be assured that it contains nothing of moment which I may inadvertently have overlooked.'

She rose, crossed to her writing-table, unlocked a drawer and produced therefrom her dead son's pocket-book, which she at once placed in Fanny's hands.

'Look carefully through it, my dear,' she said. 'There is nothing in it that you may not read.'

Fanny cast her eyes over a number of the entries, all of which bore out Mrs. Melray's description of them. Then, because a pocket-book without a pocket would in some sort be a misnomer, she turned to the Russia-leather cover and, on lifting a flap, found the receptacle she was in search of. It held nothing save a small folded paper, which, from its texture, she took at first for a bank-note. When, however, she had extracted it she saw that it was merely an ordinary piece of tissue-paper with some written characters showing through it. Without opening it she handed it to Mrs. Melray.

'What is this, my dear?' demanded the elder lady. 'I saw nothing of this when I looked through the book. But I suppose I did not look carefully enough. There seems to be writing on it, but my eyes are so weak that I must ask you to read it for me.'

Accordingly Fanny took back the paper, which proved to be an ordinary press copy of a letter, its uneven edge on one side tending to show that it had been torn out of the tissue-book after having been passed through the machine. Having unfolded it she proceeded to read aloud as follows:

'Loudwater House,
'September 4, 18—.

'Mr. John Noyes,
'Solchester.

'Sir,—I beg to enclose you Bank of England notes value three hundred and fifty pounds (viz., three of 100*l.* each and one of 50*l.*) in full discharge of the claim standing in your books against my name. This I do in preference to forwarding you a cheque for the amount. You will understand what I mean when I tell you that a few hours ago I had a long interview with our mutual friend, Mr. ——. I have retained the documents brought by him for my examination, as to the authenticity of which it is not needful that I should enter into any particulars. Kindly acknowledge the receipt of my enclosure by return, and at the same time forward, through registered post, the important document belonging to me which you have still in your possession.

'To a person of your business tact and experience I need scarcely remark that in a delicate matter like the present discretion is a most laudable virtue.

'Yours most truly,
'James Melray.'

'Well, my dear, and what do you make of it?' asked Mrs. Melray, after staring silently at Fanny for several seconds.

'On the face of it, it seems a very mysterious production, and I confess that I don't in the least know what to make of it. The date of it is just a fortnight before Mr. Melray's death.'

'So it is. That is a point which failed to strike me at the moment. But what is meant by "our mutual friend, Mr. ———"? Is the name omitted?'

'Not omitted, but owing to a fault in copying, it is so smudged as to be illegible.'

'That is a pity, but of course it can't be helped.' Then, after a few moments of silent consideration, she added: 'I think this is a case as to which it may be advisable to consult my son. What say you?'

'I quite agree with you, madam.'

'Then you are inclined to attach some importance to the paper?'

'I am inclined to attach very great importance to it.'

'In that case, will you be good enough to ring the bell?'

But Robert Melray was no more able to make head or tail of the paper found by Fanny than his mother had been. 'The name of the person to whom the letter is addressed is altogether strange to me,' he said; 'but that is hardly to be wondered at, seeing that I don't know more than half-a-dozen people in all Solchester. I think we had better ask Cray to come upstairs, and ascertain whether he can throw any light on the affair.'

But the managing clerk, when summoned, only shook his head. 'The name of Mr. Noyes is quite unknown to me,' he said. 'From the tenor of this letter, I take it to refer to some private transaction of Mr. Melray. There is certainly no entry in the books of the firm bearing on any affair of the kind.'

'I will have a copy of this copy made and forwarded to Winslade by to-night's post,' was Robert Melray's final decision. 'If he can do nothing else, he can at least establish for us the identity of Mr. John Noyes.'

CHAPTER XVI

A FRESH LINE OF INQUIRY

ONCE more Philip Winslade found himself under the necessity of journeying down to Solchester. It took him no long time after his arrival to discover that Mr. Noyes was the secretary and manager of a certain Loan and Discount Corporation well known to not a few of the good people of the town.

No sooner had he ascertained this than he made it his business to call upon Mr. Noyes. Having explained who he was and that he was prosecuting the inquiry on behalf of Mr. Robert Melray, he produced his copy of the letter of the 4th of September, and asked the manager to inform him whether he remembered the receipt of the original, to which Mr. Noyes, having glanced his eye over the copy, replied that he remembered it very well indeed.

'In that case,' resumed Winslade, 'will you be good enough to enlighten me, and Mr. Robert Melray through me, as to the precise nature of the transaction to which it refers, in view of the fact that no note or memorandum of any kind has been found among the late Mr. Melray's papers which helps in the slightest degree to explain it?'

Mr. Noyes toyed for some seconds with his watch-chain before answering. Then he said: 'I need scarcely tell you, Mr. Winslade, that it is a matter of principle with me never to open my lips about any confidential matters of which I may become the depositary in the ordinary course of business. Seeing, however, that the case to which this letter refers is of a very exceptional kind, that Mr. Melray is dead, and that the information is asked for by his brother as his partner and successor, I think that, for once, I shall be justified in taking an exceptional course. Here is the "Times." If you will kindly engage yourself with it for a matter of five or six minutes, I shall then be at liberty to tell you all I know of the affair.'

'It was about the middle of last August,' began the manager a few minutes later, as he wheeled his chair half round so as more directly to confront his auditor, 'that a young man called upon me whom I had never to my knowledge seen before. (I can verify the exact date for you, should it be necessary to do so.) His name, he told me, was Richard

Dyson, and that he was a relative of Mr. Melray, the well-known shipowner of Merehampton. His object in calling on me was to negotiate, on the part of that gentleman, a loan of three hundred pounds, of which sum, he gave me to understand, Mr. Melray was in immediate need; the security offered for the same being a fully paid-up life policy for two thousand pounds. That Mr. Melray, although in a large way of business, should be in pressing want of the sum in question did not surprise me in the least. Many prosperous merchants and tradesmen whose capital is locked up, or otherwise not available at a moment's notice, are occasionally pressed for a comparatively small amount of ready money. Consequently what I did was to take down the particulars of the required loan and tell Mr. Dyson that I would lay the application before my directors and communicate with him at the earliest possible moment.

'Well, sir, the terms of the loan having been acceded to, a communication to that effect was sent under cover to Mr. Dyson. Next day saw him at my office again, his object in coming being to settle with me the details for the completion of the affair. Mr. Melray having an objection to being seen entering or leaving an office the chief business of which was the lending of money, it was arranged between Dyson and myself that I should wait upon his relative at half-past seven on the evening of the next day but one, at the George and Dragon Hotel, where a private room would be engaged by him.

'I was at the hotel punctually at the time agreed upon, and on asking for Mr. Melray was at once ushered into his room. I found the shipowner, whom I had never seen before, to be a thin, grey-haired man, somewhat prim and old-fashioned in his attire, and wearing smoke-tinted spectacles. After a brief greeting we at once entered on the business which had taken me there. The evening was closing in and the room was in semi-darkness. I thought Mr. Melray would have rung for lights, but he did not. There were pen and ink on the table. At his request I stationed myself by him, and pointed out the particular spot on the assignment and other documents where his signature was required. That done, I folded up the papers and handed him a cheque for three hundred pounds; he, in return, presented me with the policy, which, till the sum lent should be repaid, together with interest as agreed on, would remain in my custody. The whole affair was over in five or six minutes at the most. At this distance of time there can be no harm in my confessing that I thought it rather stingy treatment on the part of Mr. Melray not to offer me as much as a glass of wine.

'Now, one of the two people who, twice every year, audit the Corporation's accounts and verify their securities, is Mr. Dunning, a lawyer well known both at Solchester and Merehampton. At the half-yearly audit, which took place about three weeks after my interview with Mr. Melray, the policy of assurance, together with other documents bearing on the transaction, came, in due course, under Mr. Dunning's inspection. You will readily imagine, then, that I was not a little surprised when he came to me with the papers in his hand and asked me to tell him all I knew of the transaction to which they referred. Taking into account his official connection with the Corporation, there was no breach of confidence in my complying with his request. It was then my turn to put certain questions to him, and the surprise I had felt before was in nowise lessened when he told me that he had been Mr. Melray's lawyer, and, in certain matters, his confidential adviser, for something like a quarter of a century; that, from his knowledge of that gentleman's affairs, he could aver that it was next to impossible that he should have been in need of such a sum as three hundred pounds; that, so far as he was aware, Mr. Melray, whose eyes were remarkably good for his age, had never worn spectacles in his life; and, finally, that he, Mr. Dunning, believed the signatures which I had witnessed to be neither more nor less than unblushing forgeries of his client's name. Thereupon it was agreed that he should take the suspected documents away with him and see Mr. Melray on the morrow.

'Of what passed between the two I have no knowledge, but when I tell you that, as far as I am concerned, the sequel of the affair was the letter of which you have this morning shown me a copy, you are at liberty, just as I was, to think what you like. Having got my "pound of flesh," as I suppose you would term it, I returned the policy as requested, and from that day to this have never sought to pry further into the affair.'

The first thing Winslade did after leaving Mr. Noyes was to despatch a telegram to Mr. Melray, which served to bring that gentleman to Solchester by the next train. It is not needful to dilate on the grieved astonishment with which he listened to the other's recital of what had passed between himself and the money-lender. Dyson had been a favourite with both the brothers, not merely because he was the only son of an orphan cousin—of whom, as a girl, they had been both proud and fond—but also by reason of certain pleasant qualities of his own, which, if they did not spring from any genuine depth or sincerity of feeling, had all the appearance of doing so and answered their purpose equally as well.

'We must go at once and find Dunning,' were Mr. Melray's first words when he had in some measure regained his composure. 'So far we have only heard half the story. It rests with him to tell us the remainder.'

They were fortunate enough to find Mr. Dunning at home and disengaged. A very few minutes sufficed to acquaint the lawyer with the nature of their errand.

'We know all that Mr. Noyes has to tell,' said Mr. Melray in conclusion. 'We want you to supplement his narrative from the point where his information comes to an end.'

'That I can very readily do,' said the lawyer. 'When I showed Mr. James Melray the loan-office documents, with what purported to be three separate signatures of his attached thereto, he at once, in the most emphatic and indignant terms, denounced the whole affair as an audacious mixture of forgery and fraud. He had never seen Noyes in his life, much less applied to him for a loan, or pledged his policy of assurance. But when he had reached that point of his disclaimer I said to him, "Would it not be as well to satisfy yourself that the policy is still in your possession?" "Why, I had it in my hand no longer ago than yesterday," was his reply. "It lies where it has always lain, on the top shelf in the large safe, one of a bundle of documents tied round with red tape." Thereupon, as if to make assurance doubly sure, he rose, crossed the room, unlocked the safe, and produced from the interior the bundle of papers of which he had spoken, and extracted from the rest a large oblong envelope, which he brought to the table. It was labelled in his own writing, "Paid-up Policy of Assurance on Own Life for 2,000l." "There," he said, with a little triumph in his tone, "whatever else the rogue may have been guilty of, he has not succeeded in making away with this." "I hope you won't think me unreasonable," I replied, "if I ask you to open the envelope and examine its contents." Scarcely had the words left my lips before, with his office knife, he had slit open one end of the envelope and drawn forth the enclosure. An instant later he sank back in his chair with a groan. All that the envelope contained was some blank sheets of engrossing paper.

'For a few moments I was afraid that Mr. Melray was about to have a seizure of some kind, so colourless was his face and so glassy were his eyes. He would not, however, let me ring for help, and gradually he came round. A careful examination of the envelope revealed the *modus operandi* by which the fictitious contents had been substituted for the genuine. The large black seal, with its impression of Mr. Melray's monogram, had not been meddled with beyond the point of detaching it bodily, probably with the help of a sharp penknife, from the thick paper of the envelope. Then, after the substitution had been effected, the seal had been reaffixed in its place with the help of a little gum ; and, finally, a thin rim of melted wax had been run round it so as completely to hide any evidence of the envelope having been tampered with. In the confidential position held by Dyson under his kinsman, he had free access to the safe and its contents. When once he had got the policy into his possession and had put everything in train with Mr. Noyes, it was a comparatively simple matter, with the aid of a wig and a few other accessories, to pass himself off in the half-light of the August evening for a man double his own age. What puzzled me then, and not only me, but Mr. Melray, and what puzzles me still, is, why he contented himself with the comparatively small sum of three hundred pounds, when he might have borrowed double that amount on the security of the policy had he been so minded. But it may have been that he saw, or thought he saw, the means of repaying a small sum, and so of redeeming the policy, while it might have been impossible for him to do so in the case of a more considerable loan.

'I have already told you, gentlemen,' continued the lawyer, 'how terribly Mr. Melray was put about by the discovery of his young relative's treachery and ingratitude, not to call his conduct by a stronger name. In the first excess of his resentment he vowed that the moment Dyson returned (just then he happened to be away on his annual holiday) he would cause him to be arrested, and would prosecute him with the most extreme rigour of the law. But, after a while, the flame of his anger began to burn less fiercely. He called to mind that the culprit was the only son of his favourite cousin, to whom he had passed his word when she lay on her death-bed that he would act a parent's part by the lad. He remembered, too, his unfortunate bringing-up, and that his father had been a dissolute spendthrift, bankrupt of all moral principle. Nor did he forget that young men often flounder into difficulties almost unwittingly and through no very grave dereliction on their part, and that, in order to get rid of one difficulty, they sometimes succumb to the first temptation that comes in their way, and thereby saddle themselves with an incubus of a far more onerous kind. Finally, he decided that on Dyson's return he would confront him with the evidences of his crime, but that, instead of handing him over to the arm of the law, he would insist on his quitting England for a certain term of years, and would forgive him to the extent of finding him the means wherewith to make a fresh start in life on the other side of the world. Me he bound to secrecy, while, either on the same or the following day, he forwarded the three hundred and fifty pounds to Noyes and thereby redeemed his policy.

'As we all know,' said Robert Melray, 'the interview between my brother and Richard never took place. The latter did not get back from his holidays till the third day after James's death; but it seems somewhat remarkable, in view of my brother's intention, as avowed to you, of confronting Richard with the evidence of his guilt, that the criminatory documents should not have been found by Mr. Cray among his papers.'

'The absence of the papers in question, as it seems to me, can only be explained by one of two suppositions. Either your brother afterwards changed his mind and himself destroyed them, or else Dyson, either suspecting or knowing that his crime had been brought to light during his absence, contrived to find and appropriate them in advance of Mr. Cray.'

'Your last supposition seems to me the more likely of the two,' said Mr. Melray. 'I recollect now that it was not till after the funeral that Mr. Cray set about a systematic examination of my brother's papers, so that, in the interim, Richard would have plenty of opportunity to search for and find what he wanted. I declare that, next to my poor brother's death, to-day's revelation is the most distressing thing I have had to contend with in the whole course of my life!'

'You say, Mr. Dunning, that my brother bound you to secrecy,' resumed Robert Melray after a pause. 'Would it not have been better if you had looked upon his death as virtually absolving you from your promise, thereby enabling you to bring under my notice certain facts which I have learnt to-day for the first time?'

'The point is one which I have debated with myself not once, but many times. The conclusion I finally came to was that, having regard to certain special features of the case, your brother's death did *not* absolve me from my promise. That a grievous crime had been committed could not be gainsaid;

P

but if Mr. Melray chose to condone it that was no business of mine. In all probability, as he said, it was the one great sin of the young man's life, and who should say that it had not been bitterly repented of? Further, how was I to be sure in what light you would look at the affair? You might have chosen to prosecute the culprit, which would have made it a very difficult matter for me ever to forgive myself. In any case his character would have been blasted, and his career, almost of necessity, ruined. Still, I am not prepared to state positively what I might or might not have done, had it been your intention to carry on the business of Melray Brothers, which, almost as a matter of course, would have involved the retention of your kinsman in your service. Knowing, however, as I have from the first, that it is your resolve to get rid of the business as speedily as possible and retire into private life, in which case you and he would part, probably for ever, I deemed it best to keep the secret of his delinquencies locked up in my own breast, where, I can assure you, it had no lack of other secrets to keep it company.'

'I will not say but that you have perhaps acted for the best,' remarked Mr. Melray. 'Still—— But at this stage of the affair it would be futile to dwell on suppositions. What I have now to decide upon is the nature of the steps which it behoves me to take after what has been told me to-day. That, however,' he added with a sigh, ' is a problem which requires consideration.'

'May I ask whether Mr. Dyson is entitled to any bequest under his late cousin's will?' It was Winslade who put the question.

'His name is down in the late Mr. Melray's will for a legacy of three thousand pounds,' replied the lawyer. 'The reason he has not been paid it before now is because the estate has not yet been finally wound up.'

Presently Mr. Melray and Winslade went their way, the former to the railway station, the latter to prosecute certain inquiries on his own account.

The first thing he did was to retrace his steps to the office of Mr. Noyes.

'I must ask you to excuse me for troubling you again,' he said to the money-lender; 'but what I am desirous of knowing is whether any communication passed between Dyson and yourself after his return from his holidays?'

'I wrote to him the day after the funeral, asking him to come and see me. He came. Thereupon I proceeded to tell him of Mr. Melray's discovery, of

p 2

the payment by the latter of the three hundred and fifty pounds (principal and interest of the loan), and of my return to him of the policy of assurance. What, however, I positively declined to tell him, although he pressed me hard to do so, was how and by whose agency the discovery had been brought about. From that day to this I have seen nothing of Mr. Dyson, neither do I care if I never set eyes on him again.'

Philip Winslade thanked Mr. Noyes and took his leave. 'There can be little doubt,' he said to himself as he walked along, 'that, as Dunning suggested, Dyson obtained access to the dead man's papers before Mr. Cray had an opportunity of going through them, and abstracted the promissory note and other documents which bore Mr. Melray's signature as forged by himself.'

In the course of the interview with Mr. Dunning the question had suggested itself to him whether it was really a fact that Dyson did not get back from his holidays till the third day after Mr. Melray's death. In order to answer it, it would be needful for him to go to Merehampton; but, as he had still another inquiry to make in Solchester, he resolved to take that in hand first.

It was not till late in the evening that he got

back to his hotel, after having brought his inquiry to a successful issue. The nature of it and its result cannot be told more succinctly than in the following note:

'My dearest Fanny,—In Mrs. Melray's statement there occurs the following passage: " Evan was an especially handsome young man, with large, black, lustrous eyes, and a dark Italian-looking face." Elsewhere she makes mention of his " ebon brows." Now, in face of this, I have ascertained to-day beyond the possibility of doubt, and not from one, but from three different sources, that Evan Wildash, instead of being a dark-complexioned man with black eyes and "ebon brows," had a particularly fair complexion, also that his eyes were blue-grey, and the colour both of his hair and eyebrows a light reddish brown.

'Solve me the problem which is involved in this contradiction if you can. For myself, I confess that it baffles me.

'For the present I have decided to say nothing of this to Mr. Melray. It would only unsettle him and cause him to imagine all sorts of things, and just now he has enough to occupy his thoughts, poor man!

'I will write you fully in the matter of R. D. in

the course of a few days. I shall be in Merehampton for an hour or two to-morrow, but it is not advisable that we should meet.

' Ever and always yours,
' PHIL.'

In the dusk of the following evening Philip Winslade alighted at Merehampton station. Thence he made his way to the head constable's office, where he was already known, and where he found awaiting him certain information which, the day before, he had asked by letter might be obtained for him.

The information thus supplied him was to the effect that Richard Dyson, at the time of Mr. Melray's death, was lodging with a widow of the name of Parkinson, at No. 5 Lydd Place, but that he had removed to fresh rooms about a month later. It was to No. 5 Lydd Place that Winslade now betook himself.

Widow Parkinson proved to be quite willing to tell all she knew, which was not much, about her late lodger, and even to adorn her somewhat bald narrative with a little fanciful embroidery of her own invention. She considered that she had a grievance against Mr. Dyson. According to her account, he had left her, without any just cause or reason, in what she was pleased to term a very shabby way, and had taken himself and his belongings elsewhere; therefore did she feel herself at liberty to throw reticence to the winds.

That from the widow's flood of talk, which at times threatened, metaphorically, to wash him off his feet, Phil contrived to eliminate the particular bit of information he was in search of goes without saying. Mr. Melray came by his death on the evening of Friday, September 18. According to his landlady, Dyson, at that time on his holidays, did not put in an appearance at his lodgings till Monday, the 21st, early on the morning of which day—that is to say, somewhere between five and six o'clock—he knocked the widow up. The account of himself which he volunteered was to the effect that he had just arrived by an early train, having lengthened out his holiday to the last possible moment, and that he was due back at the office at nine o'clock that same morning. It was the widow herself who broke to him the news of his cousin's tragical fate. 'And awfully cut up about it he was surely,' she went on to remark. ' He had always been a laughing, careless, easy-going sort of gent, and I did not think he had so much feeling in him.'

Philip Winslade left No. 5 Lydd Place no wiser

than he had entered it. While his inquiries of the last few days had served to bring to light many strange and hitherto unsuspected facts, they left the Loudwater Tragedy as much a mystery as before, and to Phil, in the mood in which he then was, it seemed likely to remain such for all time to come. But it sometimes happens that when everything seems at a standstill, when the way we would go is, as it were, blocked by a solid wall against which it would be folly to dash ourselves, silent forces of which we know nothing are at work, and in their own way and their own good time bring round the appointed end, which, as often as not, proves to be an end such as has not been dreamed of by us in any of our schemes of what the future might possibly bring to pass.

CHAPTER XVII

'A MAN I AM, CROSS'D WITH ADVERSITY'

THERE are certain persons connected with our narrative whom, although for some time we may seem to have lost sight of them, it is permissible to hope the reader has not quite forgotten. To them and their concerns we now turn for a little while.

Mrs. Winslade, since her departure from Iselford, had been living a very quiet life with her son in one of the north-western suburbs of London. It was an infinite relief to her to be able to breathe the freer and more generous air of the metropolis (where people scarcely know the names of their next-door neighbours, much less their business, and find enough to do in attending to their own concerns) after having lived for so long a time under the prying eyes of the gossip-mongers of Iselford.

On a certain chilly afternoon in early summer, as

Philip Winslade was being driven in a hansom along the Thames Embankment on an errand connected with his employers, his eyes were attracted to a solitary figure seated on a bench fronting the river. After staring for a moment or two as though doubtful whether he saw aright, he ordered the driver to pull up, and alighted. Even then he paused before advancing. Could it be possible, he asked himself, that yonder lonely figure, sitting with bowed shoulders, his clasped hands resting on the nob of his umbrella, and gazing into vacancy with the unmistakable air of a man weighed down by some secret trouble which he was unable to shake off, could be the Rev. Louth Sudlow? As he drew nearer he saw that it was indeed none other than the Vicar of St. Michael's who was sitting there.

That something was amiss, that the whilom genial, kind-hearted Vicar was suffering from the effects of a blow of some kind, Phil could no longer doubt.

Seeing that the other took no notice of his presence, he laid a hand lightly on his shoulder. 'Mr. Sudlow,' he said, 'this is indeed a surprise to meet you here.'

The Vicar started violently, straightened his back and stared up into Phil's face, as he might into that of a stranger; but presently a slow light of recognition dawned in his eyes. 'Surely—surely it must be young Mr. Winslade,' he said, as he extended his hand with something of his old urbanity.

'Yes, sir, it is I,' answered Phil as he grasped the proffered hand, which trembled like that of a very old man. 'I trust that you are quite well, sir, and that all are well at home.' Then, after a moment's hesitation: 'May I ask whether you have been sitting here long?'

'The Vicar stared around for a moment as if not quite certain how he came to be there, and stroked his cheeks with the fingers and thumb of his left hand before answering. 'Not very long, I think,' he said hesitatingly; 'but, really, I am not quite sure at what hour I left my hotel.'

If Phil, while at a distance, had been struck by the change in his appearance, he was nothing less than dismayed now that he saw him close at hand. The gold-rimmed spectacles were there as of yore, but the eyes that looked through them were dim and sunken, with a sort of vacant despair in them and that sad, heavy-lidded weariness which betokens insomnia. Then, too, it was evident that he had not been shaved for some days, which, of itself, was enough to prove that all was not well with him. His white cravat was limp and loosely tied, his hat and clothes were unbrushed, while his shoes were thick with dust and one shoe-string had come untied. The fresh healthy tints of his face were utterly gone; his cheeks had become flabby and pendulous, and, in short, the Rev. Louth Sudlow looked to the full a dozen years older than when Phil had seen him last.

The young man was at a loss what to say or do next. Presently he ventured to ask, 'Are you making much of a stay in London, Mr. Sudlow?'

Again the elder man had to pull his thoughts together before replying. 'I—I scarcely know. That is to say, I had intended going back home to-night, but—but certain things have happened, and I have not quite made up my mind what to do.'

Phil saw that his thoughts would be far away again in a moment or two, and that he must say what he had to say while he could still claim his attention.

'You are perhaps not aware, sir,' he went on, 'that my mother is keeping house for me in London; but such is the case. I need scarcely tell you how pleased she would be to see you. That is my cab waiting there. Let me persuade you to keep me company as far as where I live. We shall just be in time for a cup of my mother's tea, which I remember you used to say was the best you tasted anywhere.'

Somewhat to his surprise, the Vicar rose at once, although a little stiffly. 'I shall be very gratified indeed,' he said, 'to see Mrs. Winslade again after so long a time. I know no one for whom I have a greater respect and esteem.'

Half-an-hour later the hansom deposited the two men at Pembury Villa.

As Phil had prophesied, they were just in time for a cup of his mother's tea. After the Vicar had partaken of one, together with a few mouthfuls of thin bread-and-butter, he suddenly fell fast asleep in the easy-chair in which he was sitting on one side of the fire. It was past ten o'clock when he awoke. Scarcely had he opened his eyes and had time to call to mind where he was, before his hostess was at his side with a cup of broth in which a glass of sherry had been infused. A few minutes later he averred that he felt better and stronger than he had felt for the past week. It was too late now to think of going down to Iselford till the morrow, and he must perforce stay where he was over night.

As the Vicar sat there an irresistible longing came over him to unburden his mind of the trouble that was crushing him down—so utterly down that, as he sat on the Embankment, he had more than once been tempted to make an end of everything in the cold grey river running so swiftly within a few yards of his feet.

Well, he yielded to the longing and did unburden himself. The story he had to tell, although sad enough, was by no means an uncommon one. He had been induced—he did not say by whom or what —to invest the whole of his savings, painfully accumulated, a few pounds at a time, during a long course of years, in some American mining shares of which only half the nominal capital had been subscribed. The concern had been paying an intermittent dividend for three or four years, and there seemed no likelihood that the shareholders would ever be called upon to disburse the remainder of the capital. The sudden flooding of the mine had, however, entirely altered the complexion of affairs. A large sum was needed to enable it to be got into working order again, and a heavy call was at once made, something like six hundred pounds being demanded from the Rev. Louth Sudlow as his portion thereof. Now, the whole of the Vicar's available resources did not amount to more than one-sixth of the sum in question. The predicament was a serious one—so serious, in point of fact, that Mrs. Sudlow, in a moment of desperation, had been induced to appeal for help to her kinsman, the Earl of Beaumaris. The answer to that appeal had been a curt refusal. After that, as a last resource, the Vicar had come up to London in the hope of being able to borrow the required sum from an old college chum with whom he still kept up a desultory correspondence. Here again disappointment awaited him. His friend had gone on a voyage to the antipodes for the benefit of his health, and was not expected back for some months. Ruin stared the unhappy man in the face, and he had been wandering about the streets for some hours, lacking courage to carry back home the story of his failure, when Phil chanced to encounter him.

Such was the story poured forth by the Vicar, brokenly and with many pauses and hesitations, to his sympathising listeners. But when, an hour later, he went down on his knees in his bedroom he had been made happy by the assurance that the morrow should see his troubles at an end.

Next forenoon Mrs. Winslade went into the City and sought an interview with her broker. When, later in the day, Phil saw the Vicar off at the terminus on his way to Iselford, the heart of the latter was too full to find expression in words. There was a last handshake, a fervent 'God bless you!' and then, as the wheels of the train began to revolve, he was fain to turn away his face and hide the emotion which would no longer be controlled.

CHAPTER XVIII

AN UNLOOKED-FOR DEVELOPMENT

THAT Robert Melray was infinitely distressed by the revelations of his kinsman's delinquences we have had his own word for. He had been so much away from England that for a number of years he had seen scarcely anything of Dyson, but he knew that his brother had always had a high opinion of the young man's industry and business capacity, and that from the time of the elder Dyson's death he had stood in a sort of paternal relation to him. To James Melray, as Robert admitted, far more than to himself, must the discovery, thrust upon him by Dunning, have come as a shock—one, indeed, in his case from which he would never have wholly recovered had his life been prolonged for years.

Richard Dyson's wrongdoing was of a character so extreme that not to have taken some kind of notice of it would have seemed to Robert Melray not merely weak, but criminal. What if he were to carry out the programme as laid down by his brother to Dunning? What if he were to advance Dyson the three thousand pounds which would accrue to him presently under James Melray's will and dismiss him with ignominy? Nothing less than that did it seem possible for him to do. On the other hand, he could not afford to overlook the love borne by his mother for her dead niece's son—a love till now undarkened by the faintest shadow of a cloud. Mrs. Melray senior was seventy-six years old. The murder of her eldest son had been a blow which nothing but her indomitable spirit had enabled her to recover from. Should his be the hand, Robert Melray asked himself, to strike her another blow, which, to such a woman as she—one to whom the probity of every member of the house of Melray was as dear as her own virtue—would be only less terrible than the first? The more he thought of it the more he shrank from taking upon himself the onus of such a deed.

One other course was open to him. He had good hope of being able to dispose of the business of Melray Brothers before he was many weeks older. What if he were to go on till then and make no sign? With the turning over of the business to other hands his relations with Dyson, so far as the firm was concerned, would cease, and there would be no need ever to set eyes on him again were he minded not to do so. What if he were to keep his dark secret undivulged, unless it were to the criminal himself at their hour of parting, and allow his mother to live on for the rest of her days in happy ignorance of what, were it brought to her knowledge, might, perchance, prove well-nigh fatal to her? Yet it galled Robert Melray's strong sense of right and justice to think that a crime so flagrant should go wholly unpunished, even although the criminal were of his own flesh and blood. Willingly, then, did he accede to Dyson's written request for a ten-days' holiday on the plea of ill-health, which he found on his desk one morning shortly after his and Philip Winslade's interview with Mr. Dunning. For the time being he felt absolved from coming to a decision of any kind, and he breathed more freely in consequence.

Fanny Sudlow was another inmate of Loudwater House whose mind was beset by doubts which refused either to allow themselves to be treated as if they were of no consequence, or to furnish any ground from which they might be developed into certainties. It was Phil's last briefly-worded epistle which had served to upset Fanny's equanimity. The strange discrepancy between Evan Wildash, as described by those who had known him, and the same person as described in Mrs. Melray's statement, was one which it baffled her to reconcile, even as it had baffled her lover. When she looked at Denia and asked herself whether it were possible that the foul demon of deceit could find lodgment in so fair a frame, she could but shake her head and tell herself that such a thing was very hard to believe. And yet there was Phil's letter! In her own despite, Fanny began to feel something of that sentiment of vague distrust which the elder Mrs. Melray avowed that her daughter-in-law had inspired her with from the first.

Meanwhile Denia's smiles, as the spring days lengthened, began to come and go more frequently, and there were times when some quaint remark on Fanny's part would elicit a little burst of rippling laughter and a gay rejoinder. The cloud which had for so many months overshadowed her young life was beginning to melt and disappear. Soon the past, with all that it held of pleasure or of pain, would for her have become nothing more than a faint memory which, as time went on, would intrude itself less and less often upon her. Hers was one of those natures which no calamity can crush for long. Her heart was like one of those quiet tarns, deep-buried among the hills, high above which the tempests rave while they lie softly darkling below. She was happy as the birds are happy, because it was not in her to be otherwise: that, at least, was how Fanny Sudlow summed her up in her own thoughts.

But Denia's talk, however wide it might range, or however apparently careless it might be, was always strictly impersonal. Herself and her concerns were kept studiously in the background, and Fanny's hand was not the one to try to drag them to the front. One afternoon, however, either of set purpose or because for a moment her usual caution had deserted her, Denia said to Miss Sudlow: 'Don't these sunny, sweet-breathing spring days, when everything seems bursting with life, often make you long to have wings that you might fly away somewhere—anywhere? They do me. Oh! I am not going to bury myself in this place for ever, let who will think it. I have ideas—intentions. As soon as my husband's affairs have been wound up and I know for certain what my portion of the estate will amount to, I shall leave here and for ever. I have friends in London, and to them I shall go first of all. Afterwards—— But that is no matter.'

It was a hot close evening in mid May. There had scarcely been a breath of air all day and the night had brought no coolness. Fanny Sudlow sat in the dark at the open casement of her bedroom window, her hair unbound and a handkerchief soaked in vinegar laid across her forehead. She was suffering from one of those distressing headaches to which she had been more or less liable all her life. She heard the clock of St. Mary's strike eleven, and still she sat on, knowing of old that it was useless for her to go to bed till the pain should in some measure have abated. Her window looked into a corner of the old garden, in which, just then, the moon shone silvery bright. She had not been out of doors all day; her room felt so stifling and the garden looked so cool and inviting, that a strong desire came over her to get away from the close atmosphere of the house and pace its silent walks awhile in search of that nepenthe she was unable to find indoors. It was a desire which she let have its way.

Having tied back her hair, she flung a dark travelling cloak around her, the hood of which she could draw over her head were she so minded. Then she quitted her room and went lightly downstairs. Early hours were the rule at Loudwater House, and everybody had retired long ago. There were two exits from the house into the garden, one through the conservatory, the other by means of a glass door at the end of a side corridor. Fanny chose the latter. Having, with as little noise as possible, unlocked the door, she opened it and stepped out into the still moonlit night.

Making her way into the farther walks, she began to pace them slowly to and fro. Not a light shone anywhere in such windows of the house as were visible from the garden. The quietude was intense, but presently the silence was broken by the chiming of the quarter before twelve. The moonlight seemed to listen, and as the sound died away a low sigh breathed over the garden, and therewith half-opened leaves and bursting buds began to stir and whisper. They had awoke to the first kisses of the soft cool airs which had come as the avant-couriers of midnight.

Suddenly Fanny became as rigid as a statue. Her quick ears had caught a faint sound, as it might be of the crunching of gravel beneath someone's footsteps. Scarcely breathing, she listened. Yes, there it was again, nearer than before. Evidently someone was approaching in the direction where she was. Her first impulse was to hide herself. In a little trepidation she glanced around. Ah! there, close by her, was the well-house, as it was called. It was the one sheltered spot in the garden. A few swift noiseless strides and her form was lost among its shadows.

The old well was said to be coeval with the building of Loudwater House, to the inmates of which it had been the sole source of water supply for several generations. Of late years, however, that is to say, since the establishment of the Merehampton waterworks, it had fallen into the desuetude and neglect which become the portion of all things which outlast their uses. Nowadays its water was used for two purposes only. One was to supply the dowager Mrs. Melray's tea-kettle (there was no water anywhere, in that lady's opinion, equal to that of the old well for expressing the hidden virtues of Souchong or Bohea). The other purpose to which it was put was the irrigation of the garden. The well itself was covered in by a conical overhanging red-tiled roof, supported by thick oaken beams, with other beams inside, forming, with the windlass-rope and bucket, the needful apparatus for bringing the water to the surface. Even on a moonlight night like the present it was a home of dense shadow.

Fanny drew the hood of her cloak about her and waited in mute expectancy, her eyes fixed on the point whence the sound had come. Nearer came the footsteps—only in the intense midnight quietude could they have been heard—and presently round a curve of the path advanced a female figure, also, like Fanny, darkly cloaked; but, for all that, one glance was enough to reveal to the latter the identity of the new-comer. It was impossible to mistake either figure or gait for those of anyone save Denia Melray.

Fanny, with an arm flung round one of the beams that supported the windlass and with her other hand pressed to her bosom, watched the lithe, graceful figure pass her hiding-place and disappear round a curve of the walk a little further on. Three or four seconds later came the sound of a low whistle, which was immediately responded to by another whistle. Then, as in a flash, Fanny recalled to mind that, among other knick-knacks suspended from a chatelaine which the young widow occasionally wore, was a tiny silver dog-whistle, which had struck her as being a somewhat incongruous ornament for a person to carry who acknowledged to never having owned a dog in her life. Now, in the direction which Denia had taken was the one door by which admittance could be had to the garden from the outside; consequently, when a peculiar grating sound presently made itself heard, Fanny at once came to the conclusion that Mrs. Melray was at that moment withdrawing the bolts of the door in question. Who was her midnight visitor? Fanny's heart beat painfully. On the threshold of what mystery had she unwittingly found herself?

Evidently a change of weather was impending. By this time a fine gauzy mist had overspread the upper reaches of the sky, through which the moon shone with a chastened lustre. The evergreens babbled softly to each other of the rain that was soon to come. Presently a sound of voices reached the ears of the waiting girl, those of a man and a woman talking together in low tones, and then, half a minute later, the speakers came round a turn of the path and so towards the well-house, he with an arm round her waist and with his other hand holding one of hers pressed close to his breast. Then, while the two were still some distance away, something in the man's walk, or figure, or his way of carrying himself, revealed his identity. 'It is Richard Dyson!' exclaimed Fanny to herself, with a thrill that set every nerve tingling. 'Oh, blind, blind that I have been!'

Phil had written her a brief account of what had passed at the interviews with Messrs. Noyes and Dunning, and she was aware that Dyson had been accorded a holiday on the plea of ill-health, Mr. Melray having mentioned the fact in her hearing in reply to his mother's question, 'How is it that I have seen nothing of Richard for the last few days?' In all probability Dyson had only just returned, and his first thought, his first object had been to—— But when Fanny's thoughts had travelled thus far they veered suddenly round to his companion. 'Oh, it is dreadful—dreadful!' she murmured under her breath. 'Who would have thought it of her?—Who would have believed it possible?'

Meanwhile the two were slowly drawing nearer, talking earnestly together. The first words which reached Fanny distinctly were spoken by Denia.

'You are sure your holiday has done you good, and that you have come back better than you went?' she was saying.

'On that point I have no doubt whatever,' was Dyson's low-voiced reply. 'Only, darling, had *you* been with me I should have enjoyed my holiday infinitely more. But the day will come, and that before long, when you will be mine and I shall be yours, and no one in the wide world will have the right to come between us.'

With that he bent his head and, unreproved, pressed his lips to hers.

At that moment they were exactly opposite the well-house. Slowly they kept on to a point about a score yards beyond it, then they turned and as slowly retraced their steps. It struck Fanny that the reason why they kept to that particular walk might be because it was less overlooked from the windows of Loudwater House than any other part of the grounds. Ought she to stay and overhear more of what they might have to say to each other? Ought she not, rather, to try and get away unseen and unheard? What right had she to be there, hiding and listening? On the other hand, she could not forget that a certain dark mystery still remained unfathomed, and in consideration of the strange and undreamed-of way in which events were shaping themselves, she could not help saying to herself, 'What if by staying here and listening I should chance to overhear something which would——' She was about to add, 'bring to light the long-sought-for clue?' But her thought became dumb midway. No, whatever Denia might be, whatever she might have been guilty of otherwise, she, Fanny, could not and would not believe that she had had any hand in the bringing about of her husband's death. It was a hateful thing to be an eavesdropper, and as soon as they had passed her— they were close to the well-house again by this time —she would steal away through the shrubbery at the back.

Suddenly, with a quick movement, Denia disengaged herself from Dyson's encircling arm. 'Ah!' she exclaimed, drawing a deep breath, as she turned and confronted him, 'for the moment I had forgotten. Answer me this, and truthfully, as the breath is in your body: Did you, or did you not, just before you went away, on two occasions, take Annabel Glyn for a walk along the Solchester Road?'

There was a perceptible pause before Dyson replied. Then with a laugh which to Fanny in her hiding-place sounded wholly forced and artificial, he said: 'Why, my darling, what rubbishing nonsense is this you have got into that pretty head of yours? *I* take Annabel Glyn for a walk? The idea is preposterous.'

'Your answer is no answer. Did you, or did you not, take her?'

'I did not.'

'That you will swear?'

'That I swear.'

'Very well. I will take your word for the truth of what you tell me. It was the dusk of evening and my informant must have mistaken someone else for you. Only, I want you to understand, Dick, that if I know how to love, I know how to hate just as fervently. It is as easy to me to do one as the other.

Therefore, *cher ami*, woe be to you if you deceive me. Don't forget—never for one moment forget, that your secret is my property—that I hold your life in the hollow of my hand!'

For a moment or two longer her emotion seemed almost to choke her; then suddenly turning, she placed her hand within his arm. 'Come,' she said, and her voice was again as soft as that of a cooing dove, 'just one turn more and then you must positively go. Who can say what prying eyes may not be secretly watching us?'

With that they passed out of earshot, and the same instant Fanny turned and sped softly away through the shrubbery at the back of the well-house. As she passed the conservatory she saw that the door was ajar, but she did not pause till she reached her own room. Then she stood with her hands pressed to her head, amazed—confounded—not so much by her own blindness as by the revelation of Denia's unparalleled cunning and duplicity. It almost took her breath away to think of it. How she had hoodwinked them all!—she, with her doll's eyes and candid-seeming brow, and her smile that was almost infantine in its sweetness. What puppets they had been in her fingers—Mr. Melray, Phil, and herself!

And she loved Richard Dyson! On that point,

after what she, Fanny, had been witness to, there could be no possible doubt; and yet all along Denia had made believe that Dyson's presence was utterly repugnant to her. But over and above their love for each other was there not some dark secret between the two—some bond the nature of which was known to themselves alone? 'Your secret is my property. I hold your life in the hollow of my hand.' Those had been Denia's words, and they had been meant as a warning to Dyson. What hidden meaning lay at the back of them? Could it, after all, be possible that Denia—— ? 'No—no—even now I will not believe it!' cried Fanny when her thoughts had carried her thus far.

CHAPTER XIX

AN UNAVOIDABLE NECESSITY

LITTLE sleep had Fanny Sudlow that night. In the morning she arose weary and unrefreshed; but by that time she saw her duty clearly before her. How distasteful soever it might be to her to do so, it was evident that she must acquaint Mr. Melray with what she had seen and heard overnight in the garden. This was no commonplace instance of a pair of secret lovers, of two people meeting stealthily at midnight. With the knowledge strong upon her of what had happened under that roof one fatal September night and of all that had since occurred, no other course seemed open to her. It was a necessity from which she shrank with the most heartfelt repugnance, but she was powerless to help herself. Her first impulse had been to telegraph to Phil and ask him to meet her at Merehampton station. She would have given much, very much, to be able to confide her secret to him and so shift to his broad shoulders the responsibility of deciding what ought to be done next. But she called to mind the fact that Phil was on the Continent, having been sent there, in the interests of the *Pharos*, to work up a certain subject which was just then attracting a good deal of public attention, and that the date of his return was uncertain. It was very unfortunate, but in nowise could it be helped.

She was almost glad, when she went downstairs, to find that Mr. Melray had left home for the day on business and would not be back till a late hour. A respite, however brief, was welcome.

It was something of an ordeal for her to be compelled to meet Denia at meal times, and yet, neither by tone, nor look, nor manner, allow anything to escape her which would tend to arouse the suspicions of that sharp-witted young woman. Fortunately the day was a wet one. There was no possibility of going out, consequently no opportunity was afforded Denia for a private gossip with Miss Sudlow. The latter kept close to the school-room, and, except at table, the two saw nothing of each other. The dowager Mrs. Melray, being unaware of Richard Dyson's return, made no inquiry about him; and so the day wore itself uneventfully away. There was no slightest sign to give warning of the storm that was so soon to break.

It was close upon eleven o'clock when Robert Melray reached home. He would have been annoyed had he found anyone waiting up for him except the one man-servant who was kept at Loudwater House. His supper had been laid for him in the dining-room. 'You can fasten up, Johnson, and get to bed as soon as you like,' he said to the man as he took off his overcoat in the hall. 'I shall not want you any more to-night.'

Robert Melray had finished his supper and was glancing somewhat sleepily over the *Times*, when a low knock at the door startled him into wakefulness. His surprise was not lessened when, in response to his 'Come in,' the door opened and he saw that his untimely visitor was none other than Miss Sudlow.

Of Fanny's apologies for her intrusion, and of the narrative she presently proceeded to unfold to her wondering listener, it is not requisite that we should speak in detail. What she had to tell is already known to the reader.

'It is an odious duty, Mr. Melray, that I have taken upon myself,' she said in conclusion, with a little break in her voice, 'but I felt that no other course was open to me.'

'None whatever, Miss Sudlow. You have done your duty, and I honour you for it; indeed, I may add that I am infinitely obliged to you.'

That he was terribly pained and distressed by what had just been told him was plainly evident. Sick at heart, Fanny left him. Just then she devoutly wished that she had never set foot across the threshold of Loudwater House.

Mention has been made of a certain Miss Annabel Glyn. Till within six months of the date at which we have now arrived the young woman in question had been a milliner's assistant in one of the Merehampton shops. Then, by the death of an uncle in Australia, she had come in for a fortune of eight thousand pounds, whereupon she had at once thrown up her situation, and, till she could decide upon her future plans, had gone to lodge with the widow of a Captain Malcolm in the most fashionable part of Merehampton. Miss Glyn being of age and both her parents being dead, she was at liberty to bestow her hand and fortune on whomsoever she pleased.

Denia's information with regard to Dyson and Miss Glyn having been seen walking out together had reached her through a very simple channel. It so fell out that Charlotte Wallis (she who had been the first to find Mr. Melray's body and give the alarm), whose duties were partly those of own maid to young Mrs. Melray, had a brother who was a member of the very limited police force of Merehampton. It was through information furnished by him to his sister and passed on by the latter to her mistress, that Denia had based the interrogatory she put to Dyson in the garden. Still, she was willing to believe that Charlotte's brother might have been mistaken, more especially after Dyson's emphatic denial that he had ever been out walking with Annabel Glyn.

CHAPTER XX

'WE MUST SPEAK BY THE CARD'

IT was Thursday morning, the morning of the day following that of Mr. Melray's journey to London. Denia, Freddy, and Miss Sudlow breakfasted by themselves, Mr. Melray having requested that his tea and toast might be taken upstairs to his dressing-room. Denia had just left the table and was on her way back to her own room, when she was accosted by Charlotte. 'If you please, ma'am,' said the girl, 'I have had a note this morning from my brother. I don't know whether you would care to read it, but in case you should I have left it on your dressing-table.'

Be it noted that Charlotte was the only person, or so Denia believed, who had any knowledge or suspicion of the relations between Dyson and her mistress.

Denia nodded and passed on. Shutting the door of the room behind her, she went quickly up to the table and pounced on the note. She felt quite sure that Charlotte would not have left it for her to read had there not been something in it which nearly concerned her.

Here is what she read:

'Dear Lotty,—This comes to inform you that on Tuesday evening, between nine and ten o'clock, I see Mr. R. D. and Miss G. a-walking out together. They passed close under a lamp by which I was standing, so that I could not be mistaken about either one or the other. Still, to make quite sure, I thought I would follow them. I did so, and I see them part at Mrs. Malcolm's door. He kissed her, and then she rang the bell. Then he strolled back to his lodgings in Peelgate, I strolling after him; and that is all I know.

'Your loving brother,
'Edgar Wallis.'

(It was at midnight on Tuesday that Dyson had kissed Denia in the garden.)

Ten minutes later Denia received a message to the effect that Mr. Melray would feel obliged if she would step downstairs to his office. 'Something about money matters, I suppose,' she said wearily to herself. She went at once, presaging nothing, fearing nothing. She was as one half dazed, who, having been struck down from behind, as yet can hardly realise what has happened to him. Although she was unaware of it, the note which had been to her as a message of doom was still clutched tightly between her fingers as she entered the room. Robert Melray was at once struck by the pallor of her face, and by a certain hard, cold glitter in her eyes such as he had never noticed in them before.

'Sit down, Denia; I have something of particular moment to say to you,' he began, in no unkindly tones, indicating a chair at the table opposite his own. Then, opening the door of the outer office, he said: 'Mr. Cray, will you be good enough to see that I am not disturbed by anybody till I ring.' Then he turned the key of the door which opened into the side lane, after which he sat down facing Denia. It was evident to that clear-sighted young woman, even through her own perturbation, that he was extremely nervous and ill at ease.

With his elbows resting on the table and his fingers interlocked, he gazed at her for a few seconds with a sort of sad, wistful earnestness. Then clearing his voice he said: 'I am a poor hand at a preface, or at leading up by degrees to anything I may have to say.

In short, I cannot beat about the bush.' For a moment he paused, and again he cleared his voice. 'Denia, it has come to my knowledge that you and Richard Dyson were together in the garden at midnight on Tuesday. It was your hand that admitted him by way of the side-door.'

He ceased, as though to afford her time to recover herself. The pallor of her face gave way to a great wave of colour which surged quickly up from her bosom to her cheeks and thence to the roots of her hair. For a few moments it remained thus, at high-water mark as it were, and then began to subside.

'His arm was round you,' continued Robert, 'he kissed you and you did not repulse him. Only one inference can be drawn—that he and you are in love with each other.'

Denia's bosom rose with the slow indrawing of her breath. It was one of those supreme moments when, brought to bay, one's whole future course in life may depend on the next few sentences that fall from one's lips.

'I believed that Richard Dyson loved me, but now I know that I was mistaken,' said Denia in a low voice. 'I loved him (or, perhaps, I only dreamt I did), but now—I hate him!'

'You hate him!' exclaimed Robert. 'And yet,

less than thirty-six hours ago, you allowed him un-reproved to press his lips to yours.'

'A great deal may happen in thirty-six hours. I loved him then. I hate him now.'

'So be it. Whatever reasons may have influenced you in this sudden change of feeling are no concern of mine. What, however, does seem to concern me (and you yourself can best infer why), and what I must ask you to afford me some explanation of, is a certain threat which you made use of to Dyson on Tuesday night. You bade him beware in that his secret was your property, that you "held his life in the hollow of your hand." Now, will you be good enough to tell me to what those words referred?'

Denia's hesitation was of the briefest. For a moment or two she set her teeth hard, then with a little nod of her head she said: 'Yes, Mr. Melray, I *will* tell you—will tell you everything. From this moment there shall be no more secrets between you and me. I used those words to Richard Dyson because to his hand was due the death of my husband and your brother!'

Robert Melray sank back in his chair with a gasp. 'You have known this all along, and yet you have kept it hidden from everyone in your own breast!' he contrived to say after a time.

'I have known it all along, and yet I have kept it hidden from everyone,' came like an echo from Denia's lips.

Robert knew not what to say. Never had he been so utterly at a loss for words. There was a space of silence while the two sat confronting each other. Denia was the first to break it.

'You stare at me, Mr. Melray, as if I were some monster of wickedness,' she said with a bitter smile. 'Perhaps, before you open your lips to reproach me or to give utterance to words such as, later on, you might see reason to regret, it may be as well that you should be enlightened about certain matters as to which at present you are wholly ignorant. If you will condescend to listen to me, I will promise to be as little tedious as possible, and that, on this occasion at least, you shall hear from me the truth, the whole truth, and nothing but the truth!'

'Go on,' said Robert in a voice that was hardly raised above a whisper.

But Denia did not at once respond to the invitation. It was neither shyness nor hesitation that held her back; the former, indeed, was a quality of which she knew nothing; she was merely considering in what terms it behoved her to couch her version of what could no longer be kept back.

'It was my husband who, soon after our marriage introduced Richard Dyson to me,' at length she began, her blue eyes fixed calmly on Robert Melray's face. 'Before long he began to spend three or four evenings a week in the drawing-room, and by the time I had been half a year married it was evident to me that (not to mince my words) he had either fallen in love with me or was wishful of making me believe that he had done so. He was young and handsome and had a certain fascinating way with him; he played and sang charmingly, or so it seemed to me. I liked and respected my husband—no one could help doing that—and I strove to do my duty by him as a true wife should do; but I did not love him. Love is a very different sentiment from that which I experienced for James Melray. Is it, then, greatly to be wondered at if, at times, my heart could not help fluttering a little under the ardent glances of Richard Dyson? But, for all that, when, one day, he ventured to whisper certain words in my ear such as he had no right to whisper in the ear of any married woman, I was not slow in giving him to understand what an egregious piece of folly he had been guilty of. So strongly, indeed, did I resent the liberty he had taken that he never ventured to err in the same way again. And so matters went on as before. I continued to do my duty by my husband and guarded my feelings to the best of my ability; but, having promised that this shall be a full and frank confession, let me at once admit that deep down in my heart a germ of love lay perdu, and that it was only my strong sense of wifely obligation and the remembrance of all I owed my husband, which kept it there, frozen and half torpid, like a bulb buried deep under the snow.

'Such was the state of affairs on Friday, the 18th of September. Richard had gone for his annual holiday about ten days before. Sometimes I felt sad and lonely without him, missing his bright, vivacious talk and those half-veiled glances the meaning of which could be read by me alone; at other times I wished most devoutly that I might never set eyes on him again.

'At eight o'clock that evening I saw my husband off on his way to Mr. Arbour's for his usual rubber of whist. After that I sat down with the intention of writing a long letter to my friend, Mrs. Simpson. I was alone in the little sitting-room at the back of the drawing-room. The servants were all below stairs. Your mother had gone to her own room at the further end of the long corridor, and Miss Armishaw with her. I had got about half-way through my letter when a slight noise caused me to turn my head, and there in the open door-way I beheld Richard Dyson! Next instant he came forward and fell on his knees at my feet. His dress was disordered, his face was as white as that of corpse, while his eyes were charged with horror and fear, the like of which I have never seen in those of anyone else. "Save me! Save me!" were the first words he gave utterance to.

'I have no wish to weary you, and will relate, as succinctly as possible, the story told me by Richard on that memorable night.

'Lack of funds had brought him back from his holidays two or three days before he was due at business. He had been compelled to leave his luggage in pawn at the seaside hotel where he had been staying. Not wishing it to be known, for private reasons of his own, that he had come back before his time, he had alighted from the train at a station a couple of miles away, and was making his way through some of the back streets to his lodgings, when he came face to face with Mr. Melray. The recognition was mutual. It would seem that Richard had been guilty of something at which my husband had just cause to be offended, but of what nature the something in question was even now I have no knowledge. In any case, Mr. Melray insisted on Richard there and then accompanying him back to his office. Once there, they appear to have got to high words, one thing leading to another, till at length Mr. Melray threatened Richard with some kind of public exposure. There was a struggle for the possession of some papers, and in the result my husband unhappily came by his death. On his knees Richard swore to me by everything he held sacred that it was purely an accident. Well, I believed him. Some people might say that, instead of putting credence in what he told me, I ought there and then to have denounced him as a murderer; but to me it seemed too terrible a thing to credit that he could wilfully have been guilty of such a crime. But, be that as it may, when he appealed to me to save him I felt it impossible to reject his appeal. From Friday night till an early hour on Monday he lay hidden in the lumber-room on the top floor, which is rarely entered from one year's end to another, I supplying him with food meanwhile. On Monday morning he made his appearance at his lodgings, and, later on, at the office, no one suspecting otherwise than that he had just got back from his holidays.'

Robert Melray had not interrupted her by a word. He sat for a space after she had done with drawn brows and introverted eyes which saw nothing of what was before them. At length he roused himself with a deep sigh. 'That your narrative throws a wholly unexpected light on a mystery which has long perplexed both me and others cannot be denied, he said, 'and I am obliged to you for the frankness which has at length prompted the telling of it. Still, I altogether fail to reconcile what you have just told me with the details of certain circumstances as set down in your written statement of a fortnight ago.'

A short derisive laugh broke from Denia. 'My good sir,' she said, ' seeing that I have just told you the true history of the events of the 18th of September as far as they concern me individually, but one inference can be drawn by you with regard to my so-called statement, namely, that from beginning to end it was a simple tissue of romance.'

Mr. Melray stared at her in wide-eyed amazement. 'But surely,' he gasped, ' you don't mean to say that all which was there stated with reference to Evan Wildash and yourself was——'

'A sheer piece of rigmarole—that and nothing more. I found it impossible to resist the temptation Miss Sudlow was good enough to put in my way. Besides, I had a suspicion, which may or may not have been baseless, that she had been brought to Loudwater House purposely to watch me and spy upon my actions, so that when she gave me a certain story to read, which undoubtedly seemed to embody in rather a startling way a number of details in connection with my husband's death, I decided to accept it as a true narrative, and it was on that assumption that I wrote out my statement. I need hardly add that my object in acting thus was to divert suspicion from the real quarter, and, if it were possible thereby to do so, to bring to an end, once and for ever, the inquiry into the causes of my husband's death.'

'It is most extraordinary!' ejaculated Robert Melray. 'But do you mean to imply that Evan Wildash never came back from Africa?'

'Never, to my knowledge. He was reported to have died there, and, for anything known by me to the contrary the report was true.'

'Then, as regards the man who was killed in the railway accident?'

'I know no more about him than about the man in the moon.'

Robert Melray sat back in his chair like a man bereft of speech.

CHAPTER XXI

THE TRUTH AT LAST

SOME minutes later Robert Melray opened the door which led to the outer office, and said to his head clerk, 'Mr. Cray, will you be good enough to ask Mr. Dyson to step this way?'

When Richard Dyson entered the private office he had no prevision that he was wanted about anything more important than some ordinary business detail. Long immunity from suspicion had bred in him the belief that his dark secret was buried out of sight for ever. He glanced round as he entered. He had not the remotest suspicion that the high screen in the corner hid Denia from his view.

'Sit there,' said Robert, pointing to the chair vacated by Denia a minute before. There was something in his tone which caused Dyson to glance keenly at him, something which warned him to be

s

on his guard. The two had not met since the latter's return from his leave of absence.

'Since I saw you last to speak to,' began Robert, regarding the other with a cold steady gaze, 'certain facts have come to my knowledge which have shocked and surprised me far more than I could express to you in any words. In order that you need be under no misapprehension as to how much, or how little, I know of the circumstances in question, I will at once enlighten you on the point. Being in want of money for some purpose of which I know nothing, you abstracted my brother's life policy from the safe, and on the security of it obtained an advance of three hundred pounds from Mr. Noyes of Solchester. But, in order to carry out your nefarious purpose, you were compelled to forge James's signature to three several documents. Of the means by which you contrived to make Mr. Noyes believe that he was dealing with my brother in person, I will say nothing. Whether it was your intention ultimately to redeem the policy and put it back in the place whence you had taken it, or whether——'

'Certainly it was my intention to redeem the policy and replace it in the safe, without, as I hoped, anyone being the wiser,' broke in Dyson a little impetuously. He was pale, but composed.

Robert's exordium had allowed time for his nerves to recover from any shock which the latter's opening words might have caused them. 'The three hundred pounds was only borrowed for a term of four months, by the end of which time I had every reason to believe that I should be in ample funds. I may add that my difficulties were the result of some unfortunate operations on the Stock Exchange, but latterly I had hit on a good thing and I felt no doubt whatever about being able shortly to far more than recoup myself for all my losses.'

'I will refrain from asking you how you proposed to yourself to get out of the clutches of Mr. Noyes, and to redeem the policy in case your expectations should come to nothing. But, in all likelihood, that was a contingency which you never cared to face. In any case, it is a matter of no consequence at this time of day; so, if you have no objection, we will now come to the events of the 18th of September.'

Dyson started visibly and bit his under-lip hard, as he might have done had he been on the point of undergoing a surgical operation.

'For reasons best known to yourself,' resumed Robert in the same quiet, passionless voice in which he had spoken before, 'you arrived back from your holiday on Friday evening, although you were not due at business till the following Monday. While on your way to your lodgings you came face to face with my brother, and in consequence, doubtless, of certain representations on his part, you accompanied him back to his office—to this very room, in point of fact. A quarter of an hour later you surprised Mrs. Melray in her sitting-room. In explanation of your intrusion you gave her to understand that, through some mischance, my brother had met his death at your hands, and you appealed to her to help to save you from the consequences of your rash act. To that appeal she responded by finding you, unknown to anyone, shelter and food for three nights and two days; by which means you were enabled to appear at the office on Monday morning as if you had but just got back from your holiday. Now, Richard Dyson, I demand of you that you shall account to me for my brother! I hint no threats, but it must be plain to you on the verge of what a precipice you are standing. Let me have the truth about what happened just as it did happen. I ask for no more and I have a right to look for no less.'

It would not be easy to describe with what a strange confluence of emotions Dyson had listened to the growing indictment. Wonder as whence and how Robert had gleaned his information was, perhaps, his predominant feeling just then. Could it be possible, he asked himself, that Denia had turned traitor and betrayed him? But such was his faith in the sincerity of her love for him that he dismissed the thought almost as soon as it was formed. But it was no time for indulging in futile speculations. Robert Melray was waiting with bent brows.

Dyson's face darkened as his thoughts concentred themselves on the story he had to tell. 'Yes,' he presently began, facing Robert with the quiet and collected air of one who has nothing to hide, 'as you have stated, I unexpectedly encountered cousin James on my way from the railway station to my lodgings. Gripping me by the arm he said, "So you are back, are you? That is well. I want particularly to speak with you. Come with me at once to my office." Nothing more was said, but I pretty well guessed what was in the wind. As soon as we were inside the office, with the door shut and the gas alight, he turned upon me. As I surmised, he had found out about the abstraction of the policy and the advance obtained by means of it from Noyes. I at once admitted that it was an infamous return to have made for all that he had done for me. I explained to him, as I have explained to you, by what means it happened that I was temporarily "cornered," that not to have raised the three hundred pounds meant exposure and ruin, and that I had every expectation of being in a position to repay the amount before the bill would fall due. But by this he had worked himself into a passion and was no longer in a condition to listen to any excuses. You cannot have forgotten to what ungovernable bursts of rage he would give way on rare occasions, in one of which, when you were boys, I have been told he all but strangled you, his brother.

'He had already opened the safe and brought thence the documents to which I had forged his signature. Placing one finger on them as they lay on the table, and speaking in coldly contemptuous tones, which stung me far more than any invective on his part would have done, he said : " Here are the proofs of your guilt. Here is the evidence that will condemn you to penal servitude. In less than an hour from now the four walls of Merehampton gaol will hold your worthless carcase." It was a threat that maddened me. I dashed his hand aside and seized the papers. With a cry like that of some wild animal, he sprang from his chair and flung himself upon me. Although double my age, he was a much more powerful and muscular man than I, and when once he had got his fingers fixed firmly inside my necktie and was grinding his knuckles into my throat, I was almost as powerless in his hands as a child would have been. As it seems to me now, it was all the work of a few seconds. Backward and forward we swayed and struggled, I trying desperately, but vainly, with one hand to loosen his hold of me, but still gripping the papers fast with my other hand; he, his eyes glaring with a passion that was almost maniacal, and those terrible knuckles still compressing my windpipe. I was being slowly but surely choked. Vivid jets of flame began to dance and quiver before my eyes; my heart laboured almost to the point of bursting; the papers dropped from my fingers; I could feel myself being forced back against the table till my spine was bent half double. Suddenly my fingers, wildly clutching at nothing, came in contact with a heavy iron paperweight and closed over it. With a last effort I struck with all my force at my cousin's head. For aught I know, I may have struck more than once, but in the very act consciousness left me.

'When I regained my senses, a quarter of an hour later, I was lying on the floor. A little way off lay the body of my cousin—stone dead. Hardly had I time to realise the horror of the situation before I heard the voices of two men talking in the lane outside. With that, the instinct of self-preservation came back in full force. As in a flash, I seemed to see how hardly it would fare with me should I chance to be found there. After picking up the papers which had cost me so dearly, I put out the gas, and then a sudden impulse, for which I am unable to account, decided me to—to—— But you know already what befell afterwards.'

'And the paper-weight—what became of that?' demanded Robert Melray after a short silence.

'I dropped it into the pocket of my coat and took it upstairs with me. Later on I hid it away in the lumber-room where I myself was in hiding at the time.'

'You had better leave me now,' said Robert presently. 'I will see you again later in the day. I must have time to think over what you have told me and to decide upon some course of action which——'

But at this juncture there came a tap at the door, which was followed by the intrusion of Mr. Cray's spectacled head. 'I beg your pardon, sir,' said the chief clerk, 'but Mr. Bayliss has been waiting some time, and he says that if you can't see him at once, he will call again to-morrow, or next day.'

Now, Mr. Bayliss was the person with whom

Robert was in negotiation for the purchase of the business of Melray Brothers.

'I will see him now—at once,' was his reply.

Richard Dyson stepped quietly out without a word more, as Robert went forward into the outer office to greet his visitor. At the same moment Denia slipped out of her hiding-place, and out of the room by the other door, unseen and unheard by anyone.

CHAPTER XXII

ALL'S WELL THAT ENDS WELL

Richard Dyson went out to luncheon at his usual time, but failed to return. About five o'clock Mr. Melray asked for him, but no one knew what had become of him, nor did any authentic tidings of him come to hand till the following day. It was then discovered that he and Miss Glyn had gone off together, after having been married at an early hour by special license. Neither of them was ever seen in Merehampton again. It may be that Robert Melray was not ill-pleased to have the hard problem which circumstances would otherwise have compelled him to solve taken out of his hands and done with, as far as he was concerned, for ever.

Mrs. Melray the elder was never told that it was to the hand of her nephew that James Melray owed his death-blow. To her, as to the world at large, the Loudwater Tragedy remained an unsolved mystery.

Neither was she ever enlightened as to that secondary crime of forgery and fraud of which her nephew had been guilty. To have told her would have answered no good purpose, but might, indeed, have had a serious effect upon her health, already hardly tried by that which had gone before. It was a quite sufficient shock to her to learn of the elopement of Dyson and Miss Glyn. Womanlike, she laid the whole blame of the affair on the girl. Doubtless she was one of those double-faced, scheming hussies who seem sent into the world purposely to spoil the lives and ruin the careers of whatever young men may not be strong-minded enough to resist their siren-like blandishments. That poor dear Richard had been both weak and foolish she could not deny; still, he was to be pitied far more than blamed. He was not the first man by many, nor would he be the last, to fall a victim to the arts of a designing woman. As long as she lived Mrs. Melray continued to think and speak of Dyson with mingled pity and tenderness, and at her death it was found that she had bequeathed him half of all she had to leave.

Long before that event took place Robert Melray had paid over to Dyson, or rather to the solicitor who represented him, the three thousand pounds willed him by the man whose death lay at his door. Had it not been for those two legacies falling in one after another, Dyson, in all probability, would have lived several years longer than he did. But for them—his wife's fortune having been quickly dissipated—he would not have been able to continue in that course of fast living, combined with hard drinking, which gradually shattered his constitution and consigned him to a premature grave while he ought still to have been in the prime of life.

The Erinyes have many ways of avenging their misdeeds on the children of men.

Within twenty-four hours of Dyson's disappearance Denia had quitted Loudwater House, never to return. She announced her intention of taking up her abode, for a time at least, with certain friends in London whom she had known during her uncle's lifetime. About a year later, she married again, by which time she had received her share of the property left by her husband. Her second husband (a blackleg with the manners and education of a gentleman) was a very different type of man from James Melray, as, later on, Denia found to her cost.

It was about the time of Denia's marriage that the final mystery in connection with the Loudwater Tragedy found its solution.

One day a young American arrived at Merehampton in search of his brother, who had been missing for upwards of a year. After some difficulty he had succeeded in tracing him as far as the little seaport, but at that point he came, for the time being, to a deadlock. Like so many of his countrymen, the missing man had been fond of adventure and change of scene. For many months he had been touring about England, chiefly on foot, and, with a view of eking out his slender means, had been in the habit of writing sketches of English life and character for one or more American newspapers, as well as occasional short stories for sundry magazines.

It would be beyond the scope of this narrative to recount how Gavin Pryce, having succeeded in picking up the missing clue, was led onward step by step till at length a shred of doubt was no longer left him that the unidentified victim of the Eastwich accident was none other than his brother Evan.

The way in which the latter had acquired his intimate knowledge of the details of the Loudwater Tragedy, as set forth by him in the MS. which fell into the hands of Mr. Timmins, was as peculiar as it was simple.

It may be remembered that the alarm raised by the housemaid Charlotte, which followed immediately on her discovery of her master's body, was responded to by a constable and a couple of strangers who happened to be passing at the time. One of the strangers in question was the young American, Evan Pryce. He it was who helped the constable to examine the body with the view of ascertaining whether life was extinct, and, a little later, assisted in carrying it upstairs. At the inquest he was called as a witness, and, being a newspaper man, the case had an exceptional interest for him in so far as it furnished him with an ample supply ot 'copy' for some time to come. Having used it up as far as the newspapers were concerned, the idea would appear to have occurred to him that the main incidents of the affair, if worked up into a magazine story, would not prove ineffective. Hence, in order to supply the crime with a *raison d'être*, his invention of a lover for the young wife, who finding on his return from abroad that she is married, picks a quarrel with the husband; at which point, as the reader may remember, the manuscript broke off abruptly. Whether the author had written no further when he came by his untimely end, or whether only a part of the manuscript was recovered from the *débris* of the accident, is a question which must remain for ever unanswered. It will not have been forgotten that it was Mr. Timmins who furnished the story with an ending after a fashion of his own.

That it was as gall and wormwood to Mrs. Sudlow to have to be beholden to a woman she disliked more than anyone, and whom she had contemned and turned her back upon as the widow of a notorious felon, for the pecuniary help which had been forthcoming from no other source, may be taken for granted. But for Mrs. Winslade the Vicar would have been a ruined man. It was bitter, very bitter, to have to acknowledge that such was the indisputable fact. And then, what likelihood was there of her husband ever being in a position to pay back the sum which had been thus generously and unconditionally advanced? None at all as far as Mrs. Sudlow could see. A few pounds might be spared now and again—mere driblets, as it were—but, in the face of family expenses which could not but help growing for several years to come, it would not be possible to do more, In those days Mrs. Sudlow was a very unhappy woman.

No one, not even her husband, ever heard her mention Mrs. Winslade's name. When, half a year later, Philip and Fanny were married, no word of opposition fell from her lips; but, on the other hand, she resolutely declined to be present at the ceremony. Neither when, later on, Philip offered to find a situation for her eldest son in the counting-house of

Mr. Layland did she raise the slightest objection to his doing so. It was as though her life was burdened with the weight of an obligation from which she found it impossible to rid herself.

Finally, it may be said of the 'Vicaress' that, if from the date of a certain transaction Mrs. Winslade's name found no mention at her lips, neither did that of her kinsman, the Earl of Beaumaris. One seemed to have passed out of the sphere of her mental retina as absolutely as the other.

Once and once only did Fanny and Denia see each other again after the latter's abrupt departure from Loudwater House.

Late one autumn evening about a year and a half after Fanny's marriage, as she was sitting alone in the drawing-room, she was informed that a lady was waiting in the entrance-hall who wished particularly to see her, but who refused to send in her name. The untimely visitor proved to be none other than Denia Melray, now Mrs. Ferdinand Gascoigne. The two years which had elapsed since Fanny had seen her last had wrought a great change in her appearance, but not for the better. She had fallen away both in face and figure; there were dark half-circles under her eyes; while that expression of mingled candour and ingenuousness which had been one of her greatest charms in days gone by had given place to the anxious careworn look of one whose days and nights were full of trouble.

That Fanny was surprised to see her goes without saying. She did not know then, nor does she to this day, by what means Denia had discovered her address. When greetings were over and they were together in the drawing-room, Mrs. Gascoigne said: 'I am here this evening, my dear, on purpose to ask you a very great favour. But where is Mr. Winslade?'

Fanny explained that her husband had gone for a couple of days' shooting to the house of a bachelor friend in the shires.

'So much the better,' observed Denia in her old quick way. 'Pleased as on many accounts I should have been to see Mr. Winslade again, I am more pleased that he is not here to-night. But your eyes are asking what the favour is that I want you to grant me. It is simply this: I have left my husband, without his knowledge or consent, and I want you to give me shelter till morning.'

'You have left your husband!' exclaimed Fanny. 'Oh, Mrs. Gascoigne!'

'Yes, I have left him, never to go back,' replied Denia with a hard cold glitter in her blue-grey eyes. Then with deft fingers she unfastened a portion of her dress, and baring her left shoulder, exposed to Fanny's shocked gaze a great livid bruise. 'That is where he struck me last night with his clenched fist and felled me to the ground. It is not the first occasion by many that he has struck me. But last night was the climax. Then and there I swore an oath to leave him. He did not believe me, but when he gets home from his club at midnight he will not find me there. To-day I have been making certain arrangements which to-morrow will see completed. At ten o'clock my cousin, William Champneys—the son of my late uncle—will call here for me (you see, dear, I have taken the liberty of assuming that you won't turn me into the street), and will take me down into the country to some relatives of my mother, whom I have not seen since I was quite a child.'

It is almost needless to state that Mrs. Gascoigne was accorded the shelter she craved.

At ten o'clock next morning a hired brougham drove up at the door, and Mr. William Champneys was announced. Denia had already breakfasted (her troubles seemed in no wise to have impaired her appetite), and two minutes sufficed her to put on her outdoor things. Having introduced her cousin to Fanny, she seemed in a hurry to be gone. Her last words as she touched Fanny's cheek with her lips were:

'I shall be sure to write to you, dear, and let you know how I am getting on.' But she never did.

Two months later Mr. Ferdinand Gascoigne fell down a flight of stairs and broke his neck.

Half a year later still came an Australian newspaper, addressed to Winslade, containing an announcement of the marriage of 'Evan Wildash, Esq., formerly of Solchester, England, to Denia (*née* Lidington), widow of Ferdinand Gascoigne, Esq., of London.'

When Phil read the announcement aloud he and his wife could only stare at one another in blank bewilderment.

'Evan Wildash alive!' gasped Phil.

'And married to Denia at last!' exclaimed Fanny. 'Of all the strange developments brought about by the Loudwater case this last one is the strangest of all.'

'By the way,' remarked Phil a little later, 'you never told me, or else I omitted to ask, what kind of looking man was the cousin in whose charge Mrs. Gascoigne left here.'

Thereupon Fanny proceeded to describe Mr. William Champneys to the best of her ability.

'Your description tallies exactly with that of Evan Wildash, as given me at Solchester. And now that I begin to call things to mind, I am nearly sure I was told by somebody that Mr. Champneys, Denia's uncle, was a bachelor. Can it be possible that the man she introduced to you as her cousin was none other than Evan Wildash himself? It would be just like one of Denia's *supercheries* if it were so.'

It was a question to which no answer was ever forthcoming.

Maud Muller

"It Might Have Been."

Her Joy was Duty
And Love was Law.

MAUD MULLER.

Maud Muller, on a summer's day, raked the meadow sweet with hay.
Beneath her torn hat glowed the wealth of simple beauty and rustic health.
Singing, she wrought, and her merry glee the mock-bird echoed from his tree.
But when she glanced to the far-off town, white from its hill-slope looking down,
The sweet song died, and a vague unrest and a nameless longing filled her breast,—
A wish, that she hardly dare to own, for something better than she had known.
The Judge rode slowly down the lane, smoothing his horse's chestnut mane.
He drew his bridle in the shade of the apple-trees to greet the maid,
And asked a draught from the spring that flowed through the meadow across the road.
She stooped where the cool spring bubbled up, and filled for him her small tin cup,
And blushed as she gave it, looking down on her feet so bare, and her tattered gown.
"Thanks!" said the Judge; "a sweeter draught from a fairer hand was never quaffed."
He spoke of the grass and flowers and trees, of the singing birds and the humming bees;
Then talked of the haying, and wondered whether the cloud in the west would bring foul [weather.
And Maud forgot her brier-torn gown, and her graceful ankles bare and brown
And listened, while a pleased surprise looked from her long-lashed hazel eyes.
At last, like one who for delay seeks a vain excuse, he rode away.
Maud Muller looked and sighed: "Ah me! That I the Judge's bride might be!
" He would dress me up in silks so fine, and praise and toast me at his wine.
" My father should wear a broadcloth coat; my brother should sail a painted boat.
" I'd dress my mother so grand and gay, and the baby should have a new toy each day.
" And I'd feed the hungry and clothe the poor, and all should bless me who left our door."
The Judge looked back as he climbed the hill, and saw Maud Muller standing still.
" A form more fair, a face more sweet, ne'er hath it been my lot to meet.
" And her modest answer and graceful air show her wise and good as she is fair.
" Would she were mine, and I to-day, like her, a harvester of hay:
" No doubtful balance of rights and wrongs, nor weary lawyers with endless tongues,
" But low of cattle and song of birds, and health and quiet and loving words."
But he thought of his sisters proud and cold, and his mother vain of her rank and gold.
So, closing his heart the Judge rode on and Maud was left in the field alone.
But the lawyers smiled that afternoon, when he hummed in Court an old love tune;
And the young girl mused beside the well till the rain on the unraked clover fell.
He wedded a wife of richest dower, who lived for fashion, as he for power.
Yet oft, in his marble hearth's bright glow, he watched a picture come and go;
And sweet Maud Muller's hazel eyes looked out in their innocent surprise.
Oft, when the wine in his glass was red, he longed for the wayside well instead;
And closed his eyes on his garnished rooms to dream of meadows and clover-blooms.
And the proud man sighed, with a secret pain, " Ah, that I was free again!
" Free as when I rode that day, where the barefoot maiden raked her hay."
She wedded a man unlearned and poor, and many children played round her door.
But care and sorrow, and childbirth pain, left their traces on heart and brain.
And oft, when the summer sun shone hot on the new-mown hay in the meadow lot,
And she heard the little spring brook fall over the road side, through the wall,
In the shade of the apple-tree again she saw a rider draw his rein.
And, gazing down with timid grace, she felt his pleased eyes read her face.
Sometimes her narrow kitchen walls stretched away into stately halls;
The weary wheel to a spinnet turned, the tallow candle an astral burned,
And for him who sat by the chimney lug, dozing and grumbling o'er pipe and mug,
A manly form at her side she saw, and joy was duty and love was law.
Then she took up her burden of life again, saying only, " It might have been."
Alas for maiden, alas for Judge, for rich repiner and household drudge!
God pity them both! and pity us all, who vainly the dreams of youth recall.
For of all sad words of tongue or pen, the saddest are these: " It might have been."
Ah, well! for us all some sweet hope lies deeply buried from human eyes;
And, in the hereafter, angels may roll the stone from its grave away! WHITTIER.

What Higher aim can Man attain than Conquest over Human Pain?

The JEOPARDY OF LIFE Is IMMENSELY INCREASED without such a simple precaution as

ENO'S 'FRUIT SALT.'

How important it is to every individual to have at hand some simple, effective and palatable remedy such as 'FRUIT SALT' to check disease at the onset. Whenever a change is contemplated likely to disturb the condition of health, let it be your companion, for, under any circumstances, its use is beneficial, and never can do harm.

"It is not too much to say that its merits have been published, tested, and approved literally, from pole to pole, and that its cosmopolitan popularity to-day presents one of the most signal illustrations of commercial enterprise to be found in our trading records"—*European Mail.*
Its effect upon any Disordered, Sleepless, and Feverish condition is simply marvellous.

CAUTION.—Examine each bottle and see that the capsule is marked ENO'S 'FRUIT SALT.' Without it, you have been imposed upon by a WORTHLESS IMITATION.

Prepared only by **J. C. ENO**, Ltd., at the '**FRUIT SALT**' **WORKS**, **LONDON, S.E.**, by J. C. ENO'S Patent.

CHATTO & WINDUS'S
LIST OF 528 POPULAR NOVELS
BY THE BEST AUTHORS.
Picture Covers, TWO SHILLINGS each.

BY EDMOND ABOUT.
The Fellah.

BY HAMILTON AÏDÉ.
Carr of Carrlyon.
Confidences.

BY MARY ALBERT.
Brooke Finchley's Daughter.

BY MRS. ALEXANDER.
Maid, Wife, or Widow?
Valerie's Fate.

BY GRANT ALLEN.
Strange Stories.
Philistia.
Babylon.
The Beckoning Hand.
In All Shades.
For Maimie's Sake.
The Devil's Die.
This Mortal Coil.
The Tents of Shem.
The Great Taboo.
Dumaresq's Daughter.

BY EDWIN LESTER ARNOLD.
Phra the Phœnician.

BY FRANK BARRETT.
A Recoiling Vengeance.
For Love and Honour.
John Ford; & His Helpmate.
Honest Davie.
A Prodigal's Progress.
Folly Morrison.
Lieutenant Barnabas.
Found Guilty.
Fettered for Life.
Between Life and Death.
The Sin of Olga Zassoulich.
Little Lady Linton.

BY SHELSLEY BEAUCHAMP.
Grantley Grange.

BY BESANT AND RICE.
Ready-Money Mortiboy.
With Harp and Crown.
This Son of Vulcan.
My Little Girl.
The Case of Mr. Lucraft.
The Golden Butterfly.
By Celia's Arbour.
The Monks of Thelema.
'Twas in Trafalgar's Bay.
The Seamy Side.
The Ten Years' Tenant.
The Chaplain of the Fleet.

BY WALTER BESANT.
All Sorts and Conditions of Men.
The Captains' Room.
All in a Garden Fair.
Dorothy Forster.
Uncle Jack.
Children of Gibeon.
World went very well then.
Herr Paulus.
For Faith and Freedom.
To Call her Mine.
The Bell of St. Paul's.
The Holy Rose.
Armorel of Lyonesse.
St. Katherine's by the Tower.

BY AMBROSE BIERCE.
In the Midst of Life.

BY FREDERICK BOYLE.
Camp Notes.
Savage Life.
Chronicles of No-Man's Land.

BY HAROLD BRYDGES.
Uncle Sam at Home.

BY ROBERT BUCHANAN.
The Shadow of the Sword.
A Child of Nature.
God and the Man.
Annan Water.
The New Abelard.
The Martyrdom of Madeline.
Love Me for Ever.
Matt: a Story of a Caravan.
Foxglove Manor.
The Master of the Mine.
The Heir of Linne.

BY HALL CAINE.
The Shadow of a Crime.
A Son of Hagar.
The Deemster.

BY COMMANDER CAMERON.
Cruise of the 'Black Prince.'

BY MRS. LOVETT CAMERON.
Deceivers Ever.
Juliet's Guardian.

BY AUSTIN CLARE.
For the Love of a Lass.

BY MRS. ARCHER CLIVE.
Paul Ferroll.
Why Paul Ferroll Killed his Wife.

BY MACLAREN COBBAN.
The Cure of Souls.

BY C. ALLSTON COLLINS.
The Bar Sinister.

BY WILKIE COLLINS.
Armadale.
After Dark.
No Name.
A Rogue's Life.
Antonina.
Basil.
Hide and Seek.
The Dead Secret.
Queen of Hearts.
My Miscellanies.
The Woman in White.
The Moonstone.
Man and Wife.
Poor Miss Finch.
Miss or Mrs.?
The New Magdalen.
The Frozen Deep.
The Law and the Lady.
The Two Destinies.
The Haunted Hotel.
The Fallen Leaves.
Jezebel's Daughter.
The Black Robe.
Heart and Science.
'I say No.'
The Evil Genius.
Little Novels.
The Legacy of Cain.
Blind Love.

BY MORTIMER COLLINS.
Sweet Anne Page.
Transmigration.
From Midnight to Midnight.
A Fight with Fortune.

MORT. AND FRANCES COLLINS.
Sweet and Twenty.
Frances.
The Village Comedy.
You Play Me False.
Blacksmith and Scholar.

BY M. J. COLQUHOUN.
Every Inch a Soldier.

BY DUTTON COOK.
Leo.
Paul Foster's Daughter.

London: CHATTO & WINDUS, 214 Piccadilly, W.

TWO-SHILLING POPULAR NOVELS.

BY C. EGBERT CRADDOCK.
The Prophet of the Great Smoky Mountains.

BY MATT CRIM.
Adventures of a Fair Rebel.

BY B. M. CROKER.
Pretty Miss Neville.
Proper Pride.
A Bird of Passage.
Diana Barrington.

BY WILLIAM CYPLES.
Hearts of Gold.

BY ALPHONSE DAUDET.
The Evangelist.

BY ERASMUS DAWSON.
The Fountain of Youth.

BY JAMES DE MILLE.
A Castle in Spain.

BY J. LEITH DERWENT.
Our Lady of Tears.
Circe's Lovers.

BY CHARLES DICKENS.
Sketches by Boz.
The Pickwick Papers.
Oliver Twist.
Nicholas Nickleby.

BY DICK DONOVAN.
The Man-hunter.
Caught at Last!
Tracked and Taken.
Who Poisoned Hetty Duncan?
The Man from Manchester.
A Detective's Triumphs.
In the Grip of the Law.
Wanted!
From Information Received.
Tracked to Doom.

BY MRS. ANNIE EDWARDES.
A Point of Honour.
Archie Lovell.

BY M. BETHAM-EDWARDS.
Felicia.
Kitty.

BY EDWARD EGGLESTON.
Roxy.

BY G. MANVILLE FENN.
The New Mistress.

BY PERCY FITZGERALD.
Bella Donna.
Polly.
The Second Mrs. Tillotson.
Seventy-five Brooke Street.
Never Forgotten.
The Lady of Brantome.
Fatal Zero.

BY PERCY FITZGERALD, &c.
Strange Secrets.

BY ALBANY DE FONBLANQUE.
Filthy Lucre.

BY R. E. FRANCILLON.
Olympia.
One by One.
Queen Cophetua.
A Real Queen.
King or Knave.
Romances of the Law.

BY HAROLD FREDERIC.
Seth's Brother's Wife.
The Lawton Girl.

PREFACED BY BARTLE FRERE.
Pandurang Hári.

BY HAIN FRISWELL.
One of Two.

BY EDWARD GARRETT.
The Capel Girls.

BY CHARLES GIBBON.
Robin Gray.
For Lack of Gold.
What will the World Say?
In Honour Bound.
In Love and War.
For the King.
Queen of the Meadow.
In Pastures Green.
The Flower of the Forest.
A Heart's Problem.
The Braes of Yarrow.
The Golden Shaft.
Of High Degree.
The Dead Heart.
By Mead and Stream.
Heart's Delight.
Fancy Free.
Loving a Dream.
A Hard Knot.
Blood-Money.

BY WILLIAM GILBERT.
James Duke.
Dr. Austin's Guests.
The Wizard of the Mountain.

BY ERNEST GLANVILLE.
The Lost Heiress.
The Fossicker.

BY REV. S. BARING GOULD.
Eve.
Red Spider.

BY HENRY GREVILLE.
A Noble Woman.
Nikanor.

BY JOHN HABBERTON.
Brueton's Bayou.
Country Luck.

BY ANDREW HALLIDAY.
Every-Day Papers.

BY LADY DUFFUS HARDY.
Paul Wynter's Sacrifice.

BY THOMAS HARDY.
Under the Greenwood Tree.

BY BRET HARTE.
An Heiress of Red Dog.
The Luck of Roaring Camp.
Californian Stories.
Gabriel Conroy.
Flip.
Maruja.
A Phyllis of the Sierras.

BY J. BERWICK HARWOOD.
The Tenth Earl.

BY JULIAN HAWTHORNE.
Garth.
Ellice Quentin.
Sebastian Strome.
Dust.
Fortune's Fool.
Beatrix Randolph.
Miss Cadogna.
Love—or a Name.
David Poindexter's Disappearance.
The Spectre of the Camera.

BY SIR ARTHUR HELPS.
Ivan de Biron.

BY HENRY HERMAN.
A Leading Lady.

BY MRS. CASHEL HOEY.
The Lover's Creed.

BY MRS. GEORGE HOOPER.
The House of Raby.

BY TIGHE HOPKINS.
'Twixt Love and Duty.

BY MRS. HUNGERFORD.
In Durance Vile.
A Maiden all Forlorn.
A Mental Struggle.
Marvel.
A Modern Circe.

BY MRS. ALFRED HUNT.
Thornicroft's Model.
The Leaden Casket.
Self-Condemned.
That Other Person.

BY JEAN INGELOW.
Fated to be Free.

BY HARRIETT JAY.
The Dark Colleen.
The Queen of Connaught.

BY MARK KERSHAW.
Colonial Facts and Fictions.

London: *CHATTO & WINDUS*, 214 *Piccadilly*, W.

TWO-SHILLING POPULAR NOVELS.

BY R. ASHE KING.
A Drawn Game.
'The Wearing of the Green.'
Passion's Slave.
Bell Barry.

BY JOHN LEYS.
The Lindsays.

BY E. LYNN LINTON.
Patricia Kemball.
Atonement of Leam Dundas.
The World Well Lost.
Under which Lord?
With a Silken Thread.
The Rebel of the Family.
'My Love!'
Ione.
Paston Carew.
Sowing the Wind.

BY HENRY W. LUCY.
Gideon Fleyce.

BY JUSTIN McCARTHY.
Dear Lady Disdain.
The Waterdale Neighbours.
My Enemy's Daughter.
A Fair Saxon.
Linley Rochford.
Miss Misanthrope.
Donna Quixote.
The Comet of a Season.
Maid of Athens.
Camiola: a Girl with Fortune.

BY HUGH MacCOLL.
Mr. Stranger's Sealed Packet.

BY MRS. MACDONELL.
Quaker Cousins.

BY KATHARINE S. MACQUOID.
The Evil Eye.
Lost Rose.

BY W. H. MALLOCK.
The New Republic.

BY FLORENCE MARRYAT.
Fighting the Air.
Written in Fire.
A Harvest of Wild Oats.
Open! Sesame!

BY J. MASTERMAN.
Half-a-dozen Daughters.

BY BRANDER MATTHEWS.
A Secret of the Sea.

BY LEONARD MERRICK.
The Man who was Good.

BY JEAN MIDDLEMASS.
Touch and Go.
Mr. Dorillion.

BY MRS. MOLESWORTH.
Hathercourt Rectory.

BY J. E. MUDDOCK.
Stories Weird and Wonderful.
The Dead Man's Secret.
From the Bosom of the Deep.

BY D. CHRISTIE MURRAY.
A Life's Atonement.
Joseph's Coat.
Val Strange.
A Model Father.
Coals of Fire.
Hearts.
By the Gate of the Sea.
The Way of the World.
A Bit of Human Nature.
First Person Singular.
Cynic Fortune.
Old Blazer's Hero.

BY D. CHRISTIE MURRAY AND HENRY HERMAN.
One Traveller Returns.
Paul Jones's Alias.
The Bishops' Bible.

BY HENRY MURRAY.
A Game of Bluff.

BY KUME NISBET.
'Bail Up!'
Dr. Bernard St. Vincent.

BY ALICE O'HANLON.
The Unforeseen.
Chance? or Fate?

BY GEORGES OHNET.
Doctor Rameau.
A Last Love.
A Weird Gift.

BY MRS. OLIPHANT.
Whiteladies.
The Primrose Path.
Greatest Heiress in England.

BY MRS. ROBERT O'REILLY.
Phoebe's Fortunes.

BY OUIDA.
Held in Bondage.
Strathmore.
Chandos.
Under Two Flags.
Idalia.
Cecil Castlemaine's Gage.
Tricotrin.
Puck.
Folle Farine.
A Dog of Flanders.
Pascarèl.
Signa.
In a Winter City.
Ariadnê.
Moths.
Friendship.
Pipistrello.
Bimbi.
In Maremma.

BY OUIDA—continued.
Wanda.
Frescoes.
Princess Napraxine.
Two Little Wooden Shoes.
A Village Commune.
Othmar.
Guilderoy.
Ruffino.
Syrlin.
Wisdom, Wit, and Pathos.

BY MARGARET AGNES PAUL.
Gentle and Simple.

BY JAMES PAYN.
Lost Sir Massingberd.
A Perfect Treasure.
Bentinck's Tutor.
Murphy's Master.
A County Family.
At Her Mercy.
A Woman's Vengeance.
Cecil's Tryst.
The Clyffards of Clyffe.
The Family Scapegrace.
The Foster Brothers.
The Best of Husbands.
Found Dead.
Walter's Word.
Halves.
Fallen Fortunes.
What He Cost Her.
Humorous Stories.
Gwendoline's Harvest.
Like Father, Like Son.
A Marine Residence.
Married Beneath Him.
Mirk Abbey.
Not Wooed, but Won.
£200 Reward.
Less Black than Painted.
By Proxy.
High Spirits.
Under One Roof.
Carlyon's Year.
A Confidential Agent.
Some Private Views.
A Grape from a Thorn.
From Exile.
Kit: a Memory.
For Cash Only.
The Canon's Ward.
The Talk of the Town.
Holiday Tasks.
Glow-worm Tales.
The Mystery of Mirbridge.
The Burnt Million.
The Word and the Will.
A Prince of the Blood.
Sunny Stories.

BY C. L. PIRKIS.
Lady Lovelace.

BY EDGAR A. POE.
The Mystery of Marie Roget.

London: CHATTO & WINDUS, 214 Piccadilly, W.

TWO-SHILLING POPULAR NOVELS.

BY MRS. CAMPBELL PRAED.
The Romance of a Station.
The Soul of Countess Adrian.

BY E. C. PRICE.
Valentina.
Gerald.
Mrs. Lancaster's Rival.
The Foreigners.

BY RICHARD PRYCE.
Miss Maxwell's Affections.

BY CHARLES READE.
It is Never Too Late to Mend.
Hard Cash.
Peg Woffington.
Christie Johnstone.
Griffith Gaunt.
Put Yourself in His Place.
The Double Marriage.
Love Me Little, Love Me Long.
Foul Play.
The Cloister and the Hearth.
The Course of True Love.
The Autobiography of a Thief.
A Terrible Temptation.
The Wandering Heir.
A Simpleton.
A Woman-Hater.
Singleheart and Doubleface.
Good Stories of Men &c.
The Jilt.
A Perilous Secret.
Readiana.

BY MRS. J. H. RIDDELL.
Her Mother's Darling.
The Uninhabited House.
Weird Stories.
Fairy Water. [Party.
Prince of Wales's Garden
Mystery in Palace Gardens.
The Nun's Curse.
Idle Tales.

BY F. W. ROBINSON.
Women are Strange.
The Hands of Justice.

BY JAMES RUNCIMAN.
Skippers and Shellbacks.
Grace Balmaign's Sweetheart.
Schools and Scholars.

BY W. CLARK RUSSELL.
Round the Galley Fire.
On the Fo'k'sle Head.
In the Middle Watch.
A Voyage to the Cape.
A Book for the Hammock.
Mystery of the 'Ocean Star.'
Romance of Jenny Harlowe.
An Ocean Tragedy.
My Shipmate Louise.
Alone on a Wide Wide Sea.

BY ALAN ST. AUBYN.
A Fellow of Trinity.
The Junior Dean.

BY GEORGE AUGUSTUS SALA.
Gaslight and Daylight.

BY JOHN SAUNDERS.
Guy Waterman.
The Lion in the Path.
The Two Dreamers.

BY KATHARINE SAUNDERS.
Joan Merryweather.
The High Mills.
Margaret and Elizabeth.
Sebastian.
Heart Salvage.

BY GEORGE R. SIMS.
Rogues and Vagabonds.
The Ring o' Bells.
Mary Jane's Memoirs.
Mary Jane Married.
Tales of To-day.
Dramas of Life.
Tinkletop's Crime.
Zeph: a Circus Story.

BY ARTHUR SKETCHLEY.
A Match in the Dark.

BY HAWLEY SMART.
Without Love or Licence.

BY T. W. SPEIGHT.
The Mysteries of Heron Dyke.
The Golden Hoop.
By Devious Ways.
Hoodwinked.
Back to Life.

BY R. A. STERNDALE.
The Afghan Knife.

BY R. LOUIS STEVENSON.
New Arabian Nights.
Prince Otto.

BY BERTHA THOMAS.
Proud Maisie.
The Violin-player.
Cressida.

BY WALTER THORNBURY.
Tales for the Marines.
Old Stories Re-told.

BY ANTHONY TROLLOPE.
The Way We Live Now.
Mr. Scarborough's Family.
The Golden Lion of Granpere.
The American Senator.
Frau Frohmann.
Marion Fay.
Kept in the Dark.
The Land-Leaguers.
John Caldigate.

BY FRANCES E. TROLLOPE.
Anne Furness.
Mabel's Progress.
Like Ships upon the Sea.

BY T. ADOLPHUS TROLLOPE.
Diamond Cut Diamond.

BY J. T. TROWBRIDGE.
Farnell's Folly.

BY IVAN TURGENIEFF, &c.
Stories from Foreign Novels.

BY MARK TWAIN.
Tom Sawyer.
A Tramp Abroad.
The Stolen White Elephant.
Pleasure Trip on Continent.
The Gilded Age.
Huckleberry Finn.
Life on the Mississippi.
The Prince and the Pauper.
Mark Twain's Sketches.
A Yankee at the Court of King Arthur.

BY SARAH TYTLER.
Noblesse Oblige.
Citoyenne Jacqueline.
The Huguenot Family.
What She Came Through.
Beauty and the Beast.
The Bride's Pass.
Saint Mungo's City.
Disappeared.
Lady Bell.
Buried Diamonds.
The Blackhall Ghosts.

BY C. C. FRASER-TYTLER.
Mistress Judith.

BY ARTEMUS WARD.
Artemus Ward Complete.

BY MRS. F. H. WILLIAMSON.
A Child Widow.

BY J. S. WINTER.
Cavalry Life.
Regimental Legends.

BY H. F. WOOD.
Passenger from Scotland Yard.
Englishman of the Rue Cain.

BY LADY WOOD.
Sabina.

BY CELIA PARKER WOOLLEY.
Rachel Armstrong.

BY EDMUND YATES.
Castaway.
The Forlorn Hope.
Land at Last.

London: CHATTO & WINDUS, 214 Piccadilly, W.

AN ALPHABETICAL CATALOGUE
OF BOOKS IN FICTION AND GENERAL LITERATURE
PUBLISHED BY
CHATTO & WINDUS
111 ST. MARTIN'S LANE
CHARING CROSS
LONDON, W.C.
[MAY, 1901.]

Adams (W. Davenport), Works by.
A Dictionary of the Drama: being a comprehensive Guide to the Plays, Playwrights, Players, and Playhouses of the United Kingdom and America, from the Earliest Times to the Present Day. Crown 8vo, half-bound, 12s. 6d. [*Preparing*.
Quips and Quiddities. Selected by W. DAVENPORT ADAMS. Post 8vo, cloth limp, 2s. 6d.

Agony Column (The) of 'The Times,' from 1800 to 1870. Edited with an Introduction, by ALICE CLAY. Post 8vo, cloth limp, 2s. 6d.

Alexander (Mrs.), Novels by. Post 8vo, illustrated boards, 2s. each.
Maid, Wife, or Widow? | Blind Fate.
Crown 8vo, cloth, 3s. 6d. each; post 8vo, picture boards, 2s. each.
Valerie's Fate. | A Life Interest. | Mona's Choice. | By Woman's Wit.
Crown 8vo, cloth 3s. 6d. each.
The Cost of her Pride. | Barbara, Lady's Maid and Peeress. | A Fight with Fate.
A Golden Autumn. | Mrs. Crichton's Creditor. | The Step-mother.
A Missing Hero. Crown 8vo, cloth, gilt top, 6s.

Allen (F. M.).—Green as Grass. Crown 8vo, cloth, 3s. 6d.

Allen (Grant), Works by. Crown 8vo, cloth, 6s. each.
The Evolutionist at Large. | Moorland Idylls.
Post-Prandial Philosophy. Crown 8vo, art linen, 3s. 6d.
Crown 8vo, cloth extra, 3s. 6d. each; post 8vo, illustrated boards, 2s. each.
Babylon. 12 Illustrations. | The Devil's Die. | The Duchess of Powysland.
Strange Stories. Frontis. | This Mortal Coil. | Blood Royal.
The Beckoning Hand. | The Tents of Shem. Frontis. | Ivan Greet's Masterpiece.
For Maimie's Sake. | The Great Taboo. | The Scallywag. 24 Illusts.
Philistia. | Dumaresq's Daughter. | At Market Value.
In all Shades. | Under Sealed Orders.
Dr. Palliser's Patient. Fcap. 8vo, cloth boards, 1s. 6d.

Anderson (Mary).—Othello's Occupation. Crown 8vo, cloth, 3s. 6d.

Antrobus (C. L.), Novels by. Crown 8vo, cloth, gilt top, 6s. each.
Quality Corner: A Study of Remorse.
Wildersmoor.

Arnold (Edwin Lester), Stories by.
The Wonderful Adventures of Phra the Phœnician. Crown 8vo, cloth extra, with 12 Illustrations by H. M. PAGET, 3s. 6d.; post 8vo, illustrated boards, 2s.
The Constable of St. Nicholas. With Frontispiece by S. L. WOOD. Crown 8vo, cloth, 3s. 6d.

Artemus Ward's Works. With Portrait and Facsimile. Crown 8vo, cloth extra, 3s. 6d.—Also a POPULAR EDITION post 8vo, picture boards, 2s.

Ashton (John), Works by. Crown 8vo, cloth extra, 7s. 6d. each.
Humour, Wit, and Satire of the Seventeenth Century. With 82 Illustrations.
English Caricature and Satire on Napoleon the First. With 115 Illustrations.
Modern Street Ballads. With 57 Illustrations.
Social Life in the Reign of Queen Anne. With 85 Illustrations. Crown 8vo, cloth, 3s. 6d.
Crown 8vo, cloth, gilt top, 6s. each.
Social Life under the Regency. With 90 Illustrations.
Florizel's Folly: The Story of GEORGE IV. With Photogravure Frontispiece and 12 Illustrations.

Bacteria, Yeast Fungi, and Allied Species, A Synopsis of. By W. B. GROVE B.A. With 87 Illustrations. Crown 8vo, cloth extra, 3s. 6d.

CHATTO & WINDUS, Publishers, 111 St. Martin's Lane, London, W.C.

Bardsley (Rev. C. Wareing, M.A.), Works by.
English Surnames: Their Sources and Significations. Crown 8vo, cloth, 7s. 6d.
Curiosities of Puritan Nomenclature. Crown 8vo, cloth, 3s. 6d.

Baring Gould (Sabine, Author of 'John Herring,' &c.), Novels by.
Crown 8vo, cloth extra, 3s. 6d. each; post 8vo, illustrated boards, 2s. each.
Red Spider. | **Eve.**

Barr (Robert: Luke Sharp), Stories by. Cr. 8vo, cl., 3s. 6d. each.
In a Steamer Chair. With Frontispiece and Vignette by DEMAIN HAMMOND.
From Whose Bourne, &c. With 47 Illustrations by HAL HURST and others.
Revenge! With 12 Illustrations by LANCELOT SPEED and others.
A Woman Intervenes. With 8 Illustrations by HAL HURST.
The Unchanging East: Notes on a Visit to the Farther Edge of the Mediterranean. With a Frontispiece. Crown 8vo, cloth, gilt top, 6s.
The Adventures of a Merry Monarch. With numerous Illustrations. Crown 8vo, cloth, gilt top, 6s. [*Shortly*

Barrett (Frank), Novels by.
Post 8vo, illustrated boards, 2s. each; cloth, 2s. 6d. each.
The Sin of Olga Zassoulich. | **John Ford; and His Helpmate.**
Between Life and Death. | **A Recoiling Vengeance.**
Folly Morrison. | **Honest Davie.** | **Lieut. Barnabas.** | **Found Guilty.**
Little Lady Linton. | **For Love and Honour.**
A Prodigal's Progress.

Crown 8vo, cloth, 3s. 6d. each; post 8vo, picture boards, 2s. each; cloth limp, 2s. 6d. each.
Fettered for Life. | **The Woman of the Iron Bracelets.** | **The Harding Scandal**
A Missing Witness. With 8 Illustrations by W. H. MARGETSON.

Crown 8vo, cloth, 3s. 6d. each.
Under a Strange Mask. With 19 Illusts. by E. F. BREWTNALL. | **Was She Justified?**

Barrett (Joan).—Monte Carlo Stories. Fcap. 8vo, cloth, 1s. 6d.

Besant (Sir Walter) and James Rice, Novels by.
Crown 8vo, cloth extra, 3s. 6d. each; post 8vo, illustrated boards, 2s. each; cloth limp, 2s. 6d. each.
Ready-Money Mortiboy. | **The Golden Butterfly.** | **The Seamy Side.**
My Little Girl. | **The Monks of Thelema.** | **The Case of Mr. Lucraft.**
With Harp and Crown. | **By Celia's Arbour.** | **'Twas in Trafalgar's Bay.**
This Son of Vulcan. | **The Chaplain of the Fleet.** | **The Ten Years' Tenant.**

*** There are also LIBRARY EDITIONS of all the above, excepting **Ready-Money Mortiboy** and **The Golden Butterfly**, handsomely set in new type on a large crown 8vo page, and bound in cloth extra, 6s. each; and POPULAR EDITIONS of **The Golden Butterfly** and of **The Orange Girl**, medium 8vo, 6d. each; and of **All Sorts and Conditions of Men**, medium 8vo, 6d.; cloth, 1s.

Besant (Sir Walter), Novels by.
Crown 8vo, cloth extra, 3s. 6d. each; post 8vo, illustrated boards, 2s. each; cloth limp, 2s. 6d. each.
All Sorts and Conditions of Men. With 12 Illustrations by FRED. BARNARD.
The Captains' Room, &c. With Frontispiece by E. J. WHEELER.
All in a Garden Fair. With 6 Illustrations by HARRY FURNISS.
Dorothy Forster. With Frontispiece by CHARLES GREEN.
Uncle Jack, and other Stories. | **Children of Gibeon.**
The World Went Very Well Then. With 12 Illustrations by A. FORESTIER.
Herr Paulus: His Rise, his Greatness, and his Fall. | **The Bell of St. Paul's.**
For Faith and Freedom. With Illustrations by A. FORESTIER and F. WADDY.
To Call Her Mine, &c. With 9 Illustrations by A. FORESTIER.
The Holy Rose, &c. With Frontispiece by F. BARNARD.
Armorel of Lyonesse: A Romance of To-day. With 12 Illustrations by F. BARNARD.
St. Katherine's by the Tower. With 12 Illustrations by C. GREEN.
Verbena Camellia Stephanotis, &c. With a Frontispiece by GORDON BROWNE.
The Ivory Gate. | **The Rebel Queen.**
Beyond the Dreams of Avarice. With 12 Illustrations by W. H. HYDE.
In Deacon's Orders, &c. With Frontispiece by A. FORESTIER. | **The Revolt of Man.**
The Master Craftsman. | **The City of Refuge.**

Crown 8vo, cloth, 3s. 6d. each.
A Fountain Sealed. With a Frontispiece. | **The Changeling.**

Crown 8vo, cloth, gilt top, 6s. each.
The Orange Girl. With 8 Illustrations by F. PEGRAM. | **The Fourth Generation.**

The Charm, and other Drawing-room Plays. By Sir WALTER BESANT and WALTER H. POLLOCK. With 50 Illustrations by CHRIS HAMMOND and JULE GOODMAN. Crown 8vo, cloth, gilt edges, 6s.

CHATTO & WINDUS, Publishers, 111 St. Martin's Lane, London, W.C. 3

Beaconsfield, Lord. By T. P. O'CONNOR, M.P. Cr. 8vo, cloth, 5s.

Bechstein (Ludwig).—As Pretty as Seven, and other German Stories. With Additional Tales by the Brothers GRIMM, and 98 Illustrations by RICHTER. Square 8vo, cloth extra, 6s. 6d.; gilt edges, 7s. 6d.

Bellew (Frank).—The Art of Amusing: A Collection of Graceful Arts, Games, Tricks, Puzzles, and Charades. With 300 Illustrations. Crown 8vo, cloth extra, 4s. 6d.

Bennett (W. C. LL.D.).—Songs for Sailors. Post 8vo, cl. limp, 2s.

Bewick (Thomas) and his Pupils. By AUSTIN DOBSON. With 95 Illustrations. Square 8vo, cloth extra, 3s. 6d.

Bierce (Ambrose).—In the Midst of Life: Tales of Soldiers and Civilians. Crown 8vo, cloth extra, 3s. 6d.; post 8vo, illustrated boards, 2s.

Bill Nye's Comic History of the United States. With 146 Illustrations by F. OPPER. Crown 8vo, cloth extra, 3s. 6d.

Bindloss (Harold).—Ainslie's Ju-Ju: A Romance of the Hinterland. Crown 8vo, cloth, 3s. 6d.

Blackburn's (Henry) Art Handbooks.
Academy Notes, 1901. 200 Illustrations.
Academy Notes, 1875-79. Complete in One Vol., with 600 Illustrations. Cloth, 6s.
Academy Notes, 1890-94. Complete in One Vol., with 800 Illustrations. Cloth, 7s. 6d.
Academy Notes, 1895-99. Complete in One Vol., with 800 Illustrations. Cloth, 6s.
Grosvenor Notes, Vol. I., **1877-82.** With 300 Illustrations. Demy 8vo, cloth 6s.
Grosvenor Notes, Vol. II., **1883-87.** With 300 Illustrations. Demy 8vo, cloth, 6s.
Grosvenor Notes, Vol. III., **1888-90.** With 230 Illustrations. Demy 8vo cloth, 3s. 6d.
The New Gallery, 1888-1892. With 250 Illustrations. Demy 8vo, cloth, 6s.
English Pictures at the National Gallery. With 114 Illustrations. 1s.
Old Masters at the National Gallery. With 128 Illustrations. 1s. 6d.
Illustrated Catalogue to the National Gallery. With 242 Illusts. Demy 8vo, cloth, 3s.

Illustrated Catalogue of the Paris Salon, 1901. With 400 Illustrations. Demy 8vo, 3s.

Bodkin (M. McD., Q.C.).—Dora Myrl, the Lady Detective. Crown 8vo, cloth, 3s. 6d.

Bourget (Paul).—A Living Lie. Translated by JOHN DE VILLIERS. With special Preface for the English Edition. Crown 8vo, cloth, 3s. 6d.

Bourne (H. R. Fox), Books by.
English Merchants: Memoirs in Illustration of the Progress of British Commerce. With 32 Illustrations. Crown 8vo, cloth, 3s. 6d.
English Newspapers: Chapters in the History of Journalism. Two Vols., demy 8vo, cloth, 25s.
The Other Side of the Emin Pasha Relief Expedition. Crown 8vo, cloth, 6s.

Boyle (Frederick), Works by. Post 8vo, illustrated bds., 2s. each.
Chronicles of No-Man's Land. | **Camp Notes.** | **Savage Life.**

Brand (John).—Observations on Popular Antiquities; chiefly Illustrating the Origin of our Vulgar Customs, Ceremonies, and Superstitions. With the Additions of Sir HENRY ELLIS. Crown 8vo, cloth, 3s. 6d.

Brayshaw (J. Dodsworth).—Slum Silhouettes: Stories of London Life. Crown 8vo, cloth, 3s. 6d.

Brewer (Rev. Dr.), Works by.
The Reader's Handbook of Famous Names in Fiction, Allusions, References, Proverbs, Plots, Stories, and Poems. Together with an ENGLISH AND AMERICAN BIBLIOGRAPHY, and a LIST OF THE AUTHORS AND DATES OF DRAMAS AND OPERAS. A New Edition, Revised and Enlarged. Crown 8vo, cloth, 7s. 6d.
A Dictionary of Miracles: Imitative, Realistic, and Dogmatic. Crown 8vo, cloth, 3s. 6d.

Brewster (Sir David), Works by. Post 8vo, cloth, 4s. 6d. each.
More Worlds than One: Creed of the Philosopher and Hope of the Christian. With Plates.
The Martyrs of Science: GALILEO, TYCHO BRAHE, and KEPLER. With Portraits.
Letters on Natural Magic. With numerous Illustrations.

Brillat-Savarin.—Gastronomy as a Fine Art. Translated by R. E. ANDERSON, M.A. Post 8vo, half-bound, 2s.

Bryden (H. A.).—An Exiled Scot: A Romance. With a Frontispiece, by J. S. CROMPTON, R.I. Crown 8vo, cloth, 6s.

Brydges (Harold).—Uncle Sam at Home. With 91 Illustrations. Post 8vo, illustrated boards, 2s.; cloth limp, 2s. 6d.

4 CHATTO & WINDUS, Publishers, 111 St. Martin's Lane, London, W.C.

Buchanan (Robert), Poems and Novels by.
The Complete Poetical Works of Robert Buchanan. 2 vols., crown 8vo, buckram, with Portrait Frontispiece to each volume, 6s. each. [*Preparing.*

Crown 8vo, cloth, 6s. each.
The Devil's Case: a Bank Holiday Interlude. With 6 Illustrations.
The Earthquake; or, Six Days and a Sabbath.
The Wandering Jew: a Christmas Carol.

Crown 8vo, cloth, 3s. 6d. each.
The Outcast: a Rhyme for the Time.
The Ballad of Mary the Mother: a Christmas Carol.

St. Abe and his Seven Wives. Crown 8vo, cloth, 2s. 6d.

Crown 8vo, cloth, 3s. 6d. each; post 8vo, illustrated boards, 2s. each.
The Shadow of the Sword.	**Love Me for Ever.** With Frontispiece.
A Child of Nature. With Frontispiece.	**Annan Water.** | **Foxglove Manor.**
God and the Man. With 11 Illustrations by	**The New Abelard.** | **Rachel Dene.**
Lady Kilpatrick. [FRED. BARNARD.	**Matt:** A Story of a Caravan. With Frontispiece.
The Martyrdom of Madeline. With Frontispiece by A. W. COOPER.	**The Master of the Mine.** With Frontispiece
	The Heir of Linne. | **Woman and the Man.**

Red and White Heather. Crown 8vo, cloth, 3s. 6d.
Andromeda: An Idyll of the Great River. Crown 8vo, cloth, gilt top, 6s.
The Charlatan. By ROBERT BUCHANAN and HENRY MURRAY. Crown 8vo, cloth, with a Frontispiece by T. H. ROBINSON, 3s. 6d.; post 8vo, picture boards, 2s.

Burton (Robert).—The Anatomy of Melancholy. With Translations of the Quotations. Demy 8vo, cloth extra, 7s. 6d.
Melancholy Anatomised: An Abridgment of BURTON'S ANATOMY. Post 8vo, half-cl., 2s. 6d.

Caine (Hall), Novels by. Crown 8vo, cloth extra, 3s. 6d. each.; post
8vo, illustrated boards, 2s. each; cloth limp, 2s. 6d. each.
The Shadow of a Crime. | **A Son of Hagar.** | **The Deemster.**
Also LIBRARY EDITIONS of **The Deemster** and **The Shadow of a Crime**, set in new type, crown 8vo, and bound uniform with **The Christian**, 6s. each; and CHEAP POPULAR EDITIONS of **The Deemster**, **The Shadow of a Crime**, and **A Son of Hagar**, medium 8vo, portrait-cover, 6d. each.

Cameron (Commander V. Lovett).—The Cruise of the 'Black Prince' Privateer. Post 8vo, picture boards, 2s.

Canada (Greater): The Past, Present, and Future of the Canadian North-West. By E. B. OSBORN, B.A. With a Map. Crown 8vo, cloth, 3s. 6d.

Captain Coignet, Soldier of the Empire: An Autobiography.
Edited by LOREDAN LARCHEY. Translated by Mrs. CAREY. With 100 Illustrations. Crown 8vo, cloth, 3s. 6d.

Carlyle (Thomas).—On the Choice of Books. Post 8vo, cl., 1s. 6d.
Correspondence of Thomas Carlyle and R. W. Emerson, 1834-1872. Edited by C. E. NORTON. With Portraits. Two Vols., crown 8vo, cloth, 24s.

Carruth (Hayden).—The Adventures of Jones. With 17 Illustrations. Fcap. 8vo, cloth, 2s.

Chambers (Robert W.), Stories of Paris Life by.
The King in Yellow. Crown 8vo, cloth, 3s. 6d.; fcap. 8vo, cloth limp, 2s. 6d.
In the Quarter. Fcap. 8vo, cloth, 2s. 6d.

Chapman's (George), Works. Vol. I., Plays Complete, including the
Doubtful Ones.—Vol. II., Poems and Minor Translations, with Essay by A. C. SWINBURNE.—Vol. III., Translations of the Iliad and Odyssey. Three Vols., crown 8vo, cloth, 3s. 6d. each.

Chapple (J. Mitchell).—The Minor Chord: The Story of a Prima Donna. Crown 8vo, cloth, 3s. 6d.

Chaucer for Children: A Golden Key. By Mrs. H. R. HAWEIS. With
8 Coloured Plates and 30 Woodcuts. Crown 4to, cloth extra, 3s. 6d.
Chaucer for Schools. With the Story of his Times and his Work. By Mrs. H. R. HAWEIS. A New Edition, revised. With a Frontispiece. Demy 8vo, cloth, 2s. 6d.

Chess, The Laws and Practice of. With an Analysis of the Openings. By HOWARD STAUNTON. Edited by R. B. WORMALD. Crown 8vo, cloth, 5s.
The Minor Tactics of Chess: A Treatise on the Deployment of the Forces in obedience to Strategic Principle. By F. K. YOUNG and E. C. HOWELL. Long fcap. 8vo, cloth, 2s. 6d.
The Hastings Chess Tournament. Containing the Authorised Account of the 230 Games played Aug.-Sept., 1895. With Annotations by PILLSBURY, LASKER, TARRASCH, STEINITZ, SCHIFFERS, TEICHMANN, BARDELEBEN, BLACKBURNE, GUNSBERG, TINSLEY, MASON, and ALBIN; Biographical Sketches of the Chess Masters, and 22 Portraits. Edited by H. F. CHESHIRE. Cheaper Edition. Crown 8vo, cloth, 5s.

Clare (Austin), Stories by.
For the Love of a Lass. Post 8vo, illustrated boards, 2s.; cloth, 2s. 6d.
By the Rise of the River: Tales and Sketches in South Tynedale. Crown 8vo, cloth, 3s. 6d.

CHATTO & WINDUS, Publishers, 111 St. Martin's Lane, London, W.C. 5

Clive (Mrs. Archer), Novels by. Post 8vo, illust. boards, 2s. each.
Paul Ferroll. | Why Paul Ferroll Killed his Wife.

Clodd (Edward, F.R.A.S.).—Myths and Dreams. Cr. 8vo, 3s. 6d.

Coates (Annë).—Rie's Diary. Crown 8vo, cloth, 3s. 6d.

Cobban (J. Maclaren), Novels by.
The Cure of Souls. Post 8vo, Illustrated boards, 2s.
The Red Sultan. Crown 8vo, cloth extra, 3s. 6d. ; post 8vo, illustrated boards, 2s.
The Burden of Isabel. Crown 8vo, cloth extra, 3s. 6d.

Coleridge (M. E.).—The Seven Sleepers of Ephesus. Fcap. 8vo, leatherette, 1s. ; cloth, 1s. 6d.

Collins (C. Allston).—The Bar Sinister. Post 8vo, boards, 2s.

Collins (John Churton, M.A.), Books by.
Illustrations of Tennyson. Crown 8vo, cloth extra, 6s.
Jonathan Swift. A Biographical and Critical Study. Crown 8vo, cloth extra, 8s.

Collins (Mortimer and Frances), Novels by.
Crown 8vo, cloth extra, 3s. 6d. each ; post 8vo, illustrated boards, 2s. each.
From Midnight to Midnight. | Blacksmith and Scholar.
You Play me False. | The Village Comedy.

Post 8vo, illustrated boards, 2s. each.
Transmigration. | Sweet Anne Page. | Frances.
A Fight with Fortune. | Sweet and Twenty. |

Collins (Wilkie), Novels by.
Crown 8vo, cloth extra, many Illustrated, 3s. 6d. each ; post 8vo, picture boards, 2s. each ;
cloth limp, 2s. 6d. each.

*Antonina.   My Miscellanies.   Jezebel's Daughter.
*Basil.   Armadale.   The Black Robe.
*Hide and Seek.   Poor Miss Finch.   Heart and Science.
*The Woman in White.   Miss or Mrs.?   'I Say No.'
*The Moonstone.   The New Magdalen.   A Rogue's Life.
*Man and Wife.   The Frozen Deep.   The Evil Genius.
*The Dead Secret.   The Law and the Lady.   Little Novels.
After Dark.   The Two Destinies.   The Legacy of Cain.
The Queen of Hearts.   The Haunted Hotel.   Blind Love.
No Name.   The Fallen Leaves.

*** Marked * have been reset in new type, in uniform style.

POPULAR EDITIONS. Medium 8vo, 6d. each ; cloth, 1s. each.
The Moonstone. | Antonina. | The Dead Secret.
Medium 8vo, 6d. each.
The Woman in White. | The New Magdalen.

Colman's (George) Humorous Works: 'Broad Grins,' ' My Nightgown and Slippers,' &c. With Life and Frontispiece. Crown 8vo, cloth extra, 3s. 6d.

Colquhoun (M. J.).—Every Inch a Soldier. Crown 8vo, cloth, 3s. 6d.; post 8vo, illustrated boards, 2s.

Colt-breaking, Hints on. By W. M. HUTCHISON. Cr. 8vo, cl., 3s. 6d.

Compton (Herbert).—The Inimitable Mrs. Massingham: a Romance of Botany Bay. Crown 8vo, cloth, gilt top, 6s.

Convalescent Cookery. By CATHERINE RYAN. Cr. 8vo, 1s. ; cl., 1s. 6d.

Cooper (Edward H.).—Geoffory Hamilton. Cr. 8vo, cloth, 3s. 6d.

Cornish (J. F.).—Sour Grapes : A Novel. Cr. 8vo, cloth, gilt top, 6s.

Cornwall.—Popular Romances of the West of England; or, The Drolls, Traditions, and Superstitions of Old Cornwall. Collected by ROBERT HUNT, F.R.S. With two Steel Plates by GEORGE CRUIKSHANK. Crown 8vo, cloth, 7s. 6d.

Cotes (V. Cecil).—Two Girls on a Barge. With 44 Illustrations by F. H. TOWNSEND. Crown 8vo, cloth extra, 3s. 6d.; post 8vo, cloth, 2s. 6d.

Craddock (C. Egbert), Stories by.
The Prophet of the Great Smoky Mountains. Crown 8vo, cloth, 3s. 6d. ; post 8vo, illustrated boards, 2s.
His Vanished Star. Crown 8vo, cloth, 3s. 6d.

Cram (Ralph Adams).—Black Spirits and White. Fcap. 8vo, cloth, 1s. 6d.

6 CHATTO & WINDUS, Publishers, 111 St. Martin's Lane, London, W.C.

Crellin (H. N.), Books by.
  Romances of the Old Seraglio. With 28 Illustrations by S. L. WOOD. Crown 8vo, cloth, 3s. 6d.
  Tales of the Caliph. Crown 8vo, cloth, 2s.
  The Nazarenes: A Drama. Crown 8vo, 1s.

Crim (Matt.).—Adventures of a Fair Rebel. Crown 8vo, cloth extra, with a Frontispiece by DAN. BEARD, 3s. 6d.; post 8vo, illustrated boards, 2s.

Crockett (S. R.) and others.—Tales of Our Coast. By S. R. CROCKETT, GILBERT PARKER, HAROLD FREDERIC, 'Q.,' and W. CLARK RUSSELL. With 2 Illustrations by FRANK BRANGWYN. Crown 8vo, cloth, 3s. 6d.

Croker (Mrs. B. M.), Novels by. Crown 8vo, cloth extra, 3s. 6d. each; post 8vo, illustrated boards, 2s. each; cloth limp, 2s. 6d. each.
  Pretty Miss Neville.
  Proper Pride.
  A Bird of Passage.
  Diana Barrington.
  Two Masters.
  Interference.
  A Family Likeness.
  A Third Person.
  Mr. Jervis.
  Village Tales & Jungle Tragedies.
  The Real Lady Hilda.
  Married or Single?

  Crown 8vo, cloth extra, 3s. 6d. each.
  Some One Else.
  In the Kingdom of Kerry.
  Miss Balmaine's Past.
  Jason, &c.
  Beyond the Pale.
  Infatuation.

  'To Let,' &c. Post 8vo, picture boards, 2s.; cloth limp, 2s. 6d.
  Terence. With 6 Illustrations by SIDNEY PAGET. Crown 8vo, cloth, gilt top, 6s.

Cruikshank's Comic Almanack. Complete in Two SERIES: The FIRST, from 1835 to 1843; the SECOND, from 1844 to 1853. A Gathering of the Best Humour of THACKERAY, HOOD, MAYHEW, ALBERT SMITH, A'BECKETT, ROBERT BROUGH, &c. With numerous Steel Engravings and Woodcuts by GEORGE CRUIKSHANK, HINE, LANDELLS, &c. Two Vols., crown 8vo, cloth gilt, 7s. 6d. each.
  The Life of George Cruikshank. By BLANCHARD JERROLD. With 84 Illustrations and a Bibliography. Crown 8vo, cloth extra, 3s. 6d.

Cumming (C. F. Gordon), Works by. Large cr. 8vo, cloth, 6s. each.
  In the Hebrides. With an Autotype Frontispiece and 23 Illustrations.
  In the Himalayas and on the Indian Plains. With 42 Illustrations.
  Two Happy Years in Ceylon. With 28 Illustrations.
  Via Cornwall to Egypt. With a Photogravure Frontispiece.

Cussans (John E.).—A Handbook of Heraldry; with Instructions for Tracing Pedigrees and Deciphering Ancient MSS., &c. Fourth Edition, revised, with 408 Woodcuts and 2 Coloured Plates. Crown 8vo, cloth extra, 6s.

Cyples (William).—Hearts of Gold. Crown 8vo, cloth, 3s. 6d.

Daudet (Alphonse).—The Evangelist; or, Port Salvation. Crown 8vo, cloth extra, 3s. 6d.; post 8vo, illustrated boards, 2s.

Davenant (Francis, M.A.).—Hints for Parents on the Choice of a Profession for their Sons when Starting in Life. Crown 8vo, cloth, 1s. 6d.

Davidson (Hugh Coleman).—Mr. Sadler's Daughters. With a Frontispiece by STANLEY WOOD. Crown 8vo, cloth extra, 3s. 6d.

Davies (Dr. N. E. Yorke-), Works by. Cr. 8vo, 1s. ea.; cl., 1s. 6d. ea.
  One Thousand Medical Maxims and Surgical Hints.
  Nursery Hints: A Mother's Guide in Health and Disease.
  Foods for the Fat: The Dietetic Cure of Corpulency and of Gout.

  Aids to Long Life. Crown 8vo, 2s.; cloth limp, 2s. 6d.

Davies' (Sir John) Complete Poetical Works. Collected and Edited, with Introduction and Notes, by Rev. A. B. GROSART, D.D. Two Vols., crown 8vo, cloth, 3s. 6d. each.

Dawson (Erasmus, M.B.).—The Fountain of Youth. Crown 8vo, cloth extra, with Two Illustrations by HUME NISBET, 3s. 6d.

De Guerin (Maurice), The Journal of. Edited by G. S. TREBUTIEN. With a Memoir by SAINTE-BEUVE. Translated from the 20th French Edition by JESSIE P. FROTH INGHAM. Fcap. 8vo, half-bound, 2s. 6d.

De Maistre (Xavier).—A Journey Round my Room. Translated by HENRY ATTWELL. Post 8vo, cloth limp, 2s. 6d.

De Mille (James).—A Castle in Spain. Crown 8vo, cloth extra, with a Frontispiece, 3s. 6d.

Derby (The): The Blue Ribbon of the Turf. With Brief Accounts of THE OAKS. By LOUIS HENRY CURZON. Crown 8vo, cloth limp, 2s. 6d.

Derwent (Leith), Novels by. Crown 8vo, cloth, 3s. 6d. each.
  Our Lady of Tears. | Circe's Lovers.

Dewar (T. R.).—A Ramble Round the Globe. With 220 Illustrations. Crown 8vo, cloth extra, 7s. 6d.

De Windt (Harry), Books by.
Through the Gold-Fields of Alaska to Bering Straits. With Map and 33 full-page Illustrations. Cheaper Issue. Demy 8vo, cloth, 6s.
True Tales of Travel and Adventure. Crown 8vo, cloth, 3s. 6d.

Dickens (Charles), About England with. By ALFRED RIMMER. With 57 Illustrations by C. A. VANDERHOOF and the AUTHOR. Square 8vo, cloth, 3s. 6d.

Dictionaries.
The Reader's Handbook of Famous Names in Fiction, Allusions, References, Proverbs, Plots, Stories, and Poems. Together with an ENGLISH AND AMERICAN BIBLIOGRAPHY, and a LIST OF THE AUTHORS AND DATES OF DRAMAS AND OPERAS. By Rev. E. C. BREWER, LL.D A New Edition, Revised and Enlarged. Crown 8vo, cloth, 7s. 6d.
A Dictionary of Miracles: Imitative, Realistic, and Dogmatic. By the Rev. E. C. BREWER, LL.D. Crown 8vo, cloth, 3s. 6d.
Familiar Short Sayings of Great Men. With Historical and Explanatory Notes by SAMUEL A. BENT, A.M. Crown 8vo, cloth extra, 7s. 6d.
The Slang Dictionary: Etymological, Historical, and Anecdotal. Crown 8vo, cloth, 6s. 6d.
Words, Facts, and Phrases: A Dictionary of Curious, Quaint, and Out-of-the-Way Matters. By ELIEZER EDWARDS. Crown 8vo, cloth extra, 3s. 6d.

Dilke (Rt. Hon. Sir Charles, Bart., M.P.).—The British Empire. Crown 8vo, buckram, 3s. 6d.

Dobson (Austin), Works by.
Thomas Bewick and his Pupils. With 95 Illustrations. Square 8vo, cloth, 3s. 6d.
Four Frenchwomen. With Four Portraits. Crown 8vo, buckram, gilt top, 6s.
Eighteenth Century Vignettes. IN THREE SERIES. Crown 8vo, buckram, 6s. each.
A Paladin of Philanthropy, and other Papers. With 2 Illusts. Cr. 8vo, buckram, 6s.

Dobson (W. T.).—Poetical Ingenuities and Eccentricities. Post 8vo, cloth limp, 2s. 6d.

Donovan (Dick), Detective Stories by.
Post 8vo, illustrated boards, 2s. each; cloth limp, 2s. 6d. each.
The Man-Hunter. | Wanted! | A Detective's Triumphs.
Caught at Last. | Tracked to Doom. | In the Grip of the Law.
Tracked and Taken. | From Information Received.
Who Poisoned Hetty Duncan? | Link by Link. | Dark Deeds
Suspicion Aroused. | Riddles Read.
Crown 8vo, cloth extra, 3s. 6d. each; post 8vo, illustrated boards, 2s. each; cloth, 2s. 6d. each.
The Man from Manchester. With 23 Illustrations.
The Mystery of Jamaica Terrace. | The Chronicles of Michael Danevitch.
Crown 8vo, cloth, 3s. 6d. each.
The Records of Vincent Trill, of the Detective Service. | Tales of Terror.
The Adventures of Tyler Tatlock, Private Detective.
Deacon Brodie; or, Behind the Mask.

Dowling (Richard).—Old Corcoran's Money. Crown 8vo, cl., 3s. 6d.

Doyle (A. Conan).—The Firm of Girdlestone. Cr. 8vo, cl., 3s. 6d.

Dramatists, The Old. Cr. 8vo, cl. ex., with Portraits, 3s. 6d. per Vol.
Ben Jonson's Works. With Notes, Critical and Explanatory, and a Biographical Memoir by WILLIAM GIFFORD. Edited by Colonel CUNNINGHAM. Three Vols.
Chapman's Works. Three Vols. Vol. I. contains the Plays complete; Vol. II., Poems and Minor Translations, with an Essay by A. C. SWINBURNE; Vol. III., Translations of the Iliad and Odyssey.
Marlowe's Works. Edited, with Notes, by Colonel CUNNINGHAM. One Vol.
Massinger's Plays. From GIFFORD'S Text. Edited by Colonel CUNNINGHAM. One Vol.

Dudgeon (R. E., M.D.).—The Prolongation of Life. Crown 8vo, buckram, 3s. 6d.

Duncan (Sara Jeannette: Mrs. EVERARD COTES), Works by.
Crown 8vo, cloth extra, 7s. 6d. each.
A Social Departure. With 111 Illustrations by F. H. TOWNSEND.
An American Girl in London. With 80 Illustrations by F. H. TOWNSEND.
The Simple Adventures of a Memsahib. With 37 Illustrations by F. H. TOWNSEND.
Crown 8vo, cloth extra, 3s. 6d. each.
A Daughter of To-Day. | Vernon's Aunt. With 47 Illustrations by HAL HURST.

Dutt (Romesh C.).—England and India: A Record of Progress during One Hundred Years. Crown 8vo, cloth, 2s.

Early English Poets. Edited, with Introductions and Annotations, by Rev. A. B. GROSART, D.D. Crown 8vo, cloth boards, 3s. 6d. per Volume.
Fletcher's (Giles) Complete Poems. One Vol.
Davies' (Sir John) Complete Poetical Works. Two Vols.
Herrick's (Robert) Complete Collected Poems. Three Vols.
Sidney's (Sir Philip) Complete Poetical Works. Three Vols.

Edgcumbe (Sir E. R. Pearce).—Zephyrus: A Holiday in Brazil and on the River Plate. With 41 Illustrations. Crown 8vo, cloth extra, 5s.

Edwardes (Mrs. Annie), Novels by. Post 8vo, illust. bds., 2s. each.
Archie Lovell. | A Point of Honour.
A Plaster Saint. Crown 8vo, cloth, 3s. 6d.

Edwards (Eliezer).—Words, Facts, and Phrases: A Dictionary of Curious, Quaint, and Out-of-the-Way Matters. Cheaper Edition. Crown 8vo, cloth, 3s. 6d.

Egan (Pierce).—Life in London, With an Introduction by JOHN CAMDEN HOTTEN, and a Coloured Frontispiece. Small demy 8vo, cloth, 3s. 6d.

Egerton (Rev. J. C., M.A.).—Sussex Folk and Sussex Ways. With Introduction by Rev. Dr. H. WACE, and Four Illustrations. Crown 8vo, cloth extra, 5s.

Eggleston (Edward).—Roxy: A Novel. Post 8vo, illust. boards, 2s.

Englishman (An) in Paris. Notes and Recollections during the Reign of Louis Philippe and the Empire. Crown 8vo, cloth, 3s. 6d.

Englishman's House, The: A Practical Guide for Selecting or Building a House. By C. J. RICHARDSON. Coloured Frontispiece and 534 Illusts. Cr. 8vo, cloth, 3s. 6d.

Ewald (Alex. Charles, F.S.A.), Works by.
The Life and Times of Prince Charles Stuart, Count of Albany (THE YOUNG PRETENDER). With a Portrait. Crown 8vo, cloth extra, 7s. 6d.
Stories from the State Papers. With Autotype Frontispiece. Crown 8vo, cloth, 6s.

Eyes, Our: How to Preserve Them. By JOHN BROWNING. Cr. 8vo, 1s.

Familiar Short Sayings of Great Men. By SAMUEL ARTHUR BENT, A.M. Fifth Edition, Revised and Enlarged. Crown 8vo, cloth extra, 7s. 6d.

Faraday (Michael), Works by. Post 8vo, cloth extra, 4s. 6d. each.
The Chemical History of a Candle: Lectures delivered before a Juvenile Audience. Edited by WILLIAM CROOKES, F.C.S. With numerous Illustrations.
On the Various Forces of Nature, and their Relations to each other. Edited by WILLIAM CROOKES, F.C.S. With Illustrations.

Farrer (J. Anson).—War: Three Essays. Crown 8vo, cloth, 1s. 6d.

Fenn (G. Manville), Novels by.
Crown 8vo, cloth extra, 3s. 6d. each; post 8vo, illustrated boards, 2s. each.
The New Mistress. | Witness to the Deed. | The Tiger Lily. | The White Virgin.

Crown 8vo, cloth 3s. 6d. each.

A Woman Worth Winning. | Double Cunning. | The Story of Antony Grace.
Cursed by a Fortune. | A Fluttered Dovecote. | The Man with a Shadow.
The Case of Ailsa Gray. | King of the Castle. | One Maid's Mischief.
Commodore Junk. | The Master of the Ceremonies. | This Man's Wife.
Black Blood. | | In Jeopardy.

Crown 8vo, cloth, gilt top, 6s. each.
The Bag of Diamonds, and Three Bits of Paste.
A Crimson Crime. | Running Amok.

Fiction, A Catalogue of, with Descriptive Notices and Reviews of over NINE HUNDRED NOVELS, will be sent free by Messrs. CHATTO & WINDUS upon application.

Fin-Bec.—The Cupboard Papers: Observations on the Art of Living and Dining. Post 8vo, cloth limp, 2s. 6d.

Firework-Making, The Complete Art of; or, The Pyrotechnist's Treasury. By THOMAS KENTISH. With 267 Illustrations. Crown 8vo, cloth, 3s. 6d.

First Book, My. By WALTER BESANT, JAMES PAYN, W. CLARK RUSSELL, GRANT ALLEN, HALL CAINE, GEORGE R. SIMS, RUDYARD KIPLING, A. CONAN DOYLE, M. E. BRADDON, F. W. ROBINSON, H. RIDER HAGGARD, R. M. BALLANTYNE, I. ZANGWILL, MORLEY ROBERTS, D. CHRISTIE MURRAY, MARY CORELLI, J. K. JEROME, JOHN STRANGE WINTER, BRET HARTE, 'Q.,' ROBERT BUCHANAN, and R. L. STEVENSON. With a Prefatory Story by JEROME K. JEROME, and 185 Illustrations. A New Edition. Small demy 8vo, art linen, 3s. 6d.

Fitzgerald (Percy), Works by.
Little Essays: Passages from the Letters of CHARLES LAMB. Post 8vo, cloth, 2s. 6d.
Fatal Zero. Crown 8vo, cloth extra, 3s. 6d.; post 8vo, illustrated boards, 2s.

Post 8vo, illustrated boards, 2s. each.
Bella Donna. | The Lady of Brantome. | The Second Mrs. Tillotson.
Polly. | Never Forgotten. | Seventy-five Brooke Street.

Sir Henry Irving: Twenty Years at the Lyceum. With Portrait. Crown 8vo, cloth, 1s. 6d.

Flammarion (Camille), Works by.
Popular Astronomy: A General Description of the Heavens. Translated by J. ELLARD GORE, F.R.A.S. With Three Plates and 288 Illustrations. Medium 8vo, cloth, 10s. 6d.
Urania: A Romance. With 87 Illustrations. Crown 8vo, cloth extra, 5s.

Fletcher's (Giles, B.D.) Complete Poems: Christ's Victorie in Heaven, Christ's Victorie on Earth, Christ's Triumph over Death, and Minor Poems. With Notes by

CHATTO & WINDUS, Publishers, 111 St. Martin's Lane, London, W.C. 9

Forbes (Archibald).—The Life of Napoleon III. With Photogravure Frontispiece and Thirty-six full-page Illustrations. Cheaper Issue. Demy 8vo, cloth, 6s.

Francillon (R. E.), Novels by.
Crown 8vo, cloth extra, 3s. 6d. each; post 8vo, Illustrated boards, 2s. each.
One by One. | A Real Queen. | A Dog and his Shadow.
Ropes of Sand. Illustrated.

Post 8vo, illustrated boards, 2s. each.
Queen Cophetua. | Olympia. | Romances of the Law. | King or Knave?
Jack Doyle's Daughter. Crown 8vo, cloth, 3s. 6d.

Frederic (Harold), Novels by. Post 8vo, cloth extra, 3s. 6d. each; Illustrated boards, 2s. each.
Seth's Brother's Wife. | The Lawton Girl.

French Literature, A History of. By HENRY VAN LAUN. Three Vols., demy 8vo, cloth boards, 22s. 6d.

Fry's (Herbert) Royal Guide to the London Charities, 1900-1. Edited by JOHN LANE. Published Annually. Crown 8vo, cloth, 1s. 6d.

Gardening Books. Post 8vo, 1s. each; cloth limp. 1s. 6d. each.
A Year's Work in Garden and Greenhouse. By GEORGE GLENNY.
Household Horticulture. By TOM and JANE JERROLD. Illustrated.
The Garden that Paid the Rent. By TOM JERROLD.

Gardner (Mrs. Alan).—Rifle and Spear with the Rajpoots: Being the Narrative of a Winter's Travel and Sport in Northern India. With numerous Illustrations by the Author and F. H. TOWNSEND. Demy 4to, half-bound, 21s.

Gaulot (Paul).—The Red Shirts: A Tale of "The Terror." Translated by JOHN DE VILLIERS. With a Frontispiece by STANLEY WOOD. Crown 8vo, cloth, 3s. 6d.

Gentleman's Magazine, The. 1s. Monthly. Contains Stories, Articles upon Literature, Science, Biography, and Art, and '**Table Talk**' by SYLVANUS URBAN.
*** *Bound Volumes for recent years kept in stock, 8s. 6d. each. Cases for binding, 2s. each.*

Gentleman's Annual, The. Published Annually in November. 1s.

German Popular Stories. Collected by the Brothers GRIMM and Translated by EDGAR TAYLOR. With Introduction by JOHN RUSKIN, and 22 Steel Plates after GEORGE CRUIKSHANK. Square 8vo, cloth, 6s. 6d.; gilt edges, 7s. 6d.

Gibbon (Chas.), Novels by. Cr. 8vo, cl., 3s. 6d. ea.; post 8vo, bds., 2s. ea.
Robin Gray. With Frontispiece. | Loving a Dream. | The Braes of Yarrow.
The Golden Shaft. With Frontispiece. | Of High Degree.

Post 8vo, illustrated boards, 2s. each.
The Flower of the Forest. | A Hard Knot. | By Mead and Stream.
The Dead Heart. | Queen of the Meadow. | Fancy Free.
For Lack of Gold. | In Pastures Green. | In Honour Bound.
What Will the World Say? | In Love and War. | Heart's Delight.
For the King. | A Heart's Problem. | Blood-Money.

Gibney (Somerville).—Sentenced! Crown 8vo, cloth, 1s. 6d.

Gilbert (W. S.), Original Plays by. In Three Series, 2s. 6d. each.
The FIRST SERIES contains: The Wicked World—Pygmalion and Galatea—Charity—The Princess—The Palace of Truth—Trial by Jury.
The SECOND SERIES: Broken Hearts—Engaged—Sweethearts—Gretchen—Dan'l Druce—Tom Cobb—H.M.S. 'Pinafore'—The Sorcerer—The Pirates of Penzance.
The THIRD SERIES: Comedy and Tragedy—Foggerty's Fairy—Rosencrantz and Guildenstern—Patience—Princess Ida—The Mikado—Ruddigore—The Yeomen of the Guard—The Gondoliers—The Mountebanks—Utopia.

Eight Original Comic Operas written by W. S. GILBERT. In Two Series. Demy 8vo, cloth, 2s. 6d. each. The FIRST containing: The Sorcerer—H.M.S. 'Pinafore'—The Pirates of Penzance—Iolanthe—Patience—Princess Ida—The Mikado—Trial by Jury.
The SECOND SERIES containing: The Gondoliers—The Grand Duke—The Yeomen of the Guard—His Excellency—Utopia, Limited—Ruddigore—The Mountebanks—Haste to the Wedding.
The Gilbert and Sullivan Birthday Book: Quotations for Every Day in the Year, selected from Plays by W. S. GILBERT set to Music by Sir A. SULLIVAN. Compiled by ALEX. WATSON.

Gilbert (William).—James Duke, Costermonger. Post 8vo, illustrated boards, 2s.

Gissing (Algernon).—A Secret of the North Sea. Crown 8vo, cloth, gilt top, 6s.

Glanville (Ernest), Novels by.
Crown 8vo, cloth extra, 3s. 6d. each; post 8vo, illustrated boards, 2s. each.
The Lost Heiress: A Tale of Love, Battle, and Adventure. With Two Illustrations by H. NISBET.
The Fossicker: A Romance of Mashonaland. With Two Illustrations by HUME NISBET.
A Fair Colonist. With a Frontispiece by STANLEY WOOD.

The Golden Rock. With a Frontispiece by STANLEY WOOD. Crown 8vo, cloth extra, 3s. 6d.
Kloof Yarns. Crown 8vo cloth, 1s. 6d.
Tales from the Veld. With Twelve Illustrations by M. NISBET. Crown 8vo, cloth, 3s. 6d.
Max Thornton. With 8 Illustrations by J. S. CROMPTON, R.I. Large crown 8vo, cloth, gilt top, 6s.

Glenny (George).—A Year's Work in Garden and Greenhouse: Practical Advice as to the Management of the Flower, Fruit, and Frame Garden. Post 8vo, 1s.; cloth, 1s. 6d.

Godwin (William).—Lives of the Necromancers. Post 8vo, cl., 2s.

Golden Treasury of Thought, The: A Dictionary of Quotations from the Best Authors. By THEODORE TAYLOR. Crown 8vo, cloth, 3s. 6d.

Goodman (E. J.).—The Fate of Herbert Wayne. Cr. 8vo, 3s. 6d.

Greeks and Romans, The Life of the, described from Antique Monuments. By ERNST GUHL and W. KONER. Edited by Dr. F. HUEFFER. With 545 Illustrations. Large crown 8vo, cloth extra, 7s. 6d.

Grey (Sir George).—The Romance of a Proconsul: Being the Personal Life and Memoirs of Sir GEORGE GREY, K.C.B. By JAMES MILNE. With Portrait. SECOND EDITION. Crown 8vo, buckram, 6s.

Griffith (Cecil).—Corinthia Marazion: A Novel. Crown 8vo, cloth extra, 3s. 6d.

Gunter (A. Clavering, Author of 'Mr. Barnes of New York').—**A Florida Enchantment.** Crown 8vo, cloth, 3s. 6d.

Habberton (John, Author of 'Helen's Babies'), **Novels by.**
Post 8vo, cloth limp, 2s. 6d. each.
Brueton's Bayou. | **Country Luck.**

Hair, The: Its Treatment in Health, Weakness, and Disease. Translated from the German of Dr. J. PINCUS. Crown 8vo, 1s.; cloth, 1s. 6d.

Hake (Dr. Thomas Gordon), Poems by. Cr. 8vo, cl. ex., 6s. each.
New Symbols. | **Legends of the Morrow.** | **The Serpent Play.**
Maiden Ecstasy. Small 4to, cloth extra, 8s.

Halifax (C.).—Dr. Rumsey's Patient. By Mrs. L. T. MEADE and CLIFFORD HALIFAX, M.D. Crown 8vo, cloth, 3s. 6d.

Hall (Mrs. S. C.).—Sketches of Irish Character. With numerous Illustrations on Steel and Wood by MACLISE, GILBERT, HARVEY, and GEORGE CRUIKSHANK. Small demy 8vo, cloth extra, 7s. 6d.

Hall (Owen), Novels by. Crown 8vo, cloth, 3s. 6d. each.
The Track of a Storm. | **Jetsam.**
Eureka. Crown 8vo, cloth, gilt top, 6s.

Halliday (Andrew).—Every-day Papers. Post 8vo, boards, 2s.

Hamilton (Cosmo).—Stories by. Crown 8vo, cloth gilt, 3s. 6d. each.
The Glamour of the Impossible. | **Through a Keyhole.**

Handwriting, The Philosophy of. With over 100 Facsimiles and Explanatory Text. By DON FELIX DE SALAMANCA. Post 8vo, half-cloth, 2s. 6d.

Hanky-Panky: Easy and Difficult Tricks, White Magic, Sleight of Hand, &c. Edited by W. H. CREMER. With 200 Illustrations. Crown 8vo, cloth extra, 4s. 6d.

Hardy (Iza Duffus).—The Lesser Evil. Crown 8vo, cloth, gt. top, 6s.

Hardy (Thomas).—Under the Greenwood Tree. Post 8vo, cloth extra, 3s. 6d.; illustrated boards, 2s.; cloth limp, 2s. 6d.

CHATTO & WINDUS, Publishers, 111 St. Martin's Lane, London, W.C.   11

Harte's (Bret) Collected Works. Revised by the Author. LIBRARY
EDITION, in Ten Volumes, crown 8vo, cloth extra, 6s. each.
- Vol. I. COMPLETE POETICAL AND DRAMATIC WORKS. With Steel-plate Portrait.
- ,, II. THE LUCK OF ROARING CAMP—BOHEMIAN PAPERS—AMERICAN LEGEND.
- ,, III. TALES OF THE ARGONAUTS—EASTERN SKETCHES.
- ,, IV. GABRIEL CONROY. | Vol. V. STORIES—CONDENSED NOVELS, &c.
- ,, VI. TALES OF THE PACIFIC SLOPE.
- ,, VII. TALES OF THE PACIFIC SLOPE—II. With Portrait by JOHN PETTIE, R.A.
- ,, VIII. TALES OF THE PINE AND THE CYPRESS.
- ,, IX. BUCKEYE AND CHAPPAREL.
- ,, X. TALES OF TRAIL AND TOWN, &c.

Bret Harte's Choice Works, in Prose and Verse. With Portrait of the Author and 40 Illustrations. Crown 8vo, cloth, 3s. 6d.
Bret Harte's Poetical Works. Printed on hand-made paper. Crown 8vo, buckram, 4s. 6d.
Some Later Verses. Crown 8vo, linen gilt, 5s.

Crown 8vo, cloth extra, 3s. 6d. each; post 8vo, picture boards, 2s. each.
Gabriel Conroy.
A Waif of the Plains. With 60 Illustrations by STANLEY L. WOOD.
A Ward of the Golden Gate. With 59 Illustrations by STANLEY L. WOOD.

Crown 8vo, cloth extra, 3s. 6d. each.
A Sappho of Green Springs, &c. With Two Illustrations by HUME NISBET.
Colonel Starbottle's Client, and Some Other People. With a Frontispiece.
Susy: A Novel. With Frontispiece and Vignette by J. A. CHRISTIE.
Sally Dows, &c. With 47 Illustrations by W. D. ALMOND and others.
A Protegee of Jack Hamlin's, &c. With 26 Illustrations by W. SMALL and others.
The Bell-Ringer of Angel's, &c. With 39 Illustrations by DUDLEY HARDY and others
Clarence: A Story of the American War. With Eight Illustrations by A. JULE GOODMAN.
Barker's Luck, &c. With 39 Illustrations by A. FORESTIER, PAUL HARDY, &c.
Devil's Ford, &c. With a Frontispiece by W. H. OVEREND.
The Crusade of the "Excelsior." With a Frontispiece by J. BERNARD PARTRIDGE.
Three Partners; or, The Big Strike on Heavy Tree Hill. With 8 Illustrations by J. GULICH.
Tales of Trail and Town. With Frontispiece by G. P. JACOMB-HOOD.

Post 8vo, illustrated boards, 2s. each.
An Heiress of Red Dog, &c. | **The Luck of Roaring Camp**, &c.
Californian Stories.

Post 8vo, illustrated boards, 2s. each; cloth, 2s. 6d. each.
Flip. | **Maruja.** | **A Phyllis of the Sierras.**

Haweis (Mrs. H. R.), Books by.
The Art of Beauty. With Coloured Frontispiece and 91 Illustrations. Square 8vo, cloth bds., 6s.
The Art of Decoration. With Coloured Frontispiece and 74 Illustrations. Sq. 8vo, cloth bds., 6s.
The Art of Dress. With 32 Illustrations. Post 8vo, 1s.; cloth, 1s. 6d.
Chaucer for Schools. With the Story of his Times and his Work. A New Edition, revised. With a Frontispiece. Demy 8vo, cloth, 2s. 6d.
Chaucer for Children. With 38 Illustrations (8 Coloured). Crown 4to, cloth extra, 3s. 6d.

Haweis (Rev. H. R., M.A.).—American Humorists: WASHINGTON
IRVING, OLIVER WENDELL HOLMES, JAMES RUSSELL LOWELL, ARTEMUS WARD, MARK TWAIN, and BRET HARTE. Crown 8vo, cloth, 6s.

Hawthorne (Julian), Novels by.
Crown 8vo, cloth extra, 3s. 6d. each; post 8vo, illustrated boards, 2s. each.
Garth. | **Ellice Quentin.** | **Beatrix Randolph.** With Four Illusts.
Sebastian Strome. | **David Poindexter's Disappearance.**
Fortune's Fool, | **Dust.** Four Illusts. | **The Spectre of the Camera.**

Post 8vo, illustrated boards, 2s. each.
Miss Cadogna. | **Love—or a Name.**

Heckethorn (C. W.), Books by.
London Souvenirs. | **London Memories:** Social, Historical, and Topographical.

Helps (Sir Arthur), Books by. Post 8vo, cloth limp, 2s. 6d. each.
Animals and their Masters. | **Social Pressure.**
Ivan de Biron: A Novel. Crown 8vo, cloth extra, 3s. 6d.; post 8vo, illustrated boards, 2s.

Henderson (Isaac).—Agatha Page: A Novel. Cr. 8vo, cl., 3s. 6d.

12 CHATTO & WINDUS, Publishers, 111 St. Martin's Lane, London, W.C.

Hertzka (Dr. Theodor).—Freeland: A Social Anticipation. Translated by ARTHUR RANSOM. Crown 8vo, cloth extra, 6s.

Hesse-Wartegg (Chevalier Ernst von).— Tunis: The Land and the People. With 22 Illustrations. Crown 8vo, cloth extra, 3s. 6d.

Hill (Headon).—Zambra the Detective. Crown 8vo, cloth, 3s. 6d.; post 8vo, picture boards, 2s.

Hill (John), Works by.
Treason-Felony. Post 8vo, boards, 2s. | The Common Ancestor. Cr. 8vo, cloth, 3s. 6d.

Hoey (Mrs. Cashel).—The Lover's Creed. Post 8vo, boards, 2s.

Holiday, Where to go for a. By E. P. SHOLL, Sir H. MAXWELL, Bart., M.P., JOHN WATSON, JANE BARLOW, MARY LOVETT CAMERON, JUSTIN H. MCCARTHY, PAUL LANGE, J. W. GRAHAM, J. H. SALTER, PHŒBE ALLEN, S. J. BECKETT, L. RIVERS VINE, and C. F. GORDON CUMMING. Crown 8vo, cloth, 1s. 6d.

Hollingshead (John).—According to My Lights. With a Portrait. Crown 8vo, cloth, gilt top, 6s.

Holmes (Oliver Wendell), Works by.
The Autocrat of the Breakfast-Table. Illustrated by J. GORDON THOMSON. Post 8vo, cloth limp, 2s. 6d. Another Edition, post 8vo, cloth, 2s.
The Autocrat of the Breakfast-Table and The Professor at the Breakfast-Table. In One Vol. Post 8vo, half-bound, 2s.

Hood's (Thomas) Choice Works in Prose and Verse. With Life of the Author, Portrait, and 200 Illustrations. Crown 8vo, cloth, 3s. 6d.
Hood's Whims and Oddities. With 85 Illustrations. Post 8vo, half-bound, 2s.

Hook's (Theodore) Choice Humorous Works; including his Ludicrous Adventures, Bons Mots, Puns, and Hoaxes. With Life of the Author, Portraits, Facsimiles and Illustrations. Crown 8vo, cloth extra, 7s. 6d.

Hooper (Mrs. Geo.).—The House of Raby. Post 8vo, boards, 2s.

Hopkins (Tighe), Novels by. Crown 8vo, cloth, 6s. each.
Nell Haffenden. With 8 Illustrations by C. GREGORY. | For Freedom.
Crown 8vo, cloth, 3s. 6d. each.
'Twixt Love and Duty. With a Frontispiece. | The Incomplete Adventurer.
The Nugents of Carriconna.

Horne (R. Hengist).— Orion: An Epic Poem. With Photograph Portrait by SUMMERS. Tenth Edition. Crown 8vo, cloth extra, 7s.

Hugo (Victor).—The Outlaw of Iceland (Han d'Islande). Translated by Sir GILBERT CAMPBELL. Crown 8vo, cloth, 3s. 6d.

Hume (Fergus), Novels by.
The Lady from Nowhere. Crown 8vo, cloth, 3s. 6d.
The Millionaire Mystery. Crown 8vo, cloth, gilt top, 6s. [Shortly.

Hungerford (Mrs., Author of ' Molly Bawn '), Novels by.
Post 8vo, illustrated boards, 2s. each; cloth limp, 2s. 6d. each.
Marvel. | A Modern Circe. | Lady Patty.
In Durance Vile. | An Unsatisfactory Lover.
Crown 8vo, cloth extra, 3s. 6d. each; post 8vo, illustrated boards, 2s. each; cloth limp, 2s. 6d. each.
A Maiden All Forlorn. | Lady Verner's Flight. | The Three Graces.
April's Lady. | The Red-House Mystery. | Nora Creina.
Peter's Wife. | The Professor's Experiment. | A Mental Struggle.
Crown 8vo, cloth extra, 3s. 6d. each.
An Anxious Moment. | A Point of Conscience.
The Coming of Chloe. | Lovice.

Hunt's (Leigh) Essays: A Tale for a Chimney Corner, &c. Edited by EDMUND OLLIER. Post 8vo, half-bound, 2s.

Hunt (Mrs. Alfred), Novels by.
Crown 8vo, cloth extra, 3s. 6d. each; post 8vo, illustrated boards, 2s. each.
The Leaden Casket. | Self-Condemned. | That Other Person.
Mrs. Juliet. Crown 8vo, cloth extra, 3s. 6d.

Hutchison (W. M.).—Hints on Colt-breaking. With 25 Illustrations. Crown 8vo, cloth extra, 3s. 6d.

Hydrophobia: An Account of M. PASTEUR's System; The Technique of his Method, and Statistics. By RENAUD SUZOR, M.B. Crown 8vo, cloth extra, 6s.

CHATTO & WINDUS, Publishers, 111 St. Martin's Lane, London, W.C. 13

Impressions (The) of Aureole. Post 8vo, blush-rose paper and cloth, 2s. 6d.

Indoor Paupers. By ONE OF THEM. Crown 8vo, 1s. ; cloth, 1s. 6d.

Innkeeper's Handbook (The) and Licensed Victualler's Manual. By J. TREVOR-DAVIES. A New Edition. Crown 8vo, cloth, 2s.

Irish Wit and Humour, Songs of. Collected and Edited by A. PERCEVAL GRAVES. Post 8vo, cloth limp, 2s. 6d.

Irving (Sir Henry): A Record of over Twenty Years at the Lyceum. By PERCY FITZGERALD. With Portrait. Crown 8vo, cloth, 1s. 6d.

James (C. T. C.).—A Romance of the Queen's Hounds. Post 8vo, cloth limp, 1s. 6d.

Jameson (William).—My Dead Self. Post 8vo, cloth, 2s. 6d.

Japp (Alex. H., LL.D.).—Dramatic Pictures, &c. Cr. 8vo, cloth, 5s.

Jefferies (Richard), Books by. Post 8vo, cloth limp, 2s. 6d. each.
Nature near London. | The Life of the Fields. | The Open Air.
*** Also the HAND-MADE PAPER EDITION, crown 8vo, buckram, gilt top, 6s. each.

The Eulogy of Richard Jefferies. By Sir WALTER BESANT. With a Photograph Portrait. Crown 8vo, cloth extra, 6s.

Jennings (Henry J.), Works by.
Curiosities of Criticism. Post 8vo, cloth limp, 2s. 6d.
Lord Tennyson: A Biographical Sketch. With Portrait. Post 8vo, cloth, 1s. 6d.

Jerome (Jerome K.), Books by.
Stageland. With 64 Illustrations by J. BERNARD PARTRIDGE. Fcap. 4to, picture cover, 1s.
John Ingerfield, &c. With 9 Illusts. by A. S. BOYD and JOHN GULICH. Fcap. 8vo, pic. cov. 1s. 6d.

Jerrold (Douglas).—The Barber's Chair; and The Hedgehog Letters. Post 8vo, printed on laid paper and half-bound, 2s.

Jerrold (Tom), Works by. Post 8vo, 1s. ea. ; cloth limp, 1s. 6d. each.
The Garden that Paid the Rent.
Household Horticulture: A Gossip about Flowers. Illustrated.

Jesse (Edward).—Scenes and Occupations of a Country Life. Post 8vo, cloth limp, 2s.

Jones (William, F.S.A.), Works by. Cr. 8vo, cl. extra, 3s. 6d. each.
Finger-Ring Lore: Historical, Legendary, and Anecdotal. With Hundreds of Illustrations.
Credulities, Past and Present. Including the Sea and Seamen, Miners, Talismans, Word and Letter Divination, Exorcising and Blessing of Animals, Birds, Eggs, Luck, &c. With Frontispiece.
Crowns and Coronations: A History of Regalia. With 91 Illustrations.

Jonson's (Ben) Works. With Notes Critical and Explanatory, and a Biographical Memoir by WILLIAM GIFFORD. Edited by Colonel CUNNINGHAM. Three Vols. crown 8vo, cloth extra, 3s. 6d. each.

Josephus, The Complete Works of. Translated by WHISTON. Containing 'The Antiquities of the Jews' and 'The Wars of the Jews.' With 52 Illustrations and Maps. Two Vols., demy 8vo, half-cloth, 12s. 6d.

Kempt (Robert).—Pencil and Palette: Chapters on Art and Artists. Post 8vo, cloth limp, 2s. 6d.

Kershaw (Mark). — Colonial Facts and Fictions: Humorous Sketches. Post 8vo, illustrated boards, 2s. ; cloth, 2s. 6d.

King (R. Ashe), Novels by.

14 CHATTO & WINDUS, Publishers, 111 St. Martin's Lane, London, W.C.

Lamb's (Charles) Complete Works in Prose and Verse, including 'Poetry for Children' and 'Prince Dorus.' Edited, with Notes and Introduction, by R. H. SHEPHERD. With Two Portraits and Facsimile of the 'Essay on Roast Pig.' Crown 8vo, cloth, 3s. 6d.
The Essays of Elia. Post 8vo, printed on laid paper and half-bound, 2s.
Little Essays: Sketches and Characters by CHARLES LAMB, selected from his Letters by PERCY FITZGERALD. Post 8vo, cloth limp, 2s. 6d.
The Dramatic Essays of Charles Lamb. With Introduction and Notes by BRANDER MATTHEWS, and Steel-plate Portrait. Fcap. 8vo, half-bound, 2s. 6d.

Lambert (George).—The President of Boravia. Crown 8vo, cl., 3s. 6d.

Landor (Walter Savage).—Citation and Examination of William Shakspeare, &c. before Sir Thomas Lucy, touching Deer-stealing, 19th September, 1582. To which is added, **A Conference of Master Edmund Spenser** with the Earl of Essex, touching the State of Ireland, 1595. Fcap. 8vo, half-Roxburghe, 2s. 6d.

Lane (Edward William).—The Thousand and One Nights, commonly called in England **The Arabian Nights' Entertainments.** Translated from the Arabic, with Notes. Illustrated with many hundred Engravings from Designs by HARVEY. Edited by EDWARD STANLEY POOLE. With Preface by STANLEY LANE-POOLE. Three Vols., demy 8vo, cloth, 7s. 6d. ea.

Larwood (Jacob), Works by.
Anecdotes of the Clergy. Post 8vo, laid paper, half-bound, 2s.
Post 8vo, cloth limp, 2s. 6d. each.
Forensic Anecdotes. | **Theatrical Anecdotes.**

Lehmann (R. C.), Works by. Post 8vo, cloth, 1s. 6d. each.
Harry Fludyer at Cambridge.
Conversational Hints for Young Shooters: A Guide to Polite Talk.

Leigh (Henry S.).—Carols of Cockayne. Printed on hand-made paper, bound in buckram, 5s.

Leland (C. Godfrey).—A Manual of Mending and Repairing. With Diagrams. Crown 8vo, cloth, 5s.

Lepelletier (Edmond). — Madame Sans-Gêne. Translated from the French by JOHN DE VILLIERS. Post 8vo, cloth, 3s. 6d.; picture boards, 2s.

Leys (John K.), Novels by.
The Lindsays. Post 8vo, picture boards, 2s.
A Sore Temptation. Crown 8vo, cloth, gilt top, 6s.

Lilburn (Adam).—A Tragedy in Marble. Crown 8vo, cloth. 3s. 6d.

Lindsay (Harry, Author of 'Methodist Idylls'), Novels by.
Crown 8vo, cloth, 3s. 6d. each.
Rhoda Roberts.
The Jacobite: A Romance of the Conspiracy of 'The Forty.'

Linton (E. Lynn), Works by.
An Octave of Friends. Crown 8vo, cloth. 3s. 6d.
Crown 8vo, cloth extra, 3s. 6d. each; post 8vo, illustrated boards, 2s. each.
Patricia Kemball. | **Under which Lord?** With 12 Illustrations.
Ione. | **'My Love!'** | **Sowing the Wind.**
The Atonement of Leam Dundas. | **Paston Carew,** Millionaire and Miser.
The World Well Lost. With 12 Illusts. | **Dulcie Everton.** | **With a Silken Thread.**
The One Too Many.
The Rebel of the Family.
Post 8vo, cloth limp, 2s. 6d. each.
Witch Stories. | **Ourselves:** Essays on Women.
Freeshooting: Extracts from the Works of Mrs. LYNN LINTON.

Lowe (Charles, M.A.).—Our Greatest Living Soldiers. With 8 Portraits. Crown 8vo, cloth, 3s. 6d.

Lucy (Henry W.).—Gideon Fleyce: A Novel. Crown 8vo, cloth extra, 3s. 6d.; post 8vo, illustrated boards, 2s.

Macalpine (Avery), Novels by.
Teresa Itasca. Crown 8vo, cloth extra, 1s.
Broken Wings. With Six Illustrations by W. J. HENNESSY. Crown 8vo, cloth extra, 6s.

MacColl (Hugh), Novels by.
Mr. Stranger's Sealed Packet. Post 8vo, illustrated boards, 2s.
Ednor Whitlock. Crown 8vo, cloth extra, 6s.

Macdonell (Agnes).—Quaker Cousins. Post 8vo, boards, 2s.

MacGregor (Robert).—Pastimes and Players: Notes on Popular Games. Post 8vo, cloth limp, 2s. 6d.

Mackay (Charles, LL.D.). — Interludes and Undertones; or, Music at Twilight. Crown 8vo, cloth extra 6s.

Mackenna (Stephen J.) and J. Augustus O'Shea.—Brave Men

CHATTO & WINDUS, Publishers, 111 St. Martin's Lane, London, W.C. 15

McCarthy (Justin), Works by.

A History of Our Own Times, from the Accession of Queen Victoria to the General Election of 1880. LIBRARY EDITION. Four Vols., demy 8vo, cloth extra, 12s. each.—Also a POPULAR EDITION, in Four Vols., crown 8vo, cloth extra, 6s. each.—And the JUBILEE EDITION, with an Appendix of Events to the end of 1886, in Two Vols., large crown 8vo, cloth extra, 7s. 6d. each.
A History of Our Own Times, from 1880 to the Diamond Jubilee. Demy 8vo, cloth extra, 12s.; or crown 8vo, cloth, 6s.
A Short History of Our Own Times. One Vol., crown 8vo, cloth extra, 6s.—Also a CHEAP POPULAR EDITION, post 8vo, cloth limp, 2s. 6d.
A History of the Four Georges and of William the Fourth. By JUSTIN McCARTHY and JUSTIN HUNTLY McCARTHY. Four Vols., demy 8vo, cloth extra, 12s. each.
Reminiscences. With a Portrait. Two Vols., demy 8vo, cloth, 24s. [Vols. III. & IV. shortly.
Crown 8vo, cloth extra, 3s. 6d. each; post 8vo, illustrated boards, 2s. each; cloth limp, 2s. 6d. each.
The Waterdale Neighbours. | Donna Quixote. With 12 Illustrations.
My Enemy's Daughter. | The Comet of a Season.
A Fair Saxon. | Linley Rochford. | Maid of Athens. With 12 Illustrations.
Dear Lady Disdain. | The Dictator. | Camiola: A Girl with a Fortune.
Miss Misanthrope. With 12 Illustrations. | Red Diamonds. | The Riddle Ring.
The Three Disgraces, and other Stories. Crown 8vo, cloth, 3s. 6d.
Mononia: A Love Story of "Forty-eight." Crown 8vo, cloth, gilt top, 6s.
'The Right Honourable.' By JUSTIN McCARTHY and Mrs. CAMPBELL PRAED. Crown 8vo, cloth extra, 6s.

McCarthy (Justin Huntly), Works by.

The French Revolution. (Constituent Assembly, 1789-91). Four Vols., demy 8vo, cloth, 12s. each.
An Outline of the History of Ireland. Crown 8vo, 1s.; cloth, 1s. 6d.
Ireland Since the Union: Sketches of Irish History, 1798-1886. Crown 8vo, cloth, 6s.
Hafiz in London: Poems. Small 8vo, gold cloth, 3s. 6d.
Our Sensation Novel. Crown 8vo, picture cover, 1s.; cloth limp, 1s. 6d.
Doom: An Atlantic Episode. Crown 8vo, picture cover, 1s.
Dolly: A Sketch. Crown 8vo, picture cover, 1s.; cloth limp, 1s. 6d.
Lily Lass: A Romance. Crown 8vo, picture cover, 1s.; cloth limp, 1s. 6d.
A London Legend. Crown 8vo, cloth, 3s. 6d.
The Royal Christopher. Crown 8vo, cloth, 3s. 6d.

MacDonald (George, LL.D.), Books by.

Works of Fancy and Imagination. Ten Vols., 16mo, cloth, gilt edges, in cloth case, 21s.; or the Volumes may be had separately, in Grolier cloth, at 2s. 6d. each.
Vol. I. WITHIN AND WITHOUT.—THE HIDDEN LIFE.
" II. THE DISCIPLE.—THE GOSPEL WOMEN.—BOOK OF SONNETS.—ORGAN SONGS.
" III. VIOLIN SONGS.—SONGS OF THE DAYS AND NIGHTS.—A BOOK OF DREAMS.—ROADSIDE POEMS.—POEMS FOR CHILDREN.
" IV. PARABLES.—BALLADS.—SCOTCH SONGS.
" V. & VI. PHANTASTES: A Faerie Romance. | Vol. VII. THE PORTENT.
" VIII. THE LIGHT PRINCESS.—THE GIANT'S HEART.—SHADOWS.
" IX. CROSS PURPOSES.—THE GOLDEN KEY.—THE CARASOYN.—LITTLE DAYLIGHT.
" X. THE CRUEL PAINTER.—THE WOW O' RIVVEN.—THE CASTLE.—THE BROKEN SWORDS. —THE GRAY WOLF.—UNCLE CORNELIUS.
Poetical Works of George MacDonald. Collected and Arranged by the Author. Two Vols. crown 8vo, buckram, 12s.
A Threefold Cord. Edited by GEORGE MACDONALD. Post 8vo, cloth, 5s.
Phantastes: A Faerie Romance. With 25 Illustrations by J. BELL. Crown 8vo, cloth extra, 3s. 6d.
Heather and Snow: A Novel. Crown 8vo, cloth extra, 3s. 6d.; post 8vo, illustrated boards, 2s.
Lilith: A Romance. SECOND EDITION. Crown 8vo, cloth extra, 6s.

Maclise Portrait Gallery (The) of Illustrious Literary Characters: 85 Portraits by DANIEL MACLISE; with Memoirs—Biographical, Critical, Bibliographical, and Anecdotal—illustrative of the Literature of the former half of the Present Century, by WILLIAM BATES, B.A. Crown 8vo, cloth extra, 3s. 6d.

Macquoid (Mrs.), Works by. Square 8vo, cloth extra, 6s. each.

In the Ardennes. With 50 Illustrations by THOMAS R. MACQUOID.
Pictures and Legends from Normandy and Brittany. 34 Illusts. by T. R. MACQUOID.
Through Normandy. With 92 Illustrations by T. R. MACQUOID, and a Map.
Through Brittany. With 35 Illustrations by T. R. MACQUOID, and a Map.
About Yorkshire. With 67 Illustrations by T. R. MACQUOID.

Magician's Own Book, The: Performances with Eggs, Hats, &c. Edited by W. H. CREMER. With 200 Illustrations. Crown 8vo, cloth extra, 4s. 6d.

Magic Lantern, The, and its Management: Including full Practical Directions. By T. C. HEPWORTH. With 10 Illustrations. Crown 8vo, 1s.; cloth, 1s. 6d.

Magna Charta: An Exact Facsimile of the Original in the British Museum, 3 feet by 2 feet, with Arms and Seals emblazoned in Gold and Colours, 5s.

Mallory (Sir Thomas).—Mort d'Arthur: The Stories of King Arthur and of the Knights of the Round Table. (A Selection.) Edited by B. MONTGOMERIE RANKING. Post 8vo, cloth limp, 2s.

Mallock (W. H.), Works by.

The New Republic. Post 8vo, cloth, 3s. 6d.; picture boards, 2s.
The New Paul and Virginia: Positivism on an Island. Post 8vo, cloth, 2s. 6d.
Poems. Small 4to, parchment, 8s.
Is Life Worth Living? Crown 8vo, cloth extra, 6s.

Margueritte (Paul and Victor).—The Disaster. Translated by FREDERIC LEES. Crown 8vo, cloth, 3s. 6d.

Marlowe's Works. Including his Translations. Edited, with Notes and Introductions, by Colonel CUNNINGHAM. Crown 8vo, cloth extra, 3s. 6d.

Massinger's Plays. From the Text of WILLIAM GIFFORD. Edited by Col. CUNNINGHAM. Crown 8vo, cloth extra, 3s. 6d.

Mathams (Walter, F.R.G.S.).—Comrades All. Fcp. 8vo, cloth limp, 1s.; cloth gilt, 2s.

Matthews (Brander).—A Secret of the Sea, &c. Post 8vo, illustrated boards, 2s.; cloth limp, 2s. 6d.

Max O'Rell.—Her Royal Highness Woman. Cr. 8vo, cloth, 3s. 6d.

Meade (L. T.), Novels by.
A Soldier of Fortune. Crown 8vo, cloth, 3s. 6d.; post 8vo, illustrated boards, 2s.
Crown 8vo, cloth, 3s. 6d. each.
The Voice of the Charmer. With 8 Illustrations.
In an Iron Grip. | On the Brink of a Chasm. | A Son of Ishmael.
The Siren. | The Way of a Woman. | An Adventuress.
Dr. Rumsey's Patient. By L. T. MEADE and CLIFFORD HALIFAX, M.D.
The Blue Diamond. Crown 8vo, cloth, gilt top, 6s.
This Troublesome World. SECOND EDITION. Crown 8vo, cloth, gilt top, 6s.

Merivale (Herman).—Bar, Stage, and Platform: Autobiographic Memories. Demy 8vo, cloth, 12s. [*Shortly*

Merrick (Leonard), Novels by.
The Man who was Good. Post 8vo, picture boards, 2s.
Crown 8vo, cloth, 3s. 6d. each.
This Stage of Fools. | Cynthia: A Daughter of the Philistines.

Mexican Mustang (On a), through Texas to the Rio Grande. By A. E. SWEET and J. ARMOY KNOX. With 265 Illustrations. Crown 8vo, cloth extra, 7s. 6d.

Middlemass (Jean), Novels by. Post 8vo, illust. boards, 2s. each.
Touch and Go. | Mr. Dorillion.

Miller (Mrs. F. Fenwick).—Physiology for the Young; or, The House of Life. With numerous Illustrations. Post 8vo, cloth limp, 2s. 6d.

Milton (J. L.), Works by. Post 8vo, 1s. each; cloth, 1s. 6d. each.
The Hygiene of the Skin. With Directions for Diet, Soaps, Baths, Wines, &c.
The Bath in Diseases of the Skin.
The Laws of Life, and their Relation to Diseases of the Skin.

Minto (Wm.).—Was She Good or Bad? Crown 8vo, cloth, 1s. 6d.

Mitchell (Edmund).—The Lone Star Rush. With 8 Illustrations by NORMAN H. HARDY. Crown 8vo, cloth, gilt top, 6s.

Mitford (Bertram), Novels by. Crown 8vo, cloth extra, 3s. 6d. each.
The Gun-Runner: A Romance of Zululand. With a Frontispiece by STANLEY L. WOOD.
The Luck of Gerard Ridgeley. With a Frontispiece by STANLEY L. WOOD.
The King's Assegai. With Six full-page Illustrations by STANLEY L. WOOD.
Renshaw Fanning's Quest. With a Frontispiece by STANLEY L. WOOD.

Molesworth (Mrs.).—Hathercourt Rectory. Post 8vo, illustrated boards, 2s.

Moncrieff (W. D. Scott-).—The Abdication: An Historical Drama. With Seven Etchings by JOHN PETTIE, W. Q. ORCHARDSON, J. MACWHIRTER, COLIN HUNTER, R. MACBETH and TOM GRAHAM. Imperial 4to, buckram, 21s.

Montagu (Irving).—Things I Have Seen in War. With 16 full-page Illustrations. Crown 8vo, cloth, 6s.

Moore (Thomas), Works by.
The Epicurean; and Alciphron. Post 8vo, half-bound, 2s.
Prose and Verse; including Suppressed Passages from the MEMOIRS OF LORD BYRON. Edited by R. H. SHEPHERD. With Portrait. Crown 8vo, cloth extra, 7s. 6d.

Morrow (W. C.).—Bohemian Paris of To-Day. With 106 Illustrations by EDOUARD CUCUEL. Small demy 8vo, cloth, gilt top, 6s.

Muddock (J. E.), Stories by.
Crown 8vo, cloth extra, 3s. 6d. each.
Maid Marian and Robin Hood. With 12 Illustrations by STANLEY WOOD.
Basile the Jester. With Frontispiece by STANLEY WOOD.
Young Lochinvar. | The Golden Idol.

Post 8vo, illustrated boards, 2s. each.
The Dead Man's Secret. | From the Bosom of the Deep.
Stories Weird and Wonderful. Post 8vo, illustrated boards, 2s.; cloth, 2s. 6d.

CHATTO & WINDUS, Publishers, 111 St. Martin's Lane, London, W.C. 17

Murray (D. Christie), Novels by.
Crown 8vo, cloth extra, 3s. 6d. each; post 8vo, illustrated boards, 2s. each.
A Life's Atonement. | A Model Father. | Bob Martin's Little Girl.
Joseph's Coat. 12 Illusts. | Old Blazer's Hero. | Time's Revenges.
Coals of Fire. 3 Illusts. | Cynic Fortune. Frontisp. | A Wasted Crime.
Val Strange. | By the Gate of the Sea. | In Direst Peril.
Hearts. | A Bit of Human Nature. | Mount Despair.
The Way of the World. | First Person Singular. | A Capful o' Nails.
The Making of a Novelist: An Experiment in Autobiography. With a Collotype Portrait Cr 8vo, buckram, 3s. 6d.
My Contemporaries in Fiction. Crown 8vo, buckram, 3s. 6d.
 Crown 8vo, cloth, 3s. 6d. each.
This Little World. | A Race for Millions.
Tales in Prose and Verse. With Frontispiece by ARTHUR HOPKINS.
The Church of Humanity. Crown 8vo, cloth, gilt top, 6s.

Murray (D. Christie) and Henry Herman, Novels by.
Crown 8vo, cloth extra, 3s. 6d. each; post 8vo, illustrated boards, 2s. each.
One Traveller Returns. | The Bishops' Bible.
Paul Jones's Alias, &c. With Illustrations by A. FORESTIER and G. NICOLET.

Murray (Henry), Novels by.
Post 8vo, cloth, 2s. 6d. each.
A Game of Bluff. | A Song of Sixpence.

Newbolt (H.).—Taken from the Enemy. Post 8vo, leatherette, 1s.

Nisbet (Hume), Books by.
'Bail Up.' Crown 8vo, cloth extra, 3s. 6d.; post 8vo, illustrated boards, 2s.
Dr. Bernard St. Vincent. Post 8vo, illustrated boards, 2s.
Lessons in Art. With 21 Illustrations. Crown 8vo, cloth extra, 2s. 6d.

Norris (W. E.), Novels by. Crown 8vo, cloth, 3s. 6d. each; post 8vo, picture boards, 2s. each.
Saint Ann's.
Billy Bellew. With a Frontispiece by F. H. TOWNSEND.
Miss Wentworth's Idea. Crown 8vo, cloth, 3s. 6d.

Oakley (John).—A Gentleman in Khaki: A Story of the South African War. Demy 8vo, picture cover, 1s.

Ohnet (Georges), Novels by. Post 8vo, illustrated boards, 2s. each.
Doctor Rameau. | A Last Love.
A Weird Gift. Crown 8v cloth, 3s. 6d.; post 8vo, picture boards, 2s.
Love's Depths. Translated by F. ROTHWELL. Crown 8vo, cloth, 3s. 6d.

Oliphant (Mrs.), Novels by. Post 8vo, illustrated boards, 2s. each.
The Primrose Path. | Whiteladies.
The Greatest Heiress in England.
The Sorceress. Crown 8vo, cloth, 3s. 6d.

O'Shaughnessy (Arthur), Poems by:
Fcap. 8vo, cloth extra, 7s. 6d. each.
Music and Moonlight. | Songs of a Worker.
Lays of France. Crown 8vo, cloth extra, 10s. 6d.

Ouida, Novels by. Cr. 8vo, cl., 3s. 6d. ea.; post 8vo, illust. bds., 2s. ea.
Held in Bondage. | A Dog of Flanders. | In Maremma. | Wanda.
Tricotrin. | Pascarel. | Signa. | Bimbi. | Syrlin.
Strathmore. | Chandos. | Two Wooden Shoes. | Frescoes. | Othmar.
Cecil Castlemaine's Gage | In a Winter City. | Princess Napraxine.
Under Two Flags. | Ariadne. | Friendship. | Guilderoy. | Ruffino.
Puck. | Idalia. | A Village Commune. | Two Offenders.
Folle-Farine. | Moths. | Pipistrello. | Santa Barbara.
 POPULAR EDITIONS. Medium 8vo, 6d. each; cloth, 1s. each.
Under Two Flags. | Moths.
 Medium 8vo, 6d. each.
Held in Bondage. | Puck.
The Waters of Edera. Crown 8vo, cloth, 3s. 6d.
Wisdom, Wit, and Pathos, selected from the Works of OUIDA by F. SYDNEY MORRIS. Post 8vo, cloth extra, 5s.—CHEAP EDITION, illustrated boards, 2s.

Page (H. A.).—Thoreau: His Life and Aims. With Portrait. Post 8vo, cloth, 2s. 6d.

Pandurang Hari; or, Memoirs of a Hindoo. With Preface by Sir BARTLE FRERE. Post 8vo, illustrated boards, 2s.

Pascal's Provincial Letters. A New Translation, with Historical Introduction and Notes by T. M'CRIE, D.D. Post 8vo, half-cloth, 2s.

Paul (Margaret A.).—Gentle and Simple. Crown 8vo, cloth, with Frontispiece by HELEN PATERSON, 3s. 6d.; post 8vo, illustrated boards, 2s.

CHATTO & WINDUS, Publishers, 111 St. Martin's Lane, London, W.C.

Payn (James), Novels by.
Crown 8vo, cloth extra, 3s. 6d. each; post 8vo, illustrated boards, 2s. each.

Lost Sir Massingberd.
Walter's Word. | A County Family.
Less Black than We're Painted.
By Proxy. | For Cash Only.
High Spirits.
A Confidential Agent. With 12 Illusts.
A Grape from a Thorn. With 12 Illusts.

Holiday Tasks.
The Talk of the Town. With 12 Illusts.
The Mystery of Mirbridge.
The Word and the Will.
The Burnt Million.
Sunny Stories. | A Trying Patient.

Post 8vo illustrated boards, 2s. each.

Humorous Stories. | From Exile.
The Foster Brothers.
The Family Scapegrace.
Married Beneath Him.
Bentinck's Tutor.
A Perfect Treasure.
Like Father, Like Son.
A Woman's Vengeance.
Carlyon's Year. | Cecil's Tryst.
Murphy's Master. | At Her Mercy.
The Clyffards of Clyffe.

Found Dead. | Gwendoline's Harvest
Mirk Abbey. | A Marine Residence.
Some Private Views.
The Canon's Ward.
Not Wooed, But Won.
Two Hundred Pounds Reward.
The Best of Husbands.
Halves. | What He Cost Her.
Fallen Fortunes. | Kit: A Memory.
Under One Roof. | Glow-worm Tales.
A Prince of the Blood.

A Modern Dick Whittington; or, A Patron of Letters. With a Portrait of the Author. Crown 8vo, cloth, 3s. 6d.
In Peril and Privation. With 17 Illustrations. Crown 8vo, cloth, 3s. 6d.
Notes from the 'News.' Crown 8vo, cloth, 1s. 6d.
By Proxy. POPULAR EDITION, medium 8vo, 6d.; cloth, 1s.

Payne (Will).—Jerry the Dreamer. Crown 8vo, cloth, 3s. 6d.

Pennell (H. Cholmondeley), Works by. Post 8vo, cloth, 2s. 6d. ea.
Puck on Pegasus. With Illustrations.
Pegasus Re-Saddled. With Ten full-page Illustrations by G. DU MAURIER.
The Muses of Mayfair: Vers de Société. Selected by H. C. PENNELL.

Phelps (E. Stuart), Works by. Post 8vo, cloth, 1s. 6d. each.
An Old Maid's Paradise. | Burglars in Paradise.
Beyond the Gates. Post 8vo, picture cover, 1s.; cloth, 1s. 6d.
Jack the Fisherman. Illustrated by C. W. REED. Crown 8vo, cloth, 1s. 6d.

Phil May's Sketch-Book. Containing 54 Humorous Cartoons. Crown folio, cloth, 2s. 6d.

Phipson (Dr. T. L.), Books by. Crown 8vo, art canvas, gilt top, 5s. ea.
Famous Violinists and Fine Violins.
Voice and Violin: Sketches, Anecdotes, and Reminiscences.

Planche (J. R.), Works by.
The Pursuivant of Arms. With Six Plates and 209 Illustrations. Crown 8vo, cloth, 7s. 6d.
Songs and Poems, 1819-1879. With Introduction by Mrs. MACKARNESS. Crown 8vo, cloth, 6s.

Plutarch's Lives of Illustrious Men. With Notes and a Life of Plutarch by JOHN and WM. LANGHORNE, and Portraits. Two Vols., demy 8vo, half-cloth 10s. 6d.

Poe's (Edgar Allan) Choice Works: Poems, Stories, Essays. With an Introduction by CHARLES BAUDELAIRE. Crown 8vo, cloth, 3s. 6d.

Pollock (W. H.).—The Charm, and other Drawing-room Plays. By Sir WALTER BESANT and WALTER H. POLLOCK. With 50 Illustrations. Crown 8vo, cloth gilt, 6s.

Pond (Major J. B.).—Eccentricities of Genius: Memories of Famous Men and Women of the Platform and the Stage. With 91 Portraits. Demy 8vo, cloth, 12s.

Pope's Poetical Works. Post 8vo, cloth limp, 2s.

Porter (John).—Kingsclere. Edited by BYRON WEBBER. With 19 full-page and many smaller Illustrations. Cheaper Edition. Demy 8vo, cloth, 7s. 6d.

Praed (Mrs. Campbell), Novels by. Post 8vo, illust. bds., 2s. each.
The Romance of a Station. | The Soul of Countess Adrian.
Crown 8vo, cloth, 3s. 6d. each; post 8vo, boards, 2s. each.
Outlaw and Lawmaker. | Christina Chard. With Frontispiece by W. PAGET
Mrs. Tregaskiss. With 8 Illustrations by ROBERT SAUBER.
Crown 8vo, cloth, 3s. 6d. each.
Nulma. | Madame Izan.
'As a Watch in the Night.' Crown 8vo, cloth, gilt top, 6s.

Price (E. C.), Novels by. Crown 8vo, cloth, 3s. 6d. each.
Valentina. | The Foreigners. | Mrs. Lancaster's Rival.

Princess Olga.—Radna: A Novel. Crown 8vo, cloth extra, 6s.

CHATTO & WINDUS, Publishers, 111 St. Martin's Lane, London, W.C. 19

Proctor (Richard A.), Works by.
 Flowers of the Sky. With 55 Illustrations. Small crown 8vo, cloth extra, 3s. 6d.
 Easy Star Lessons. With Star Maps for every Night in the Year. Crown 8vo, cloth, 6s.
 Familiar Science Studies. Crown 8vo, cloth extra, 6s.
 Saturn and its System. With 13 Steel Plates. Demy 8vo, cloth extra, 10s. 6d.
 Mysteries of Time and Space. With numerous Illustrations. Crown 8vo, cloth extra, 6s.
 The Universe of Suns, &c. With numerous Illustrations. Crown 8vo, cloth extra, 6s.
 Wages and Wants of Science Workers. Crown 8vo, 1s. 6d.

Pryce (Richard).—Miss Maxwell's Affections. Crown 8vo, cloth, with Frontispiece by HAL LUDLOW, 3s. 6d.; post 8vo, illustrated boards, 2s.

Rambosson (J.).—Popular Astronomy. Translated by C. B. PITMAN. With 10 Coloured Plates and 63 Woodcut Illustrations. Crown 8vo, cloth, 3s. 6d.

Randolph (Col. G.).—Aunt Abigail Dykes. Crown 8vo, cloth, 7s. 6d.

Read (General Meredith).—Historic Studies in Vaud, Berne, and Savoy. With 31 full-page Illustrations. Two Vols., demy 8vo, cloth, 28s.

Reade's (Charles) Novels.
 The New Collected LIBRARY EDITION, complete in Seventeen Volumes, set in new long primer type, printed on laid paper, and elegantly bound in cloth, price 3s. 6d. each.
 1. Peg Woffington; and Christie Johnstone.
 2. Hard Cash.
 3. The Cloister and the Hearth. With a Preface by Sir WALTER BESANT.
 4. 'It is Never Too Late to Mend.'
 5. The Course of True Love Never Did Run Smooth; and Singleheart and Doubleface.
 6. The Autobiography of a Thief; Jack of all Trades; A Hero and a Martyr; and The Wandering Heir.
 7. Love Me Little, Love me Long.
 8. The Double Marriage.
 9. Griffith Gaunt.
 10. Foul Play.
 11. Put Yourself in His Place.
 12. A Terrible Temptation.
 13. A Simpleton.
 14. A Woman-Hater.
 15. The Jilt, and other Stories; and Good Stories of Man and other Animals.
 16. A Perilous Secret.
 17. Readiana; and Bible Characters.

 In Twenty-one Volumes, post 8vo, illustrated boards, 2s. each.
 Peg Woffington. | Christie Johnstone.
 'It is Never Too Late to Mend.'
 The Course of True Love Never Did Run Smooth.
 The Autobiography of a Thief; Jack of all Trades; and James Lambert.
 Love Me Little, Love Me Long.
 The Double Marriage.
 The Cloister and the Hearth.
 Hard Cash. | Griffith Gaunt.
 Foul Play. | Put Yourself in His Place.
 A Terrible Temptation.
 A Simpleton. | The Wandering Heir.
 A Woman-Hater.
 Singleheart and Doubleface.
 Good Stories of Man and other Animals.
 The Jilt, and other Stories.
 A Perilous Secret. | Readiana.

 POPULAR EDITIONS. Medium 8vo, 6d. each; cloth, 1s. each.
 Peg Woffington; and Christie Johnstone. | Hard Cash.
 Medium 8vo, 6d. each.
 'It is Never Too Late to Mend.' | The Cloister and the Hearth.

 Christie Johnstone. With Frontispiece. Choicely printed in Elzevir style. Fcap. 8vo, half-Roxb. 2s. 6d.
 Peg Woffington. Choicely printed in Elzevir style. Fcap. 8vo, half-Roxburghe, 2s. 6d.
 The Cloister and the Hearth. In Four Vols., post 8vo, with an Introduction by Sir WALTER BESANT, and a Frontispiece to each Vol., buckram, gilt top, 6s. the set.—Also the LARGE TYPE, FINE PAPER EDITION, pott 8vo, cloth, 2s. net; leather, 3s. net.
 Bible Characters. Fcap. 8vo, leatherette, 1s.
 Selections from the Works of Charles Reade. With an Introduction by Mrs. ALEX. IRELAND. Post 8vo, cloth limp, 2s. 6d.

Riddell (Mrs. J. H.), Novels by.
 A Rich Man's Daughter. Crown 8vo, cloth, 3s. 6d.
 Weird Stories. Crown 8vo, cloth extra, 3s. 6d.; post 8vo, illustrated boards, 2s.
 Post 8vo, illustrated boards, 2s. each.
 The Uninhabited House.
 The Prince of Wales's Garden Party.
 The Mystery in Palace Gardens.
 Fairy Water.
 Her Mother's Darling.
 The Nun's Curse. | Idle Tales.

Rimmer (Alfred), Works by. Large crown 8vo, cloth, 3s. 6d. each.
 Rambles Round Eton and Harrow. With 52 Illustrations by the Author.
 About England with Dickens. With 58 Illustrations by C. A. VANDERHOOF and A. RIMMER.

Rives (Amelie, Author of 'The Quick or the Dead?'), Stories by.
 Crown 8vo, cloth, 3s. 6d. each.
 Barbara Dering. | Meriel: A Love Story.

Robinson Crusoe. By DANIEL DEFOE. With 37 Illustrations by GEORGE CRUIKSHANK. Post 8vo, half-cloth, 2s.

Robinson (F. W.), Novels by.
 Women are Strange. Post 8vo, illustrated boards, 2s.
 The Hands of Justice. Crown 8vo, cloth extra, 3s. 6d.; post 8vo illustrated boards, 2s.

20 CHATTO & WINDUS, Publishers, 111 St. Martin's Lane, London, W.C.

Robinson (Phil), Works by. Crown 8vo, cloth extra, 6s. each.
The Poets' Birds. | The Poets' Beasts.
The Poets and Nature: Reptiles, Fishes, and Insects.

Roll of Battle Abbey, The: A List of the Principal Warriors who came from Normandy with William the Conqueror, 1066. Printed in Gold and Colours, 5s.

Rosengarten (A.).—A Handbook of Architectural Styles. Translated by W. COLLETT-SANDARS. With 630 Illustrations. Crown 8vo, cloth extra, 7s. 6d.

Ross (Albert).—A Sugar Princess. Crown 8vo, cloth, 3s. 6d.

Rowley (Hon. Hugh), Works by. Post 8vo, cloth, 2s. 6d. each.
Puniana: Riddles and Jokes. With numerous Illustrations.
More Puniana. Profusely Illustrated.

Runciman (James), Stories by. Post 8vo, cloth, 2s. 6d. each.
Grace Balmaign's Sweetheart. | Schools & Scholars.
Skippers and Shellbacks. Crown 8vo, cloth, 3s. 6d.

Russell (Dora), Novels by.
A Country Sweetheart. Post 8vo, picture boards, 2s.
The Drift of Fate. Crown 8vo, cloth, 3s. 6d.

Russell (Herbert).—True Blue; or, 'The Lass that Loved a Sailor.'
Crown 8vo, cloth, 3s. 6d.

Russell (W. Clark), Novels, &c., by.
Crown 8vo, cloth extra, 3s. 6d. each; post 8vo, illustrated boards, 2s. each; cloth limp, 2s. 6d. each.
Round the Galley-Fire. | An Ocean Tragedy.
In the Middle Watch. | My Shipmate Louise.
On the Fo'k'sle Head. | Alone on a Wide Wide Sea.
A Voyage to the Cape. | The Good Ship 'Mohock.'
A Book for the Hammock. | The Phantom Death.
The Mystery of the 'Ocean Star.' | Is He the Man? | The Convict Ship.
The Romance of Jenny Harlowe. | Heart of Oak. | The Last Entry.
The Tale of the Ten.
Crown 8vo, cloth, 3s. 6d. each.
A Tale of Two Tunnels. | The Death Ship.
The Ship: Her Story. With 50 Illustrations by H. C. SEPPINGS WRIGHT. Small 4to, cloth, 6s.
The "Pretty Polly": A Voyage of Incident. With 12 Illustrations by G. E. ROBERTSON. Large crown 8vo, cloth, gilt edges, 5s.

Saint Aubyn (Alan), Novels by.
Crown 8vo, cloth extra, 3s. 6d. each; post 8vo, illustrated boards, 2s. each.
A Fellow of Trinity. With a Note by OLIVER WENDELL HOLMES and a Frontispiece.
The Junior Dean. | The Master of St. Benedict's. | To His Own Master.
Orchard Damerel. | In the Face of the World. | The Tremlett Diamonds.
Fcap. 8vo, cloth boards, 1s. 6d. each.
The Old Maid's Sweetheart. | Modest Little Sara.
Crown 8vo, cloth, 3s. 6d. each.
The Wooing of May. | A Tragic Honeymoon. | A Proctor's Wooing.
Fortune's Gate. | Gallantry Bower. | Bonnie Maggie Lauder.
Mary Unwin. With 8 Illustrations by PERCY TARRANT.
Mrs. Dunbar's Secret. Crown 8vo, cloth, gilt top, 6s.

Saint John (Bayle).—A Levantine Family. A New Edition.
Crown 8vo, cloth, 3s. 6d.

Sala (George A.).—Gaslight and Daylight. Post 8vo, boards, 2s.

Scotland Yard, Past and Present: Experiences of Thirty-seven Years.
By Ex-Chief-Inspector CAVANAGH. Post 8vo, illustrated boards, 2s.; cloth, 2s. 6d.

Secret Out, The: One Thousand Tricks with Cards; with Entertaining Experiments in Drawing-room or 'White' Magic. By W. H. CREMER. With 300 Illustrations. Crown 8vo, cloth extra, 4s. 6d.

Seguin (L. G.), Works by.
The Country of the Passion Play (Oberammergau) and the Highlands of Bavaria. With Map and 37 Illustrations. Crown 8vo, cloth extra, 3s. 6d.
Walks in Algiers. With Two Maps and 16 Illustrations. Crown 8vo, cloth extra, 6s.

Senior (Wm.).—By Stream and Sea. Post 8vo, cloth, 2s. 6d.

Sergeant (Adeline), Novels by. Crown 8vo, cloth, 3s. 6d. each.
Under False Pretences. | Dr. Endicott's Experiment.

Shakespeare for Children: Lamb's Tales from Shakespeare.
With Illustrations, coloured and plain, by J. MOYR SMITH. Crown 4to, cloth gilt, 3s. 6d.

Shakespeare the Boy. With Sketches of the Home and School Life, the Games and Sports, the Manners, Customs, and Folk-lore of the Time. By WILLIAM J. ROLFE, Litt.D. A New Edition, with 42 Illustrations, and an INDEX OF PLAYS AND PASSAGES REFERRED TO. Crown 8vo, cloth gilt, 3s. 6d.

Sharp (William).—Children of To-morrow. Crown 8vo, cloth, 6s.

CHATTO & WINDUS, Publishers, 111 St. Martin's Lane, London, W.C. 21

Shelley's (Percy Bysshe) Complete Works in Verse and Prose.
Edited, Prefaced, and Annotated by R. HERNE SHEPHERD. Five Vols., crown 8vo, cloth, 3s. 6d. each.
Poetical Works, in Three Vols.:
  Vol. I. Introduction by the Editor; Posthumous Fragments of Margaret Nicholson; Shelley's Correspondence with Stockdale; The Wandering Jew; Queen Mab, with the Notes; Alastor, and other Poems; Rosalind and Helen; Prometheus Unbound; Adonais, &c.
  „ II. Laon and Cythna: The Cenci; Julian and Maddalo; Swellfoot the Tyrant; The Witch of Atlas; Epipsychidion; Hellas.
  „ III. Posthumous Poems; The Masque of Anarchy; and other Pieces.
Prose Works, in Two Vols.:
  Vol. I. The Two Romances of Zastrozzi and St. Irvyne; the Dublin and Marlow Pamphlets; A Refutation of Deism; Letters to Leigh Hunt, and some Minor Writings and Fragments.
  II. The Essays; Letters from Abroad; Translations and Fragments, edited by Mrs. SHELLEY. With a Biography of Shelley, and an Index of the Prose Works.

Sherard (R. H.).—Rogues: A Novel. Crown 8vo, cloth, 1s. 6d.

Sheridan's (Richard Brinsley) Complete Works, with Life and Anecdotes. Including his Dramatic Writings, his Works in Prose and Poetry, Translations, Speeches, and Jokes. Crown 8vo, cloth, 3s. 6d.
The Rivals, The School for Scandal, and other Plays. Post 8vo, half-bound, 2s.
Sheridan's Comedies: The Rivals and **The School for Scandal**. Edited, with an Introduction and Notes to each Play, and a Biographical Sketch, by BRANDER MATTHEWS. With Illustrations. Demy 8vo, half-parchment, 12s. 6d.

Shiel (M. P.).—The Purple Cloud. By the Author of "The Yellow Danger." Crown 8vo, cloth, gilt top, 6s. [*Preparing.*]

Sidney's (Sir Philip) Complete Poetical Works, including all those in 'Arcadia.' With Portrait, Memorial-Introduction, Notes, &c., by the Rev. A. B. GROSART, D.D. Three Vols., crown 8vo, cloth boards, 3s. 6d. each.

Signboards: Their History, including Anecdotes of Famous Taverns and Remarkable Characters. By JACOB LARWOOD and JOHN CAMDEN HOTTEN. With Coloured Frontispiece and 94 Illustrations. Crown 8vo, cloth extra, 3s. 6d.

Sims (George R.), Works by.
Post 8vo, illustrated boards, 2s. each; cloth limp, 2s. 6d. each.
The Ring o' Bells.	Dramas of Life. With 60 Illustrations.
Mary Jane's Memoirs.	Memoirs of a Landlady.
Tinkletop's Crime.	My Two Wives.
Zeph: A Circus Story, &c.	Scenes from the Show.
Tales of To-day.	The Ten Commandments: Stories.

Crown 8vo, picture cover, 1s. each; cloth, 1s. 6d. each.
The Dagonet Reciter and Reader: Being Readings and Recitations in Prose and Verse, selected from his own Works by GEORGE R. SIMS.
The Case of George Candlemas. | **Dagonet Ditties.** (From *The Referee*.)
How the Poor Live; and **Horrible London.** With a Frontispiece by F. BARNARD. Crown 8vo, leatherette, 1s.
Dagonet Dramas of the Day. Crown 8vo, 1s.

Crown 8vo, cloth, 3s. 6d. each; post 8vo, picture boards, 2s. each; cloth limp, 2s. 6d. each.
Mary Jane Married. | **Rogues and Vagabonds.** | **Dagonet Abroad.**

Crown 8vo, cloth, 3s. 6d. each.
Once upon a Christmas Time. With 8 Illustrations by CHARLES GREEN, R.I.
In London's Heart: A Story of To-day.
Without the Limelight: Theatrical Life as it is.
The Small-part Lady, &c.

Sister Dora: A Biography. By MARGARET LONSDALE. With Four Illustrations. Demy 8vo, picture cover, 4d.; cloth, 6d.

Sketchley (Arthur).—A Match in the Dark. Post 8vo, boards, 2s.

Slang Dictionary (The): Etymological, Historical, and Anecdotal. Crown 8vo, cloth extra, 6s. 6d.

Smart (Hawley), Novels by.
Crown 8vo, cloth 3s. 6d. each; post 8vo, picture boards, 2s. each.
Beatrice and Benedick.	Long Odds.
Without Love or Licence.	The Master of Rathkelly.

Crown 8vo, cloth, 3s. 6d. each.
The Outsider. | **A Racing Rubber.**
The Plunger. Post 8vo, picture boards, 2s.

Smith (J. Moyr), Works by.
The Prince of Argolis. With 130 Illustrations. Post 8vo, cloth extra, 3s. 6d.
The Wooing of the Water Witch. With numerous Illustrations. Post 8vo, cloth, 6s.

Snazelleparilla. Decanted by G. S. EDWARDS. With Portrait of G. H. SNAZELLE, and 65 Illustrations by C. LYALL. Crown 8vo, cloth, 3s. 6d.

Society in London. Crown 8vo, 1s.; cloth, 1s. 6d.

Somerset (Lord Henry).—Songs of Adieu. Small 4to, Jap. vel., 6s.

Spalding (T. A., LL.B.).—Elizabethan Demonology: An Essay on the Belief in the Existence of Devils. Crown 8vo, cloth extra, 5s.

Speight (T. W.), Novels by.
Post 8vo, illustrated boards, 2s. each.
The Mysteries of Heron Dyke.
By Devious Ways, &c.
Hoodwinked; & Sandycroft Mystery.
The Golden Hoop.
Back to Life.
The Loudwater Tragedy.
Burgo's Romance.
Quittance in Full.
A Husband from the Sea.

Post 8vo, cloth limp, 1s. 6d. each.
A Barren Title. | Wife or No Wife?

Crown 8vo, cloth extra, 3s. 6d. each.
A Secret of the Sea. | The Grey Monk. | The Master of Trenance.
A Minion of the Moon: A Romance of the King's Highway.
The Secret of Wyvern Towers.
The Doom of Siva. | The Web of Fate.
The Strange Experiences of Mr. Verschoyle.

Spenser for Children. By M. H. Towry. With Coloured Illustrations by WALTER J. MORGAN. Crown 4to, cloth extra, 3s. 6d.

Spettigue (H. H.).—The Heritage of Eve. Crown 8vo, cloth, 6s.

Stafford (John), Novels by.
Doris and I. Crown 8vo, cloth, 3s. 6d.
Carlton Priors. Crown 8vo, cloth, gilt top, 6s.

Starry Heavens (The): A POETICAL BIRTHDAY BOOK. Royal 16mo, cloth extra, 2s. 6d.

Stedman (E. C.).—Victorian Poets. Crown 8vo, cloth extra, 9s.

Stephens (Riccardo, M.B.).—The Cruciform Mark: The Strange Story of RICHARD TREGENNA, Bachelor of Medicine (Univ. Edinb.) Crown 8vo, cloth, 3s. 6d.

Stephens (Robert Neilson).—Philip Winwood: A Sketch of the Domestic History of an American Captain in the War of Independence; embracing events that occurred between and during the years 1763 and 1786, in New York and London; written by His Enemy in War, HERBERT RUSSELL, Lieutenant in the Loyalist Forces. With Six Illustrations by E. W. D. HAMILTON. Crown 8vo, cloth, gilt top, 6s.

Sterndale (R. Armitage).—The Afghan Knife: A Novel. Post 8vo, cloth, 3s. 6d.; illustrated boards, 2s.

Stevenson (R. Louis), Works by.
Crown 8vo, buckram, gilt top, 6s. each.
Travels with a Donkey. With a Frontispiece by WALTER CRANE.
An Inland Voyage. With a Frontispiece by WALTER CRANE.
Familiar Studies of Men and Books.
The Silverado Squatters. With Frontispiece by J. D. STRONG.
The Merry Men. | Underwoods: Poems.
Memories and Portraits.
Virginibus Puerisque, and other Papers. | Ballads. | Prince Otto.
Across the Plains, with other Memories and Essays.
Weir of Hermiston. | In the South Seas.
A Lowden Sabbath Morn. With 27 Illustrations by A. S. BOYD. Fcap. 8vo, cloth, 6s.
Songs of Travel. Crown 8vo, buckram, 5s.
New Arabian Nights. Crown 8vo, buckram, gilt top, 6s.; post 8vo, illustrated boards, 2s.
—POPULAR EDITION, medium 8vo, 6d. [Shortly.
The Suicide Club; and The Rajah's Diamond. (From NEW ARABIAN NIGHTS.) With Eight Illustrations by W. J. HENNESSY. Crown 8vo, cloth, 3s. 6d.
The Stevenson Reader: Selections from the Writings of ROBERT LOUIS STEVENSON. Edited by LLOYD OSBOURNE. Post 8vo, cloth, 2s. 6d.; buckram, gilt top, 3s. 6d.
Robert Louis Stevenson: A Life Study in Criticism. By H. BELLYSE BAILDON. With 2 Portraits. Crown 8vo, buckram, gilt top, 6s.

Stockton (Frank R.).—The Young Master of Hyson Hall. With numerous Illustrations by VIRGINIA H. DAVISSON and C. H. STEPHENS. Crown 8vo, cloth, 3s. 6d.

Storey (G. A., A.R.A.).—Sketches from Memory. With 93 Illustrations by the Author. Demy 8vo, cloth, gilt top, 12s. 6d.

Stories from Foreign Novelists. With Notices by HELEN and ALICE ZIMMERN. Crown 8vo, cloth extra 3s. 6d.

Strange Manuscript (A) Found in a Copper Cylinder. Crown 8vo, cloth extra, with 19 Illustrations by GILBERT GAUL, 3s. 6d.; post 8vo, illustrated boards, 2s.

Strange Secrets. Told by PERCY FITZGERALD, CONAN DOYLE, FLORENCE MARRYAT, &c. Post 8vo, illustrated boards, 2s.

Strutt (Joseph).—The Sports and Pastimes of the People of England; including the Rural and Domestic Recreations, May Games, Mummeries, Shows, &c., from the Earliest Period to the Present Time. Edited by WILLIAM HONE. With 140 Illustrations. Crown 8vo, cloth extra, 3s. 6d.

CHATTO & WINDUS, Publishers, 111 St. Martin's Lane, London, W.C. 23

Sundowner.—Told by the Taffrail. Crown 8vo, cloth, 3s. 6d.

Surtees (Robert).—Handley Cross; or, Mr. Jorrocks's Hunt. With 79 Illustrations by JOHN LEECH. A New Edition. Post 8vo, cloth, 2s.

Swift's (Dean) Choice Works, in Prose and Verse. With Memoir, Portrait, and Facsimiles of the Maps in 'Gulliver's Travels.' Crown 8vo, cloth, 3s. 6d.
Gulliver's Travels, and **A Tale of a Tub.** Post 8vo, half-bound, 2s.
Jonathan Swift: A Study. By J. CHURTON COLLINS. Crown 8vo, cloth extra, 8s.

Swinburne (Algernon C.), Works by.
Selections from the Poetical Works of A. C. Swinburne. Fcap. 8vo 6s.
Atalanta in Calydon. Crown 8vo, 6s.
Chastelard: A Tragedy. Crown 8vo, 7s.
Poems and Ballads. FIRST SERIES. Crown 8vo, or fcap. 8vo, 9s.
Poems and Ballads. SECOND SER. Cr.8vo,9s.
Poems & Ballads. THIRD SERIES. Cr. 8vo, 7s.
Songs before Sunrise. Crown 8vo, 10s. 6d.
Bothwell: A Tragedy. Crown 8vo, 12s. 6d.
Songs of Two Nations. Crown 8vo, 6s.
George Chapman. (See Vol. II. of G. CHAPMAN'S Works.) Crown 8vo, 3s. 6d.
Essays and Studies. Crown 8vo, 12s.
Erechtheus: A Tragedy. Crown 8vo, 6s.
A Note on Charlotte Bronte. Cr. 8vo, 6s.
A Study of Shakespeare. Crown 8vo, 8s.
Songs of the Springtides. Crown 8vo, 6s.
Studies in Song. Crown 8vo, 7s.
Mary Stuart: A Tragedy. Crown 8vo, 8s.
Tristram of Lyonesse. Crown 8vo, 9s.
A Century of Roundels. Small 4to, 8s.
A Midsummer Holiday. Crown 8vo, 7s.
Marino Faliero: A Tragedy. Crown 8vo, 6s.
A Study of Victor Hugo. Crown 8vo, 6s.
Miscellanies. Crown 8vo, 12s.
Locrine: A Tragedy. Crown 8vo, 6s.
A Study of Ben Jonson. Crown 8vo, 7s.
The Sisters: A Tragedy. Crown 8vo, 6s.
Astrophel, &c. Crown 8vo, 7s.
Studies in Prose and Poetry. Cr.8vo, 9s.
The Tale of Balen. Crown 8vo, 7s.
Rosamund, Queen of the Lombards: A Tragedy. SECOND EDITION, with a DEDICATORY POEM. Crown 8vo, 6s.

Syntax's (Dr.) Three Tours: In Search of the Picturesque, in Search of Consolation, and in Search of a Wife. With ROWLANDSON'S Coloured Illustrations, and Life of the Author by J. C. HOTTEN. Crown 8vo, cloth extra, 7s. 6d.

Taine's History of English Literature. Translated by HENRY VAN LAUN. Four Vols., small demy 8vo, cloth boards, 30s.—POPULAR EDITION, Two Vols., large crown 8vo, cloth extra, 15s.

Taylor (Bayard). — Diversions of the Echo Club: Burlesques of Modern Writers. Post 8vo, cloth limp, 2s.

Taylor (Tom).—Historical Dramas: 'JEANNE DARC,' 'TWIXT AXE AND CROWN,' 'THE FOOL'S REVENGE,' 'ARKWRIGHT'S WIFE,' 'ANNE BOLEYNE,' 'PLOT AND PASSION.' Crown 8vo, 1s. each.

Temple (Sir Richard, G.C.S.I.).—A Bird's-eye View of Picturesque India. With 32 Illustrations by the Author. Crown 8vo, cloth, gilt top, 6s.

Thackerayana: Notes and Anecdotes. With Coloured Frontispiece and Hundreds of Sketches by WILLIAM MAKEPEACE THACKERAY. Crown 8vo, cloth extra, 3s. 6d.

Thames, A New Pictorial History of the. By A. S. KRAUSSE. With 340 Illustrations. Post 8vo, cloth, 1s. 6d.

Thomas (Annie), Novels by.
The Siren's Web: A Romance of London Society. Crown 8vo, cloth, 3s. 6d.
Comrades True. Crown 8vo, cloth, gilt top, 6s.

Thomas (Bertha), Novels by.
Crown 8vo, cloth, 3s. 6d. each.
The Violin-Player. | **The House on the Scar.** [Preparing
Crown 8vo, cloth, gilt top, 6s. each.
In a Cathedral City. | **The Son of the House.**

Thomson's Seasons, and The Castle of Indolence. With Introduction by ALLAN CUNNINGHAM, and 48 Illustrations. Post 8vo, half-bound, 2s.

Thornbury (Walter), Books by.
The Life and Correspondence of J. M. W. Turner. With Eight Illustrations in Colours and Two Woodcuts. New and Revised Edition. Crown 8vo, cloth, 3s. 6d.
Tales for the Marines. Post 8vo, illustrated boards, 2s.

Timbs (John), Works by. Crown 8vo, cloth, 3s. 6d. each.
Clubs and Club Life in London: Anecdotes of its Famous Coffee-houses, Hostelries, an Taverns. With 41 Illustrations.
English Eccentrics and Eccentricities: Stories of Delusions, Impostures, Sporting Scenes Eccentric Artists, Theatrical Folk, &c. With 48 Illustrations.

Trollope (Anthony), Novels by.
Crown 8vo, cloth extra, 3s. 6d. each; post 8vo, illustrated boards, 2s. each.
The Way We Live Now. | **Mr. Scarborough's Family.**
Frau Frohmann. | **Marion Fay.** | **The Land-Leaguers.**
Post 8vo, illustrated boards, 2s. each.
Kept in the Dark. | **The American Senator.**
The Golden Lion of Granpere.

24   CHATTO & WINDUS, Publishers, 111 St. Martin's Lane, London, W.C.

Trollope (Frances E.), Novels by.
Crown 8vo, cloth extra, 3s. 6d. each; post 8vo, illustrated boards, 2s. each.
Like Ships upon the Sea. | Mabel's Progress. | Anne Furness.

Trollope (T. A.).—Diamond Cut Diamond. Post 8vo, illust. bds., 2s.

Twain's (Mark) Books.
The Author's Edition de Luxe of the Works of Mark Twain, in 22 Volumes (limited to 600 Numbered Copies for sale in Great Britain and its Dependencies), price £13 15s. net the Set; or, 12s. 6d. net per Volume, is now complete, and a detailed Prospectus may be had. The First Volume of the Set is SIGNED BY THE AUTHOR. (Sold only in Sets.)

UNIFORM LIBRARY EDITION OF MARK TWAIN'S WORKS.
Crown 8vo, cloth extra, 3s. 6d. each.
Mark Twain's Library of Humour. With 197 Illustrations by E. W. KEMBLE.
Roughing It; and The Innocents at Home. With 200 Illustrations by F. A. FRASER.
The American Claimant. With 81 Illustrations by HAL HURST and others.
*The Adventures of Tom Sawyer. With 111 Illustrations.
Tom Sawyer Abroad. With 26 Illustrations by DAN BEARD.
Tom Sawyer, Detective, &c. With Photogravure Portrait of the Author.
Pudd'nhead Wilson. With Portrait and Six Illustrations by LOUIS LOEB.
*A Tramp Abroad. With 314 Illustrations.
*The Innocents Abroad; or, The New Pilgrim's Progress. With 234 Illustrations. (The Two Shilling Edition is entitled Mark Twain's Pleasure Trip.)
*The Gilded Age. By MARK TWAIN and C. D. WARNER With 212 Illustrations.
*The Prince and the Pauper. With 190 Illustrations.
*Life on the Mississippi. With 300 Illustrations.
*The Adventures of Huckleberry Finn. With 174 Illustrations by E. W. KEMBLE.
*A Yankee at the Court of King Arthur. With 220 Illustrations by DAN BEARD.
*The Stolen White Elephant. | *The £1,000,000 Bank-Note.
The Choice Works of Mark Twain. Revised and Corrected throughout by the Author. With Life, Portrait, and numerous Illustrations.
*** The books marked * may be had also in post 8vo. picture boards, at 2s. each.

Crown 8vo, cloth, gilt top, 6s. each.
Personal Recollections of Joan of Arc. With Twelve Illustrations by F. V. DU MOND.
More Tramps Abroad.
The Man that Corrupted Hadleyburg, and other Stories and Sketches. With a Frontispiece.
Mark Twain's Sketches. Post 8vo, illustrated boards, 2s.

Tytler (C. C. Fraser-).—Mistress Judith: A Novel. Crown 8vo, cloth extra, 3s. 6d.; post 8vo, illustrated boards, 2s.

Tytler (Sarah), Novels by.
Crown 8vo, cloth extra, 3s. 6d. each; post 8vo, illustrated boards, 2s. each.
Lady Bell. | Buried Diamonds. | The Blackhall Ghosts. | What She Came Through.

Post 8vo, illustrated boards, 2s. each.
Citoyenne Jacqueline. | The Huguenot Family.
The Bride's Pass. | Noblesse Oblige. | Disappeared.
Saint Mungo's City. | Beauty and the Beast.

Crown 8vo, cloth, 3s. 6d. each.
The Macdonald Lass. With Frontispiece. | Mrs. Carmichael's Goddesses.
The Witch-Wife. | Rachel Langton. | Sapphira. | A Honeymoon's Eclipse.
A Young Dragon.

Upward (Allen), Novels by.
A Crown of Straw. Crown 8vo, cloth, 6s.
The Queen Against Owen. Crown 8vo, cloth, 3s. 6d.; post 8vo, picture boards, 2s.
The Prince of Balkistan. Post 8vo, picture boards, 2s.

Vandam (Albert D.).—A Court Tragedy. With 6 Illustrations by J. BARNARD DAVIS. Crown 8vo, cloth, 3s. 6d.

Vashti and Esther. By 'Belle' of *The World*. Cr. 8vo, cloth, 3s. 6d.

Vizetelly (Ernest A.), Books by. Crown 8vo, cloth, 3s. 6d. each.
The Scorpion: A Romance of Spain. With a Frontispiece.
With Zola in England: A Story of Exile. With 4 Portraits.
A Path of Thorns. Crown 8vo, cloth, gilt top, 6s.

Wagner (Leopold).—How to Get on the Stage, and how to Succeed there. Crown 8vo, cloth, 2s. 6d.

Walford's County Families of the United Kingdom (1901).
Containing Notices of the Descent, Birth, Marriage, Education, &c., of more than 12,000 Distinguished Heads of Families, their Heirs Apparent or Presumptive, the Offices they hold or have held, their Town and Country Addresses, Clubs, &c. Royal 8vo, cloth gilt, 50s.

Waller (S. E.).—Sebastiani's Secret. With 9 Illusts. Cr. 8vo, cl., 6s.

Walton and Cotton's Complete Angler. With Memoirs and Notes by Sir HARRIS NICOLAS, and 61 Illustrations. Crown 8vo, cloth antique, 7s. 6d.

Walt Whitman, Poems by. Edited, with Introduction, by WILLIAM M. ROSSETTI. With Portrait. Crown 8vo, hand-made paper and buckram, 6s.

Warden (Florence).—Joan, the Curate. Crown 8vo, cloth, 3s. 6d.

CHATTO & WINDUS, Publishers, 111 St. Martin's Lane, London, W.C. 25

Warman (Cy).—**The Express Messenger**, and other Tales of the Rail. Crown 8vo, cloth, 3s. 6d.

Warner (Charles Dudley).—**A Roundabout Journey.** Crown 8vo, cloth extra, 6s.

Wassermann (Lillias).—**The Daffodils.** Crown 8vo, cloth, 1s. 6d.

Warrant to Execute Charles I. A Facsimile, with the 59 Signatures and Seals. Printed on paper 22 in. by 14 in. 2s.
Warrant to Execute Mary Queen of Scots. A Facsimile, including Queen Elizabeth's Signature and the Great Seal. 2s.

Weather, How to Foretell the, with the Pocket Spectroscope. By F. W. CORY. With Ten Illustrations. Crown 8vo, 1s.; cloth, 1s. 6d.

Werner (A.).—**Chapenga's White Man.** Crown 8vo, cloth, 3s. 6d.

Westall (William), Novels by.
Trust Money. Crown 8vo, cloth, 3s. 6d.; post 8vo, Illustrated boards, 2s.

Crown 8vo, cloth, 6s. each.
| As a Man Sows. | A Red Bridal. | As Luck would have it. |
| | Her Ladyship's Secret. | |

Crown 8vo, cloth 3s. 6d. each.
A Woman Tempted Him.	Nigel Fortescue.	The Phantom City.
For Honour and Life.	Ben Clough.	Birch Dene.	Ralph Norbreck's Trust.
Her Two Millions.	The Old Factory.	A Queer Race.
Two Pinches of Snuff.	Sons of Belial.	Red Ryvington.
	With the Red Eagle.	

Roy of Roy's Court. With 6 Illustrations. Crown 8vo, cloth, 3s. 6d.
Strange Crimes. (True Stories.) Crown 8vo, cloth, 3s. 6d.
The Old Factory. POPULAR EDITION. Medium 8vo, 6d.

Westbury (Atha).—**The Shadow of Hilton Fernbrook:** A Romance of Maoriland. Crown 8vo, cloth, 3s. 6d.

Whishaw (Fred.).—**A Forbidden Name:** A Story of the Court of Catherine the Great. Crown 8vo, cloth, gilt top, 6s.

White (Gilbert).—**The Natural History of Selborne.** Post 8vo, printed on laid paper and half-bound, 2s.

Wilde (Lady). — **The Ancient Legends, Mystic Charms, and** Superstitions of Ireland; with Sketches of the Irish Past. Crown 8vo, cloth, 3s. 6d.

Williams (W. Mattieu, F.R.A.S.), Works by.
Science in Short Chapters. Crown 8vo, cloth extra, 7s. 6d.
A Simple Treatise on Heat. With Illustrations. Crown 8vo, cloth, 2s. 6d.
The Chemistry of Cookery. Crown 8vo, cloth extra, 6s.
A Vindication of Phrenology. With Portrait and 43 Illusts. Demy 8vo, cloth extra, 12s. 6d.

Williamson (Mrs. F. H.).—**A Child Widow.** Post 8vo, bds., 2s.

Wills (C. J.), Novels by.
An Easy-going Fellow. Crown 8vo, cloth, 3s. 6d. | His Dead Past. Crown 8vo, cloth, 6s.

Wilson (Dr. Andrew, F.R.S.E.), Works by.
Chapters on Evolution. With 259 Illustrations. Crown 8vo, cloth extra, 7s. 6d.
Leaves from a Naturalist's Note-Book. Post 8vo, cloth limp, 2s. 6d.
Leisure-Time Studies. With Illustrations. Crown 8vo, cloth extra, 6s.
Studies in Life and Sense. With 36 Illustrations. Crown 8vo, cloth. 3s. 6d.
Common Accidents: How to Treat Them. With Illustrations. Crown 8vo, 1s.; cloth, 1s. 6d.
Glimpses of Nature. With 35 Illustrations. Crown 8vo, cloth extra, 3s. 6d.

Winter (John Strange), Stories by. Post 8vo, illustrated boards, 2s. each; cloth limp, 2s. 6d. each.
Cavalry Life. | Regimental Legends.
Cavalry Life and Regimental Legends. LIBRARY EDITION, set in new type and handsomely bound. Crown 8vo, cloth, 3s. 6d.
A Soldier's Children. With 34 Illustrations by E. G. THOMSON and E. STUART HARDY. Crown 8vo, cloth extra, 3s. 6d.

Wissmann (Hermann von). — **My Second Journey through** Equatorial Africa. With 92 Illustrations. Demy 8vo, cloth, 16s.

Wood (H. F.), Detective Stories by. Post 8vo, boards, 2s. each.
The Passenger from Scotland Yard. | The Englishman of the Rue Cain.

Woolley (Celia Parker).—**Rachel Armstrong;** or, Love and Theology. Post 8vo, cloth, 2s. 6d.

Wright (Thomas, F.S.A.), Works by.
Caricature History of the Georges; or, Annals of the House of Hanover. Compiled from Squibs, Broadsides, Window Pictures, Lampoons, and Pictorial Caricatures of the Time. With over 300 Illustrations. Crown 8vo, cloth, 3s. 6d.
History of Caricature and of the Grotesque in Art, Literature, Sculpture, and Painting. Illustrated by F. W. FAIRHOLT, F.S.A. Crown 8vo, cloth, 7s. 6d.

Wynman (Margaret).—**My Flirtations.** With 13 Illustrations by

26   CHATTO & WINDUS, Publishers, 111 St. Martin's Lane, London, W.C.

Zola (Emile), Novels by. Crown 8vo, cloth extra, 3s. 6d. each.

The Fortune of the Rougons. Edited by ERNEST A. VIZETELLY.
Abbe Mouret's Transgression. Edited by ERNEST A. VIZETELLY.
The Conquest of Plassans Edited by ERNEST A. VIZETELLY.
Germinal; or, Master and Man. Edited by ERNEST A. VIZETELLY.
The Honour of the Army. and other Stories. Edited by ERNEST A. VIZETELLY, [Shortly.
His Excellency (Eugene Rougon). With an Introduction by ERNEST A. VIZETELLY.
The Dram-Shop (L'Assommoir). With Introduction by E. A. VIZETELLY.
The Fat and the Thin. Translated by ERNEST A. VIZETELLY.
Money. Translated by ERNEST A. VIZETELLY.
The Downfall. Translated by E. A. VIZETELLY.
The Dream. Translated by ELIZA CHASE. With Eight Illustrations by JEANNIOT.
Doctor Pascal. Translated by E. A. VIZETELLY. With Portrait of the Author.
Lourdes. Translated by ERNEST A. VIZETELLY.
Rome. Translated by ERNEST A. VIZETELLY.
Paris. Translated by ERNEST A. VIZETELLY.
Fruitfulness (Fécondité). Translated and Edited, with an Introduction, by E. A. VIZETELLY.
Work. Translated by ERNEST A. VIZETELLY.

With Zola in England. By ERNEST A. VIZETELLY. With Four Portraits. Crown 8vo, cloth, 3s. 6d.

'ZZ' (L. Zangwill).—A Nineteenth Century Miracle. Cr. 8vo, 3s. 6d.

SOME BOOKS CLASSIFIED IN SERIES.
⁎ *For fuller cataloguing, see alphabetical arrangement, pp. 1-26.*

The Mayfair Library. Post 8vo, cloth limp, 2s. 6d. per Volume.

Quips and Quiddities. By W. D. ADAMS.
The Agony Column of 'The Times.'
A Journey Round My Room. By X. DE MAISTRE.
 Translated by HENRY ATTWELL.
Poetical Ingenuities. By W. T. DOBSON.
The Cupboard Papers. By FIN-BEC.
W. S. Gilbert's Plays. Three Series.
Songs of Irish Wit and Humour.
Animals and their Masters. By Sir A HELPS.
Social Pressure. By Sir A. HELPS.
Autocrat of Breakfast-Table. By O. W. HOLMES.
Curiosities of Criticism. By H. J. JENNINGS.
Pencil and Palette. By R. KEMPT.
Little Essays: from LAMB'S LETTERS.
Forensic Anecdotes. By JACOB LARWOOD.
Theatrical Anecdotes. By JACOB LARWOOD.
Ourselves. By E. LYNN LINTON.
Witch Stories. By E. LYNN LINTON.
Pastimes and Players. By R. MACGREGOR.
New Paul and Virginia. By W. H. MALLOCK.
Muses of Mayfair. Edited by H. C. PENNELL.
Thoreau: His Life and Aims. By H. A. PAGE.
Puck on Pegasus. By H. C. PENNELL.
Pegasus Re-saddled. By H. C. PENNELL.
Puniana. By Hon. HUGH ROWLEY.
More Puniana. By Hon. HUGH ROWLEY.
By Stream and Sea. By WILLIAM SENIOR.
Leaves from a Naturalist's Note-Book. By Dr. ANDREW WILSON.

The Golden Library. Post 8vo, cloth limp, 2s. per Volume.

Songs for Sailors. By W. C. BENNETT.
Lives of the Necromancers. By W. GODWIN.
The Autocrat of the Breakfast Table. By OLIVER WENDELL HOLMES.
Tale for a Chimney Corner. By LEIGH HUNT.
Scenes of Country Life. By EDWARD JESSE.
La Mort d'Arthur: Selections from MALLORY.
The Poetical Works of Alexander Pope.
Diversions of the Echo Club. BAYARD TAYLOR.

Handy Novels. Fcap. 8vo, cloth boards, 1s. 6d. each.

Dr. Palliser's Patient. By GRANT ALLEN
Monte Carlo Stories. By JOAN BARRETT.
Black Spirits and White. By R. A. CRAM.
Seven Sleepers of Ephesus. M. E. COLERIDGE.
The Old Maid's Sweetheart. By A. ST. AUBYN.
Modest Little Sara. By ALAN ST. AUBYN.

My Library. Printed on laid paper, post 8vo, half-Roxburghe, 2s. 6d. each.

The Journal of Maurice de Guerin.
The Dramatic Essays of Charles Lamb.
Citation and Examination of William Shakspeare. By W. S. LANDOR.
Christie Johnstone. By CHARLES READE.
Peg Woffington. By CHARLES READE.

The Pocket Library. Post 8vo, printed on laid paper and hf.-bd., 2s. each.

Gastronomy. By BRILLAT-SAVARIN.
Robinson Crusoe. Illustrated by G. CRUIKSHANK
Autocrat of the Breakfast-Table and The Professor at the Breakfast-Table. By O. W. HOLMES.
Provincial Letters of Blaise Pascal.
Whims and Oddities. By THOMAS HOOD.
Leigh Hunt's Essays. Edited by E. OLLIER.
The Barber's Chair. By DOUGLAS JERROLD.
The Essays of Elia. By CHARLES LAMB.
Anecdotes of the Clergy. By JACOB LARWOOD.
The Epicurean, &c. By THOMAS MOORE.
Plays by RICHARD BRINSLEY SHERIDAN.
Gulliver's Travels, &c. By Dean SWIFT.
Thomson's Seasons. Illustrated.
White's Natural History of Selborne.

POPULAR SIXPENNY NOVELS.

The Orange Girl. By WALTER BESANT.
All Sorts and Conditions of Men. By WALTER BESANT. (and JAMES RICE.
The Golden Butterfly. By WALTER BESANT
The Deemster. By HALL CAINE.
The Shadow of a Crime. By HALL CAINE.
A Son of Hagar. By HALL CAINE.
Antonina. By WILKIE COLLINS.
The Moonstone. By WILKIE COLLINS.
The Woman in White. By WILKIE COLLINS.
The Dead Secret. By WILKIE COLLINS.
The New Magdalen. By WILKIE COLLINS.
Held in Bondage. By OUIDA.
Moths. By OUIDA.
Under Two Flags. By OUIDA.
Puck. By OUIDA.
By Proxy By JAMES PAYN.
Peg Woffington; and Christie Johnstone. By CHARLES READE. [READE.
The Cloister and the Hearth. By CHARLES
Never Too Late to Mend. By CHARLES READE.
Hard Cash. By CHARLES READE.
New Arabian Nights. By R. L. STEVENSON.
The Old Factory. By WILLIAM WESTALL.

THE PICCADILLY NOVELS.

LIBRARY EDITIONS OF NOVELS, many Illustrated, crown 8vo, cloth extra, 3s. 6d. each.

By Mrs. ALEXANDER.
Valerie's Fate. | Barbara
A Life Interest. | A Fight with Fate.
Mona's Choice. | A Golden Autumn.
By Woman's Wit. | Mrs. Crichton's Creditor.
The Cost of Her Pride. | The Step-mother.

By F. M. ALLEN.—Green as Grass.

By GRANT ALLEN.
Philistia. | Babylon. | The Great Taboo.
Strange Stories. | Dumaresq's Daughter.
For Maimie's Sake, | Duchess of Powysland.
In all Shades. | Blood Royal.
The Beckoning Hand. | I. Greet's Masterpiece.
The Devil's Die. | The Scallywag.
This Mortal Coil. | At Market Value.
The Tents of Shem. | Under Sealed Orders.

By M. ANDERSON.—Othello's Occupation.

By EDWIN L. ARNOLD.
Phra the Phœnician. | Constable of St. Nicholas.

By ROBERT BARR.
In a Steamer Chair. | A Woman Intervenes.
From Whose Bourne. | Revenge!

By FRANK BARRETT.
Woman of Iron Bracelets. | Under a Strange Mask.
Fettered for Life. | A Missing Witness.
The Harding Scandal. | Was She Justified?

By 'BELLE.'—Vashti and Esther.

By Sir W. BESANT and J. RICE.
Ready-Money Mortiboy. | By Celia's Arbour.
My Little Girl. | Chaplain of the Fleet.
With Harp and Crown. | The Seamy Side.
This Son of Vulcan. | The Case of Mr. Lucraft.
The Golden Butterfly. | In Trafalgar's Bay.
The Monks of Thelema. | The Ten Years' Tenant.

By Sir WALTER BESANT.
All Sorts & Conditions. | Armorel of Lyonesse.
The Captains' Room. | S.Katherine's by Tower
All in a Garden Fair. | Verbena Camellia, &c.
Dorothy Forster. | The Ivory Gate.
Uncle Jack. | Holy Rose | The Rebel Queen.
World Went Well Then. | Dreams of Avarice.
Children of Gibeon. | In Deacon's Orders.
Herr Paulus. | The Master Craftsman.
For Faith and Freedom. | The City of Refuge.
To Call Her Mine. | A Fountain Sealed.
The Revolt of Man. | The Changeling.
The Bell of St. Paul's. | The Charm.

By AMBROSE BIERCE—In Midst of Life.
By HAROLD BINDLOSS, Ainslie's Ju-Ju.
By M. McD. BODKIN.—Dora Myrl.
By PAUL BOURGET.—A Living Lie.
By J. D. BRAYSHAW.—Slum Silhouettes.

By ROBERT BUCHANAN.
Shadow of the Sword. | The New Abelard.
A Child of Nature. | Matt. | Rachel Dene
God and the Man. | Master of the Mine.
Martyrdom of Madeline | The Heir of Linne.
Love Me for Ever. | Woman and the Man.
Annan Water. | Red and White Heather.
Foxglove Manor. | Lady Kilpatrick.
The Charlatan.

R. W. CHAMBERS.—The King in Yellow.
By J. M. CHAPPLE.—The Minor Chord.

By HALL CAINE.
Shadow of a Crime. | Deemster. | Son of Hagar.

By AUSTIN CLARE.—By Rise of River.
By ANNE COATES.—Rie's Diary.

By MACLAREN COBBAN.
The Red Sultan. | The Burden of Isabel.

By MORT. & FRANCES COLLINS.
Blacksmith & Scholar. | You Play me False.
The Village Comedy. | Midnight to Midnight.

By WILKIE COLLINS.
Armadale. | After Dark. | The Woman in White.
No Name. | Antonina | The Law and the Lady.
Basil. | Hide and Seek. | The Haunted Hotel.
The Dead Secret. | The Moonstone.
Queen of Hearts. | Man and Wife.
My Miscellanies. | Poor Miss Finch.

By WILKIE COLLINS—continued.
Miss or Mrs.? | Jezebel's Daughter.
The New Magdalen. | The Black Robe.
The Frozen Deep. | Heart and Science.
The Two Destinies. | The Evil Genius.
'I Say No.' | The Legacy of Cain.
Little Novels. | A Rogue's Life.
The Fallen Leaves. | Blind Love.

M. J. COLQUHOUN.—Every Inch Soldier.
By E. H. COOPER.—Geoffory Hamilton.
By V. C. COTES.—Two Girls on a Barge.

By C. E. CRADDOCK.
The Prophet of the Great Smoky Mountains.
His Vanished Star.

By H. N. CRELLIN.
Romances of the Old Seraglio.

By MATT CRIM.
The Adventures of a Fair Rebel.

By S. R. CROCKETT and others.
Tales of Our Coast.

By B. M. CROKER.
Diana Barrington. | The Real Lady Hilda.
Proper Pride. | Married or Single?
A Family Likeness. | Two Masters.
Pretty Miss Neville. | In the Kingdom of Kerry
A Bird of Passage. | Interference.
Mr. Jervis. | A Third Person.
Village Tales. | Beyond the Pale.
Some One Else. | Jason. | Miss Balmaine's Past.
Infatuation.

By W. CYPLES.—Hearts of Gold.

By ALPHONSE DAUDET.
The Evangelist; or, Port Salvation.
H. C. DAVIDSON.—Mr. Sadler's Daughters
By E. DAWSON.—The Fountain of Youth.
By J. DE MILLE.—A Castle in Spain.

By J. LEITH DERWENT.
Our Lady of Tears. | Circe's Lovers.

By HARRY DE WINDT.
True Tales of Travel and Adventure.

By DICK DONOVAN.
Man from Manchester. | Tales of Terror.
Records of Vincent Trill | Chronicles of Michael
The Mystery of | Danevitch. | Detective.
Jamaica Terrace. | Tyler Tatlock, Private
Deacon Brodie.

By RICHARD DOWLING.
Old Corcoran's Money.

By A. CONAN DOYLE.
The Firm of Girdlestone.

By S. JEANNETTE DUNCAN.
A Daughter of To-day. | Vernon's Aunt.

By A. EDWARDES.—A Plaster Saint.
By G. S. EDWARDS.—Snazelleparilla.

By G. MANVILLE FENN.
Cursed by a Fortune. | A Fluttered Dovecote.
The Case of Ailsa Gray. | King of the Castle
Commodore Junk. | Master of Ceremonies.
The New Mistress. | Eve at the Wheel, &c.
Witness to the Deed. | The Man with a Shadow
The Tiger Lily. | One Maid's Mischief.
The White Virgin. | Story of Antony Grace.
Black Blood. | This Man's Wife.
Double Cunning. | In Jeopardy. | In'ng.
Bag of Diamonds, &c. | A Woman Worth Win-

By PERCY FITZGERALD.—Fatal Zero

By R. E. FRANCILLON.
One by One. | Ropes of Sand.
A Dog and his Shadow. | Jack Doyle's Daughter.
A Real Queen.

By HAROLD FREDERIC.
Seth's Brother's Wife. | The Lawton Girl.

By GILBERT GAUL.
A Strange Manuscript Found in a Copper Cylinder

By PAUL GAULOT.—The Red Shirts.

By CHARLES GIBBON.
Robin Gray. | The Golden Shaft.
Loving a Dream. | The Braes of Yarrow.
Of High Degree

THE PICCADILLY (3/6) NOVELS—*continued.*

By E. GLANVILLE.
The Lost Heiress. | The Golden Rock.
Fair Colonist | Fossicker | Tales from the Veld.

By E. J. GOODMAN.
The Fate of Herbert Wayne.

By Rev. S. BARING GOULD.
Red Spider. | Eve.

CECIL GRIFFITH.—Corinthia Marazion.

By A. CLAVERING GUNTER.
A Florida Enchantment.

By OWEN HALL.
The Track of a Storm. | Jetsam.

By COSMO HAMILTON.
Glamour of Impossible. | Through a Keyhole.

By THOMAS HARDY.
Under the Greenwood Tree.

By BRET HARTE.
A Waif of the Plains. | A Protégée of Jack Hamlin's.
A Ward of the Golden Gate. | Clarence.
A Sappho of Green Springs. | Barker's Luck.
Col. Starbottle's Client. | Devil's Ford. [celsior.'
Susy. | Sally Dows. | The Crusade of the 'Ex-
Bell-Ringer of Angel's. | Three Partners.
Tales of Trail and Town | Gabriel Conroy.

By JULIAN HAWTHORNE.
Garth. | Dust. | Beatrix Randolph.
Ellice Quentin. | David Poindexter's Dis-
Sebastian Strome. | appearance.
Fortune's Fool. | Spectre of Camera.

By Sir A. HELPS.—Ivan de Biron.

By I. HENDERSON.—Agatha Page.

By G. A. HENTY.
Dorothy's Double. | The Queen's Cup.

By HEADON HILL.
Zambra the Detective.

By JOHN HILL. The Common Ancestor.

By TIGHE HOPKINS.
'Twixt Love and Duty. | Nugents of Carriconna.
The Incomplete Adventurer.

VICTOR HUGO.—The Outlaw of Iceland.

FERGUS HUME.—Lady from Nowhere.

By Mrs. HUNGERFORD.
A Mental Struggle. | A Maiden all Forlorn.
Lady Verner's Flight. | The Coming of Chloe.
The Red-House Mystery | Nora Creina.
The Three Graces. | An Anxious Moment.
Professor's Experiment. | April's Lady.
A Point of Conscience. | Peter's Wife. | Lovice.

By Mrs. ALFRED HUNT.
The Leaden Casket. | Self-Condemned.
That Other Person. | Mrs. Juliet.

By C. J. CUTCLIFFE HYNE.
Honour of Thieves.

By R. ASHE KING.—A Drawn Game.

By GEORGE LAMBERT.
The President of Boravia.

By EDMOND LEPELLETIER.
Madame Sans-Gêne.

By ADAM LILBURN. 'A Tragedy in Marble

By HARRY LINDSAY.
Rhoda Roberts. | The Jacobite.

By HENRY W. LUCY.—Gideon Fleyce.

By E. LYNN LINTON.
Patricia Kemball. | The Atonement of Leam
Under which Lord? | Dundas.
'My Love!' | Ione. | The One Too Many.
Paston Carew. | Dulcie Everton.
Sowing the Wind. | Rebel of the Family.
With a Silken Thread. | An Octave of Friends.
The World Well Lost.

By JUSTIN McCARTHY.
A Fair Saxon. | Donna Quixote.
Linley Rochford. | Maid of Athens.
Dear Lady Disdain. | The Comet of a Season.
Camiola. | The Dictator.
Waterdale Neighbours. | Red Diamonds.
My Enemy's Daughter. | The Riddle Ring.
Miss Misanthrope. | The Three Disgraces.

By JUSTIN H. McCARTHY.
A London Legend. | The Royal Christopher

By GEORGE MACDONALD.
Heather and Snow. | Phantastes.

W. H. MALLOCK.—The New Republic.

P. & V. MARGUERITTE.—The Disaster.

By L. T. MEADE.
A Soldier of Fortune | On Brink of a Chasm.
In an Iron Grip. | The Siren.
Dr. Rumsey's Patient. | The Way of a Woman.
The Voice of the Charmer | A Son of Ishmael.
An Adventuress.

By LEONARD MERRICK.
This Stage of Fools. | Cynthia.

By BERTRAM MITFORD.
The Gun-Runner. | The King's Assegai.
Luck of Gerard Ridgeley. | Rensh. Fanning's Quest.

By J. E. MUDDOCK.
Maid Marian and Robin Hood. | Golden Idol.
Basile the Jester. | Young Lochinvar.

By D. CHRISTIE MURRAY.
A Life's Atonement. | The Way of the World.
Joseph's Coat. | Bob Martin's Little Girl
Coals of Fire. | Time's Revenges.
Old Blazer's Hero. | A Wasted Crime.
Val Strange. | Hearts. | In Direct Peril.
A Model Father. | Mount Despair.
By the Gate of the Sea. | A Capful o' Nails.
A Bit of Human Nature. | Tales in Prose & Verse
First Person Singular. | A Race for Millions.
Cynic Fortune. | This Little World.

By MURRAY and HERMAN.
The Bishops' Bible. | Paul Jones's Alias.
One Traveller Returns.

By HUME NISBET.—'Bail Up!'

By W. E. NORRIS.
Saint Ann's. | Billy Bellew.
Miss Wentworth's Idea.

By G. OHNET.
A Weird Gift. | Love's Depths.

By Mrs. OLIPHANT.—The Sorceress.

By OUIDA.
Held in Bondage. | In a Winter City.
Strathmore. | Chandos. | Friendship.
Under Two Flags. | Moths. | Ruffino.
Idalia. | Gage. | Pipistrello. | Ariadne.
Cecil Castlemaine's | A Village Commune.
Tricotrin. | Puck. | Bimbi. | Wanda.
Folle Farine. | Frescoes. | Othmar.
A Dog of Flanders. | In Maremma.
Pascarel. | Signa. | Syrlin. | Guilderoy.
Princess Napraxine. | Santa Barbara.
Two Wooden Shoes. | Two Offenders.
The Waters of Edera.

By MARGARET A. PAUL.
Gentle and Simple.

By JAMES PAYN.
Lost Sir Massingberd. | The Talk of the Town.
A County Family. | Holiday Tasks.
Less Black than We're | For Cash Only.
Painted. | The Burnt Million.
A Confidential Agent. | The Word and the Will
A Grape from a Thorn. | Sunny Stories.
In Peril and Privation. | A Trying Patient.
Mystery of Mirbridge. | A Modern Dick Whit
Walter's Word. | tington.
High Spirits. | By Proxy.

By WILL PAYNE.—Jerry the Dreamer.

By Mrs. CAMPBELL PRAED.
Outlaw and Lawmaker. | Mrs. Tregaskiss.
Christina Chard. | Nulma. | Madame Izan

By E. C. PRICE.
Valentina. | Foreigners. | Mrs. Lancaster's Rival
Miss Maxwell's Affections.

By RICHARD PRYCE.

By Mrs. J. H. RIDDELL.
Weird Stories. | A Rich Man's Daughter

By AMELIE RIVES.
Barbara Dering. | Meriel.

By F. W. ROBINSON.
The Hands of Justice. | Woman in the Dark.

CHATTO & WINDUS, Publishers, 111 St. Martin's Lane, London, W.C. 29

THE PICCADILLY (3/6) NOVELS—*continued.*
By ALBERT ROSS.—A Sugar Princess.
By HERBERT RUSSELL. True Blue
By CHARLES READE.
Peg Woffington; and Christie Johnstone.
Hard Cash.
Cloister & the Hearth.
Never Too Late to Mend
The Course of True Love; and Singleheart & Doubleface.
Autobiography of a Thief; Jack of all Trades; A Hero and a Martyr; and The Wandering Heir.
Griffith Gaunt.
Love Little, Love Long.
The Double Marriage.
Foul Play.
Put Y'rself in His Place
A Terrible Temptation.
A Simpleton.
A Woman-Hater.
The Jilt, & otherStories; & GoodStories of Man.
A Perilous Secret.
Readiana; and Bible Characters.
J. RUNCIMAN.—Skippers and Shellbacks.
By W. CLARK RUSSELL.
Round the Galley-Fire.
In the Middle Watch.
On the Fo'k'sle Head
A Voyage to the Cape.
Book for the Hammock.
Mystery of 'Ocean Star'
Jenny Harlowe.
An Ocean Tragedy.
A Tale of Two Tunnels.
The Death Ship.
My Shipmate Louise.
Alone on WideWide Sea.
The Phantom Death.
Is He the Man?
Good Ship 'Mohock.'
The Convict Ship.
Heart of Oak.
The Tale of the Ten.
The Last Entry.
By DORA RUSSELL.—Drift of Fate.
BAYLE ST. JOHN.—A Levantine Family.
By ADELINE SERGEANT.
Dr. Endicott's Experiment.
Under False Pretences.
By GEORGE R. SIMS.
Dagonet Abroad.
Once Upon a Christmas Time.
Without the Limelight.
Rogues and Vagabonds.
In London's Heart
Mary Jane Married.
The Small-part Lady.
By HAWLEY SMART.
Without Love or Licence.
The Master of Rathkelly.
Long Odds.
The Outsider.
Beatrice & Benedick.
A Racing Rubber.
By T. W. SPEIGHT.
A Secret of the Sea.
The Grey Monk.
The Master of Trenance.
The Web of Fate.
The Strange Experiences of Mr. Verschoyle.
A Minion of the Moon.
Secret Wyvern Towers.
The Doom of Siva.
By ALAN ST. AUBYN.
A Fellow of Trinity.
The Junior Dean.
Master of St.Benedict's.
To his Own Master.
Gallantry Bower.
In Face of the World.
Orchard Damerel.
The Tremlett Diamonds.
The Wooing of May.
A Tragic Honeymoon.
A Proctor's Wooing.
Fortune's Gate.
Bonnie Maggie Lauder.
Mary Unwin.
By JOHN STAFFORD.—Doris and I.
By R. STEPHENS.—The Cruciform Mark.
R. A. STERNDALE.—The Afghan Knife.
R. L. STEVENSON.—The Suicide Club.
By FRANK STOCKTON.
The Young Master of Hyson Hall.
By SUNDOWNER.—Told by the Taffrail.

By ANNIE THOMAS.—The Siren's Web.
BERTHA THOMAS.—The Violin-Player
By FRANCES E. TROLLOPE
Like Ships upon Sea.
Anne Furness.
Mabel's Progress.
By ANTHONY TROLLOPE.
The Way we Live Now.
Frau Frohmann.
Marion Fay.
Scarborough's Family.
The Land-Leaguers.
By IVAN TURGENIEFF, &c.
Stories from Foreign Novelists.
By MARK TWAIN.
Choice Works.
Library of Humour.
The Innocents Abroad.
Roughing It; and The Innocents at Home.
A Tramp Abroad.
The American Claimant.
AdventuresTomSawyer
Tom Sawyer Abroad.
Tom Sawyer, Detective
Pudd'nhead Wilson.
The Gilded Age.
Prince and the Pauper.
Life on the Mississippi.
The Adventures of Huckleberry Finn.
A Yankee at the Court of King Arthur.
Stolen White Elephant
£1,000,000 Bank-note.
C. C. F.-TYTLER.—Mistress Judith.
By SARAH TYTLER.
WhatShe CameThrough
Buried Diamonds.
The Blackhall Ghosts.
The Macdonald Lass.
Witch-Wife. | Sapphira
Mrs. Carmichael's Goddesses. | Lady Bell.
Rachel Langton.
A Honeymoon's Eclipse
A Young Dragon.
By ALLEN UPWARD.
The Queen against Owen.
By ALBERT D. VANDAM.
A Court Tragedy.
By E. A. VIZETELLY.—The Scorpion.
By F. WARDEN.—Joan, the Curate.
By CY WARMAN.—Express Messenger.
By A. WERNER.
Chapenga's White Man.
By WILLIAM WESTALL.
For Honour and Life.
A Woman Tempted Him
Her Two Millions.
Two Pinches of Snuff.
Nigel Fortescue.
Birch Dene.
The Phantom City.
A Queer Race.
Ben Clough.
The Old Factory.
Red Ryvington.
Ralph Norbreck's Trust
Trust-money
Sons of Belial.
Roy of Roy's Court.
With the Red Eagle.
Strange Crimes (True Stories).
By ATHA WESTBURY.
The Shadow of Bilton Fernbrook.
By C. J. WILLS.—An Easy-going Fellow.
By JOHN STRANGE WINTER.
Cavalry Life; and Regimental Legends.
A Soldier's Children.
By E. ZOLA.
The Fortune of the Rougons.
Abbe Mouret's Transgression.
The Conquest of Plassans. | Germinal.
The Honour of the Army.
The Downfall.
The Dream. | Money.
Dr. Pascal. | Lourdes.
The Fat and the Thin.
His Excellency.
The Dram-Shop.
Rome. | Paris.
Fruitfulness. | Work
By 'ZZ.'—A Nineteenth Century Miracle.

CHEAP EDITIONS OF POPULAR NOVELS.
Post 8vo, Illustrated boards, 2s. each.

By ARTEMUS WARD.
Artemus Ward Complete.
By Mrs. ALEXANDER.
Maid, Wife, or Widow? | A Life Interest.
Blind Fate. | Mona's Choice.
Valerie's Fate. | By Woman's Wit.
By E. LESTER ARNOLD.
Phra the Phœnician.

By GRANT ALLEN.
Philistia. | Babylon.
Strange Stories.
For Maimie's Sake.
In all Shades.
The Beckoning Hand.
The Devil's Die.
The Tents of Shem.
The Great Taboo.
Dumaresq's Daughter.
Duchess of Powysland.
Blood Royal. [piece.
Ivan Greet's Master-
The Scallywag.
This Mortal Coil.
At Market Value.
Under Sealed Orders.

CHATTO & WINDUS, Publishers, 111 St. Martin's Lane, London, W.C.

TWO-SHILLING NOVELS—*continued.*

BY FRANK BARRETT.
Fettered for Life.
Little Lady Linton.
Between Life & Death.
Sin of Olga Zassoulich.
Folly Morrison.
Lieut. Barnabas.
Honest Davie.
A Prodigal's Progress.
Found Guilty.
A Recoiling Vengeance.
For Love and Honour.
John Ford, &c.
Woman of Iron Bracelets
The Harding Scandal.
A Missing Witness.

By FREDERICK BOYLE.
Camp Notes.
Savage Life.
Chronicles of No-man's Land.

By Sir W. BESANT and J. RICE.
Ready-Money Mortiboy
My Little Girl.
With Harp and Crown.
This Son of Vulcan.
The Golden Butterfly.
The Monks of Thelema.
By Celia's Arbour.
Chaplain of the Fleet.
The Seamy Side.
The Case of Mr. Lucraft.
In Trafalgar's Bay.
The Ten Years' Tenant.

By Sir WALTER BESANT.
All Sorts and Conditions of Men.
The Captains' Room.
All in a Garden Fair.
Dorothy Forster.
Uncle Jack.
The World Went Very Well Then.
Children of Gibeon.
Herr Paulus.
For Faith and Freedom.
T Call Her Mine.
The Master Craftsman.
The Bell of St. Paul's.
The Holy Rose.
Armorel of Lyonesse.
S. Katherine's by Tower
Verbena Camellia Stephanotis.
The Ivory Gate.
The Rebel Queen.
Beyond the Dreams of Avarice.
The Revolt of Man.
In Deacon's Orders.
The City of Refuge.

By AMBROSE BIERCE.
In the Midst of Life.

BY BRET HARTE.
Californian Stories.
Gabriel Conroy.
Luck of Roaring Camp.
An Heiress of Red Dog.
Flip. | Maruja.
A Phyllis of the Sierras.
A Waif of the Plains.
Ward of Golden Gate.

By ROBERT BUCHANAN.
Shadow of the Sword.
A Child of Nature.
God and the Man.
Love Me for Ever.
Foxglove Manor.
The Master of the Mine.
Annan Water.
The Martyrdom of Madeline.
The New Abelard.
The Heir of Linne.
Woman and the Man.
Rachel Dene. | Matt.
Lady Kilpatrick.

By BUCHANAN and MURRAY.
The Charlatan.

By HALL CAINE.
The Shadow of a Crime. | The Deemster.
A Son of Hagar.

By Commander CAMERON.
The Cruise of the 'Black Prince.'

By HAYDEN CARRUTH.
The Adventures of Jones.

By AUSTIN CLARE.
For the Love of a Lass.

By Mrs. ARCHER CLIVE.
Paul Ferroll.
Why Paul Ferroll Killed his Wife.

By MACLAREN COBBAN.
The Cure of Souls. | The Red Sultan.

By C. ALLSTON COLLINS.
The Bar Sinister.

By MORT. & FRANCES COLLINS.
Sweet Anne Page.
Transmigration.
From Midnight to Midnight.
A Fight with Fortune.
Sweet and Twenty.
The Village Comedy.
You Play me False.
Blacksmith and Scholar
Frances.

By WILKIE COLLINS.
Armadale. | AfterDark.
No Name.
Antonina.
Basil.
Hide and Seek.
The Dead Secret.
Queen of Hearts.
Miss or Mrs.?
The New Magdalen.
The Frozen Deep.
The Law and the Lady
The Two Destinies.
The Haunted Hotel.
A Rogue's Life.
My Miscellanies.
The Woman in White.
The Moonstone.
Man and Wife.
Poor Miss Finch.
The Fallen Leaves.
Jezebel's Daughter.
The Black Robe.
Heart and Science.
'I Say No!'
The Evil Genius.
Little Novels.
Legacy of Cain.
Blind Love.

By M. J. COLQUHOUN.
Every Inch a Soldier.

By C. EGBERT CRADDOCK.
The Prophet of the Great Smoky Mountains.

By MATT CRIM.
The Adventures of a Fair Rebel.

By B. M. CROKER.
Pretty Miss Neville.
Diana Barrington.
'To Let.'
A Bird of Passage.
Proper Pride.
A Family Likeness.
A Third Person.
Village Tales and Jungle Tragedies.
Two Masters.
Mr. Jervis.
The Real Lady Hilda.
Married or Single?
Interference.

By ALPHONSE DAUDET.
The Evangelist; or, Port Salvation.

By DICK DONOVAN.
The Man-Hunter.
Tracked and Taken.
Caught at Last!
Wanted!
Who Poisoned Hetty Duncan?
Man from Manchester.
A Detective's Triumphs
The Mystery of Jamaica Terrace.
The Chronicles of Michael Danevitch.
In the Grip of the Law.
From Information Received.
Tracked to Doom.
Link by Link
Suspicion Aroused.
Dark Deeds.
Riddles Read.

By Mrs. ANNIE EDWARDES.
A Point of Honour. | Archie Lovell.

By EDWARD EGGLESTON.
Roxy.

By G. MANVILLE FENN.
The New Mistress.
Witness to the Deed.
The Tiger Lily.
The White Virgin.

By PERCY FITZGERALD.
Bella Donna.
Never Forgotten.
Polly.
Fatal Zero.
Second Mrs. Tillotson.
Seventy-five Brooke Street.
The Lady of Brantome.

By P. FITZGERALD and others.
Strange Secrets.

By R. E. FRANCILLON.
Olympia.
One by One.
A Real Queen.
Queen Cophetua.
King or Knave?
Romances of the Law.
Ropes of Sand.
A Dog and his Shadow

By HAROLD FREDERIC.
Seth's Brother's Wife. | The Lawton Girl.

Prefaced by Sir BARTLE FRERE.
Pandurang Hari.

By GILBERT GAUL.
A Strange Manuscript.

By CHARLES GIBBON.
Robin Gray.
Fancy Free.
For Lack of Gold.
What will World Say?
In Love and War.
For the King.
In Pastures Green.
Queen of the Meadow.
A Heart's Problem.
The Dead Heart.
In Honour Bound.
Flower of the Forest.
The Braes of Yarrow.
The Golden Shaft.
Of High Degree.
By Mead and Stream.
Loving a Dream.
A Hard Knot.
Heart's Delight.
Blood-Money.

CHATTO & WINDUS, Publishers, 111 St. Martin's Lane, London, W.C. 31

Two-Shilling Novels—*continued.*

By WILLIAM GILBERT.
James Duke.

By ERNEST GLANVILLE.
The Lost Heiress. | The Fossicker
A Fair Colonist.

By Rev. S. BARING GOULD.
Red Spider. | Eve.

By ANDREW HALLIDAY.
Every-day Papers.

By THOMAS HARDY.
Under the Greenwood Tree.

By JULIAN HAWTHORNE.
Garth. | Beatrix Randolph.
Ellice Quentin. | Love—or a Name.
Fortune's Fool. | David Poindexter's Disappearance.
Miss Cadogna. |
Sebastian Strome. | The Spectre of the Camera.
Dust. |

By Sir ARTHUR HELPS.
Ivan de Biron.

By G. A. HENTY.
Rujub the Juggler.

By HEADON HILL.
Zambra the Detective.

By JOHN HILL.
Treason Felony.

By Mrs. CASHEL HOEY.
The Lover's Creed.

By Mrs. GEORGE HOOPER.
The House of Raby.

By Mrs. HUNGERFORD.
A Maiden all Forlorn. | Lady Verner's Flight.
In Durance Vile. | The Red-House Mystery
Marvel. | The Three Graces.
A Mental Struggle. | Unsatisfactory Lover.
A Modern Circe. | Lady Patty.
April's Lady. | Nora Creina.
Peter's Wife. | Professor's Experiment.

By Mrs. ALFRED HUNT.
That Other Person. | The Leaden Casket.
Self-Condemned.

By MARK KERSHAW.
Colonial Facts and Fictions.

By R. ASHE KING.
A Drawn Game. | Passion's Slave.
'The Wearing of the | Bell Barry.
Green.'

By EDMOND LEPELLETIER
Madame Sans-Gene.

By JOHN LEYS.
The Lindsays.

By E. LYNN LINTON.
Patricia Kemball. | The Atonement of Leam
The World Well Lost. | Dundas.
Under which Lord? | Rebel of the Family.
Paston Carew. | Sowing the Wind.
'My Love!' | The One Too Many.
Ione. | Dulcie Everton.
With a Silken Thread.

By HENRY W. LUCY.
Gideon Fleyce.

By JUSTIN McCARTHY.
Dear Lady Disdain. | Donna Quixote.
Waterdale Neighbours. | Maid of Athens.
My Enemy's Daughter | The Comet of a Season.
A Fair Saxon. | The Dictator.
Linley Rochford. | Red Diamonds.
Miss Misanthrope. | The Riddle Ring.
Camiola

By HUGH MACCOLL.
Mr. Stranger's Sealed Packet.

By GEORGE MACDONALD.
Heather and Snow

By AGNES MACDONELL.
Quaker Cousins.

By W. H. MALLOCK.
The New Republic.

By BRANDER MATTHEWS.
A Secret of the Sea.

By L. T. MEADE.
A Soldier of Fortune.

By LEONARD MERRICK.
The Man who was Good.

By JEAN MIDDLEMASS.
Touch and Go. | Mr. Dorillion.

By Mrs. MOLESWORTH.
Hathercourt Rectory.

By J. E. MUDDOCK.
Stories Weird and Wonderful. | From the Bosom of the Deep.
The Dead Man's Secret. |

By D. CHRISTIE MURRAY.
A Model Father. | A Bit of Human Nature.
Joseph's Coat. | First Person Singular.
Coals of Fire. | Bob Martin's Little Girl.
Val Strange. | Hearts. | Time's Revenges.
Old Blazer's Hero. | A Wasted Crime.
The Way of the World | In Direst Peril.
Cynic Fortune. | Mount Despair.
A Life's Atonement. | A Capful o' Nails
By the Gate of the Sea. |

By MURRAY and HERMAN.
One Traveller Returns. | The Bishops' Bible.
Paul Jones's Alias.

By HUME NISBET.
'Bail Up!' | Dr. Bernard St. Vincent.

By W. E. NORRIS.
Saint Ann's. | Billy Bellew.

By GEORGES OHNET.
Dr. Rameau. | A Weird Gift.
A Last Love.

By Mrs. OLIPHANT.
Whiteladies. | The Greatest Heiress in
The Primrose Path. | England.

By OUIDA.
Held in Bondage. | Two Lit. Wooden Shoes.
Strathmore. | Moths.
Chandos. | Bimbi.
Idalia. | Pipistrello.
Under Two Flags. | A Village Commune.
Cecil Castlemaine's Gage | Wanda.
Tricotrin. | Othmar.
Puck. | Frescoes.
Folle Farine. | In Maremma.
A Dog of Flanders. | Guilderoy.
Pascarel. | Ruffino.
Signa. | Syrlin.
Princess Napraxine. | Santa Barbara.
In a Winter City. | Two Offenders.
Ariadne. | Ouida's Wisdom, Wit,
Friendship. | and Pathos.

By MARGARET AGNES PAUL.
Gentle and Simple.

By Mrs. CAMPBELL PRAED.
The Romance of a Station.
The Soul of Countess Adrian.
Outlaw and Lawmaker. | Mrs. Tregaskiss
Christina Chard. |

32   CHATTO & WINDUS, Publishers, 111 St. Martin's Lane, London, W.C.

Two-Shilling Novels—*continued.*

By RICHARD PRYCE.
Miss Maxwell's Affections.

By JAMES PAYN.
Bentinck's Tutor.
Murphy's Master.
A County Family.
At Her Mercy.
Cecil's Tryst.
The Clyffards of Clyffe.
The Foster Brothers.
Found Dead.
The Best of Husbands.
Walter's Word.
Halves.
Fallen Fortunes.
Humorous Stories.
£200 Reward.
A Marine Residence.
Mirk Abbey
By Proxy.
Under One Roof.
High Spirits.
Carlyon's Year.
From Exile.
For Cash Only.
Kit.
The Canon's Ward.
The Talk of the Town.
Holiday Tasks.
A Perfect Treasure.
What He Cost Her.
A Confidential Agent.
Glow-worm Tales.
The Burnt Million.
Sunny Stories.
Lost Sir Massingberd.
A Woman's Vengeance.
The Family Scapegrace.
Gwendoline's Harvest.
Like Father, Like Son.
Married Beneath Him.
Not Wooed, but Won.
Less Black than We're Painted.
Some Private Views.
A Grape from a Thorn.
The Mystery of Mirbridge.
The Word and the Will.
A Prince of the Blood.
A Trying Patient.

By CHARLES READE.
It is Never Too Late to Mend.
Christie Johnstone.
The Double Marriage.
Put Yourself in His Place
Love Me Little, Love Me Long.
The Cloister and the Hearth.
Course of True Love.
The Jilt.
The Autobiography of a Thief.
A Terrible Temptation.
Foul Play.
The Wandering Heir.
Hard Cash.
Singleheart and Doubleface.
Good Stories of Man and other Animals.
Peg Woffington.
Griffith Gaunt.
A Perilous Secret.
A Simpleton.
Readiana.
A Woman-Hater.

By Mrs. J. H. RIDDELL.
Weird Stories.
Fairy Water.
Her Mother's Darling.
The Prince of Wales's Garden Party.
The Uninhabited House.
The Mystery in Palace Gardens.
The Nun's Curse.
Idle Tales.

By F. W. ROBINSON.
Women are Strange.
The Hands of Justice.
The Woman in the Dark

By W. CLARK RUSSELL.
Round the Galley Fire.
On the Fo'k'sle Head.
In the Middle Watch.
A Voyage to the Cape.
A Book for the Hammock.
The Mystery of the 'Ocean Star.'
The Romance of Jenny Harlowe.
An Ocean Tragedy.
My Shipmate Louise.
Alone on Wide Wide Sea.
Good Ship 'Mohock.'
The Phantom Death.
Is He the Man?
Heart of Oak.
The Convict Ship.
The Tale of the Ten.
The Last Entry.

By DORA RUSSELL.
A Country Sweetheart.

By GEORGE AUGUSTUS SALA.
Gaslight and Daylight.

By GEORGE R. SIMS.
The Ring o' Bells.
Mary Jane's Memoirs.
Mary Jane Married.
Tales of To-day.
Dramas of Life.
Tinkletop's Crime.
My Two Wives.
Zeph.
Memoirs of a Landlady.
Scenes from the Show.
The 10 Commandments.
Dagonet Abroad.
Rogues and Vagabonds.

By ARTHUR SKETCHLEY.
A Match in the Dark.

By HAWLEY SMART.
Without Love or Licence.
Beatrice and Benedick.
The Master of Rathkelly.
The Plunger.
Long Odds.

By T. W. SPEIGHT.
The Mysteries of Heron Dyke.
The Golden Hoop.
Hoodwinked.
By Devious Ways.
Back to Life.
The Loudwater Tragedy.
Burgo's Romance.
Quittance in Full.
A Husband from the Sea.

By ALAN ST. AUBYN.
A Fellow of Trinity.
The Junior Dean.
Master of St. Benedict's
To His Own Master.
Orchard Damerel.
In the Face of the World.
The Tremlett Diamonds.

By R. A. STERNDALE.
The Afghan Knife.

By R. LOUIS STEVENSON.
New Arabian Nights.

By ROBERT SURTEES.
Handley Cross.

By BERTHA THOMAS.
The Violin-Player.

By WALTER THORNBURY.
Tales for the Marines.

By T. ADOLPHUS TROLLOPE.
Diamond Cut Diamond.

By F. ELEANOR TROLLOPE.
Like Ships upon the Sea.
Anne Furness.
Mabel's Progress.

By ANTHONY TROLLOPE.
Frau Frohmann.
Marion Fay.
Kept in the Dark.
The Way We Live Now.
The Land-Leaguers.
The American Senator.
Mr. Scarborough's Family.
Golden Lion of Granpere

By MARK TWAIN.
A Pleasure Trip on the Continent.
The Gilded Age.
Huckleberry Finn.
Mark Twain's Sketches.
Tom Sawyer.
A Tramp Abroad.
Stolen White Elephant.
Life on the Mississippi.
The Prince and the Pauper.
A Yankee at the Court of King Arthur.
£1,000,000 Bank-Note.

By C. C. FRASER-TYTLER.
Mistress Judith.

By SARAH TYTLER.
Bride's Pass
Buried Diamonds.
St. Mungo's City.
Noblesse Oblige.
Disappeared.
Lady Bell
The Huguenot Family
The Blackhall Ghosts
What She Came Through
Beauty and the Beast.
Citoyenne Jaqueline.

By ALLEN UPWARD.
The Queen against Owen. | Prince of Balkistan.

By WILLIAM WESTALL.
Trust-Money.

By Mrs. F. H. WILLIAMSON.
A Child Widow.

By J. S. WINTER.
Cavalry Life. | Regimental Legends.

By H. F. WOOD.
The Passenger from Scotland Yard.
The Englishman of the Rue Cain.

Unwin Brothers, Printers, 27, Pilgrim Street, London, E.C.

ESTABLISHED 1851.

BIRKBECK BANK

Southampton Buildings, Chancery Lane, London, W.C.

2%   **CURRENT ACCOUNTS**   **2%**
on the minimum monthly balances, when not drawn below **£100**.

2½%   **DEPOSIT ACCOUNTS**   **2½%**
or Deposits, repayable on demand.

STOCKS AND SHARES.

Stocks and Shares purchased and sold for customers.

The **BIRKBECK ALMANACK**, with full particulars, post free.

FRANCIS RAVENSCROFT, *Manager.*

Telephone No. 5 *Holborn.*
Telegraphic Address: "BIRKBECK, LONDON."

INVALUABLE, ALIKE FOR THE ROBUST OR INVALIDS.

PARRISH'S
GOLD MEDAL
CHEMICAL FOOD

CAUTION.—The only Chemical Food officially recognised as "**Parrish's**" by a jury of Medical Experts is "**Parrish's GOLD MEDAL Chemical Food.**" The Proprietors would respectfully ask the public to refuse all substitutes and highly injurious imitations, and to see their name is on the label.

LORIMER'S
COMPOUND SYRUP
of the HYPOPHOSPHITES

Recommended by the Medical Profession throughout the World for its Vitalising and Strengthening Powers.

SOLE PROPRIETORS AND MANUFACTURERS—

LORIMER & Cº Britannia Row, London, N.

Oetzmann & Co
HAMPSTEAD ROAD, W.
(Continuation North of Tottenham Court Road.

60 & 61 Grafton St., Dublin.   75 Union St., R

AN IMMENSE SAVING in the COST of HOUSE FURNIS
CAN BE EFFECTED BY CONSULTING

OETZMANN & CO.'S
Illustrated Guide to House Furni
GRATIS AND POST FREE.

Comfortable Box Ottoman Couch, with pillow head and spring seat, with cretonne, interior of box neatly lined, **29 6**.   Superior quality, ditto, 5

ALL CARPETS MADE UP FREE.

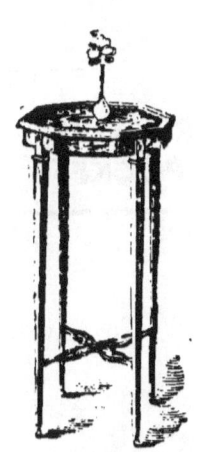

Handsome Inlaid Urnstand or Pedestal, 32 6

The "Sheraton" Easy Chair, with spr upholstered and covered in tapestry, and finish brass or copper nails, **27 6**

PR
5470
S35L6

Speight, Thomas Wilkinson
The Loudwater tragedy.

TWENTY HIGHEST AWARDS

PEARS

SOAP MAKERS

By Special Appointment

TO HER  MAJEST'

THE QUEEN

AND

HIS ROYAL HIGHNESS THI

PRINCE OF WALES

www.ingramcontent.com/pod-product-compliance
Lightning Source LLC
Chambersburg PA
CBHW021209230426
43667CB00006B/624